An Introduction to
Criminological Theory

Roger Hopkins Burke

WILLAN
PUBLISHING

Published by

Willan Publishing
Culmcott House
Mill Street, Uffculme
Cullompton, Devon
EX15 3AT, UK
Tel: +44(0)1884 840337
Fax: +44(0)1884 840251
e-mail: info@willanpublishing.co.uk

Published simultaneously in the USA and Canada by

Willan Publishing
c/o ISBS, 5824 N.E. Hassalo St,
Portland, Oregon 97213-3644, USA
Tel: +001(0)503 287 3093
Fax: +001(0)503 280 8832

© Roger Hopkins Burke

First published 2001

ISBN 1-903240-46-8 (paperback)
ISBN 1-903240-47-6 (hardback)

British Library Cataloguing-in-Publication Data
A catalogue record for this book is available from the British Library

Printed and bound by T.J. International, Padstow, Cornwall

Contents

Acknowledgements

I would like to offer my sincerest thanks to those who have offered help, advice and support during the researching and writing of this book. It has all been most appreciated. Thanks to my old friends and colleagues at the Scarman Centre at the University of Leicester where this project was first mooted and during my tenure there commenced – some of whom, like myself, have subsequently moved on to different challenges. In particular, thanks to John Benyon (who first suggested that I write this book), Martin Gill, Anthea Hucklesby, Chris Crowther, Simon Bennett, Ivan Horrocks, Ken Livingstone, Mike Rowe, Jon Garland, Martin Hemming, Claire Lawrence and of course Adam Edwards who is here with me as my deputy as Director of The Nottingham Crime Research Unit. Thanks to my current colleagues who have helped and supported me in their very different ways, Cecile Wright, Terry Gillespie, Matt Hopkins, Paul Sparrow, Graham Smith, David Webb, Nick Tilley, Mick Gregson and of course Mike Ahearne who both share my office and the trials and tribulations of support for West Ham United FC. Thanks to the reviewers of the first draft for their most encouraging comments and constructive suggestions. They were most welcome. Special thanks too to Karen Gill for her assistance during the early stages of this project, and especially for introducing me to Brian Willan. He has been quite splendid throughout as the publisher of this book, proposing suggestions in a calm but gently persuasive manner. Finally, but by no means least, thanks to my wife Kristan and our two young children, Thomas and Oliver (the latter born just after the completion of the first draft) for just being there.

Chapter 1

Introduction: crime and modernity

This is a book about the different ways in which crime and criminal behaviour have been explained in modern times. It will be seen that there are different explanations – or theories – which have been proposed at various times during the past 200 years by, among others, legal philosophers, biologists, psychologists, sociologists and political scientists. Moreover, these theories – in particular the earlier variants – have tended to reflect the various concerns and professional interests of the discipline to which the theorist or theorists has belonged. For example, biologists have sought explanations for criminality in terms of the biology of the individual criminal, while psychologists have directed our attention to the mind or personality of the person. Increasingly, however, explanations have come to incorporate elements from more than one discipline. Thus, for example, many biologists have come to recognise that individuals with specific biological profiles will behave differently depending on the social circumstances in which they have been raised and educated.

All of the theories discussed in this book nevertheless share one common characteristic. They are all products of a particular period and a way of life that has come to be termed the modern age. As such these different explanations of crime and criminal behaviour are themselves very much a reflection of the dominant ideas in that era. It is therefore a useful starting point for this book to briefly consider how crime and criminal behaviour was explained and dealt with in pre-modern times.

Pre-modern crime and criminal justice

Pre-modern judicial systems were very much influenced by religion and spirituality. Thus, the most influential explanation of crime and criminal behaviour was *demonology*, which proposed that criminals were possessed by demons that forced them to do wicked things beyond their control (Vold, Bernard and Snipes, 1998). At the same time, the law was mainly the product of judicial interpretation and caprice with few written laws. The accused often faced torture and closed trials. Punishment was both arbitrary and harsh with the emphasis being very much on the physical body. This was because the bulk of the population possessed little else on which the power to punish could be usefully exercised (Foucault, 1977). Moreover, the law was predominantly applied to those many poorer members of society who were not part of the aristocracy.

From the seventeenth to the early eighteenth century the English ruling class or aristocracy sought to protect their property interests through the exercise of the criminal law (Koestler and Rolph, 1961). Thus, a vast number of property crimes came to be punished by death in accordance with a body of legislation enacted during that period and which later came to be known as the 'the bloody code'. Furthermore, capital punishment was administered *en masse* and in public with the intention that this visual display would strike fear into the hearts of potential miscreants and thus deter them from offending. Hanging was the standard form of execution and the typical punishment for offences ranging from murder to stealing turnips, writing threatening letters or impersonating an outpatient of Greenwich Hospital (Radzinowicz, 1948). By 1800 there were more than 250 such capital offences (Lofland, 1973).

The full weight of the law was, however, not always applied. The rural aristocracy, who sat as judges and 'justices of the peace' (JPs), used their prerogative of clemency and leniency in order to demonstrate their power over the 'lower orders'. Hence, evidence of 'respectability' in the form of references from a benevolent landowner, confirmation of significant religious observance and piety, or the simple discretionary whim of a JP could lead to a lesser sentence. These alternatives included transportation to a colony, a non-fatal, if brutal, corporal punishment or even release (Thompson, 1975).

In short, the administration of criminal justice was chaotic, predominantly non-codified, thus irrational and irregular, and at the whim of individual judgement. It was the emergence and establishment of the modern era and the subsequent new ways of seeing and responding to the world that provided the preconditions for a major break in the way in which crime and criminal behaviour was both conceptualised and dealt with.

The rise of modern society

The idea of the modern originated as a description of the forms of thought and action that began to emerge with the decline of medieval society in Western Europe. Fundamentally, it involved a secular rational tradition with the following origins.

First, there was the emergence of humanist ideas and Protestantism in the sixteenth century. Previously the common people had been encouraged by the established church to accept unquestioningly their position in life and look for salvation in the afterlife. It was with the rise of the 'protestant ethic' that people came to expect success in return for hard work in this world. At the same time assumptions about the natural superiority – or the divine right – of the powerful aristocracy came to be questioned.

Second, there was the scientific revolution of the seventeenth century where our understanding of the world around us was first explained by reference to natural laws.

Third, there was the eighteenth-century philosophical Enlightenment where it was proposed that the social world could similarly be explained and regulated by natural laws; political systems should be developed that embraced new ideas of individual rationality and free will. Indeed, inspired by such ideas and responding to dramatically changing economic and political circumstances, revolutions occurred in the American colonies and in France. These were widely influential and ideas concerning human rights were championed in many European countries by the merchant, professional and middle classes. Subsequently, there were significant changes in the nature of systems of government, administration and law.

Fourth, there was the increasingly evident power of industrial society and the prestige afforded to scientific explanation in the nineteenth and twentieth centuries that seemed to confirm the superiority of the modernist intellectual tradition over all others (Harvey, 1989).

The principal features that characterise the idea of modern society can be identified in three main areas. First, in the area of economics there was the development of a market economy involving the growth of production for profit, rather than immediate local use, the development of industrial technology with a considerable extension of the division of

3

labour, with wage labour becoming the principal form of employment. Second, in the area of politics there was the growth and consolidation of the centralised nation state and the extension of bureaucratic forms of administration, systematic forms of surveillance and control, the development of representative democracy and political party systems. Third, in the area of culture there was a challenge to tradition in the name of rationality, with the emphasis on scientific and technical knowledge.

The modern world was consequently a very different place to its pre-modern predecessor. Not surprisingly, therefore, modern explanations of crime and criminal behaviour – and the nature of criminal justice interventions – were different from those that existed in pre-modern times. However, a word of caution should be considered at this point.

The eminent contemporary criminologist David Garland notes similarities between traditional accounts of criminality – whether they were religious or otherwise – and those of the modern era:

> Stories of how the offender fell in with bad company, became lax in his habits and was sorely tried by temptation, was sickly, or tainted by bad blood, or neglected by unloving parents, became too fond of drink or too idle to work, lost her reputation and found it hard to get employment, was driven by despair or poverty or simply driven to crime by avarice and lust – these seem to provide the well-worn templates from which our modern theories of crime are struck, even if we insist upon a more neutral language in which to tell the tale, and think that a story's plausibility should be borne out by evidence as well as intuition.
>
> (Garland, 1997: 22–3)

Garland notes that there were plenty of secular explanations of the roots of crime to place alongside the spiritual in pre-modern society. What was lacking, however, was a developed sense of differential explanation. Crime was widely recognised as a universal temptation to which we are all susceptible, but when it came to explaining why it is that some of us succumb and others resist, explanations tended to drift off into the metaphysical and spiritual.

Furthermore, we should note that 'traditional' ways of explaining crime have not entirely disappeared with the triumph of modernity, though they may nowadays be accorded a different status in the hierarchy of credibility. We do nevertheless continue to acknowledge the force of moral, religious and 'commonsensical' ways of discussing crime.

Defining and the extent of crime

It will become increasingly apparent to the reader of this book that developments in what has come to be termed criminological theorising have tended to reflect the economic, political and cultural developments that have occurred in modern society. In fact, definitions of crime and thus criminality are also closely linked to such socio-political factors and how we view the nature of society.

Crime includes many different activities such as theft, fraud, robbery, corruption, assault, rape and murder. However, we might usefully ask what these disparate activities – and their even more disparate perpetrators – have in common.

Some might simply define crime as the doing of wrong: this is a commonly used approach related to notions of morality. Yet not all actions or activities that might be considered immoral are considered crimes. For example, poverty and social deprivation might be considered 'crimes against humanity' but are not usually seen to be crimes. Conversely, actions that are crimes, for example parking on a yellow line or in some cases tax evasion, are not seen as immoral (Croall, 1998).

The simplest way of defining crime is that it is an act that contravenes the criminal law. This is nevertheless a problematic definition, for many people break the criminal law but are not considered to be 'criminals'. In English law, for example, some offences such as murder, theft or serious assaults are described as *mala in se* or wrong in themselves. These are often seen as 'real' crimes in contrast to acts that are *mala prohibita*, prohibited not because they are morally wrong but for the protection of the public (Lacey, Wells and Meure, 1990). Thus the criminal law is used to enforce regulations concerning public health or pollution not because they are morally wrong but because it is considered to be the most effective way of ensuring that regulations are complied with.

Legal definitions also change over time and vary across culture. For example, in some countries the sale and consumption of alcohol is a crime, in others the sale and consumption of opium heroin or cannabis is perfectly legal. There have recently been arguments in Britain for the use of some soft drugs such as cannabis to be legalised. On the other hand, there has been a demand for other activities – in recent years these have included 'stalking', racially motivated crime and knowingly passing on the aids virus – to be criminalised. The way that crime is defined is therefore a social construction and part of political processes.

This construction can be exemplified by considering what is included and excluded. Thus, Mars (1982) observes that 'crime', 'theft' and 'offence' are 'hard' words that can be differentiated from 'softer' words

5

such as 'fiddle' or 'perk' that are often used to describe and diminish criminal activities conducted in the workplace. In the same context, the terms 'creative accounting' or 'fiddling the books' do not sound quite as criminal as 'fraud'. Furthermore, incidents in which people are killed or injured in a train crash or as a result of using unsafe equipment are generally described as 'accidents' or 'disasters' rather than as 'crimes', albeit they often result from a failure of transport operators or managers to comply with safety regulations (Wells, 1993). Thus different words denote different kinds of crime, with some activities being totally excluded from the social construction of crime (Croall, 1998).

Crime is usually associated with particular groups such as young men or the unemployed, some of who become folk devils, and are identified with certain kinds of offences. This social construction of crime is reflected in media discussions and portrayals of what constitutes the 'crime problem'. Thus, for example, rising crime rates or policies are introduced to 'crack down' on crimes such as burglary or violent street crime rather than on environmental crimes such as pollution, corporate crimes or major frauds.

The vast majority of criminological research – and thus the explanations or theories of criminal behaviour that emanate from those studies and which are discussed in this book – have been conducted on those from the lower socio-economic groups and their activities. For it is concerns about this apparently 'dangerous class' that have dominated criminological thought since at least the beginning of modern society. The substitution of determinate prison sentences for those of capital punishment and transportation came to mean in reality the existence of a growing population of convicted criminals that frightened many in 'respectable society'. It is therefore perhaps not surprising that both the law and criminology has subsequently targeted this group.

The problem of 'white collar', business or corporate crime has nonetheless been recognised since at least the beginning of the twentieth century, although it has continued to be neglected and under-researched by criminologists (Clinard and Yeager, 1980; Kramer, 1984; Croall, 1992). Moreover, there has also been a tendency for much of the research conducted in this area to be atheoretical, with white collar and corporate crime seen as a phenomenon completely separate from 'normal', that is, predatory 'street' crime. This criminological neglect does, however, appear at first sight to be somewhat surprising.

It has been estimated that, for example, in the USA the economic losses from various white collar crimes are about ten times those that arise from 'ordinary' economic crime (Conklin, 1977) with corporate crime killing and maiming more people than any violence committed by the poor (Liazos, 1972). In the same country 100,000 people have died each year from occupationally related diseases that have mostly been contracted as a result of wilful violation of laws designed to protect workers (Swartz, 1975); defective products have killed another 30,000 US citizens annually (Kramer, 1984), while US manufacturers have been observed to dump drugs and medical equipment in developing countries after they have been banned from the home market (Braithwaite, 1984). Croall (1992) observes that the activities of the corporate criminal are not only greater in impact that those of the ordinary offender, but they are also longer lasting in effect.

There has been a real problem in actually defining the concept of white collar or corporate crime (Geis and Meier, 1977). Sutherland (1949) had proposed that 'white collar crime may be defined approximately as a crime committed by a person of respectability and high social status in the course of his occupation'. However, this is a restricted definition. White-collar crime can occur when an individual commits crime against an organisation in which they work or, for example, when a self-employed person evades income tax. Corporate crime, on the other hand, involves illegal acts carried out in the furtherance of the goals of an organisation and is therefore a particular form of white-collar crime. Schrager and Short (1978: 409) propose that organisational crime should be defined as 'illegal acts of omission of an individual or a group of individuals in a legitimate formal organisation in accordance with the operative goals of the organisation which have a serious physical or economic impact on employees, consumers or the general public'.

This is a definition that goes beyond that of economic impact and includes crimes of omission – failing to act – as well as those of commission. Others go further and include serious harms, which, though not proscribed, are in breach of human rights (Schwendinger and Schwendinger, 1970). In this book we will consider how the various explanations – or theories – of criminal behaviour that have usually been developed and applied to the socio-economically less powerful can be, and have on occasion been, applied to these crimes of the powerful and relatively powerful.

The structure of the book

The book is divided into four parts. Each of the first three parts considers a different model – or tradition – of explaining crime and criminal behaviour that has been developed during the modern era. Different explanations or theories can generally be located in terms of one of these models and these are here introduced chronologically in order of their emergence and development. It is shown how each later theory helped to revive, develop and/or rectify identified weaknesses in the ideas and prescriptions of their predecessors within that tradition.

A word of caution needs to be signposted at this point. Explanations of criminal behaviour have become increasingly complex as researchers have become aware that crime is a more complicated and perplexing matter than their criminological predecessors had previously recognised. Thus, some readers might consider that a particular theory introduced here as being central to the development of a particular tradition might also be considered in terms of a different model. In such instances attention is directed to that ambiguity. For clearly, as each tradition has developed there has been an increasing recognition by researchers of a need to address previously identified weaknesses internal to the model. The solution has invariably encompassed recognition of the at least partial strengths contained within alternative approaches. Hence, biologists have come increasingly to recognise the influence of environmental factors while some psychologists have embraced the previously alien notion of individual choice. Some more recent theoretical initiatives are in fact impossible to locate in any one of the three models. In short, their proponents have consciously sought to cross model boundaries by developing integrated theoretical approaches. These developments provide the focus of the fourth part of the book.

This book is structured in the following manner. *Part One* introduces the rational actor model. Central to this tradition is the notion that people have free will and make the choice to commit crime in very much the same way as they choose to indulge in any other form of behaviour. It is a tradition with two central intellectual influences. First, *social contract* theories challenged the notion of the 'natural' political authority previously asserted by the aristocracy. Human beings were now viewed as freely choosing to enter into contracts with others to perform interpersonal or civic duties (Hobbes, 1968 originally 1651; Locke, 1970 originally 1686, 1975 originally 1689; Rousseau, 1964 originally 1762, 1978 originally 1775). Second, *utilitarianism* sought to assess the applicability of policies and legislation to promote the 'happiness' of those citizens affected by them (Bentham, 1970 originally 1789; Mill, 1963–84 originally 1859).

Chapter 2 considers the ideas of the Classical School that provide the central theoretical foundations of the rational actor tradition. It was argued that people are rational creatures who seek pleasure while avoiding pain. Thus, the level of punishment inflicted must outweigh any pleasure that might be derived from a criminal act in order to deter people from resorting to crime. It was nevertheless a model of criminal behaviour that was to go into steep decline for many years. The increasing recognition that children, 'idiots' and the insane did not enjoy the capacity of perfect rational decision-making seemed best explained by the predestined actor model of human behaviour – or positivism – that is the focus of the second part of this book. The Classical School has nonetheless had a major and enduring influence on the contemporary criminal justice process epitomised by notions of 'due process' (Packer, 1968) and 'just deserts' (von Hirsch, 1976).

Chapter 3 considers the later revival of the rational actor model of explaining crime and criminal behaviour that occurred with the rise of the political 'new right' – or populist conservatives – both in the USA and the UK during the 1970s. This body of thought was highly critical of both the then orthodox predestined actor model with its prescriptions of treatment rather than punishment and the even more radical 'victimised' actor model – the focus of the third part of this book – with its proposals of forgiveness and non-intervention (Morgan, 1978; Dale, 1984; Scruton, 1980; 1985). These rational actor model revivalists argued that crime would be reduced if the costs of involvement were increased so that legal activities become comparatively more attractive (Wilson, 1975; Wilson and Herrnstein, 1985; Felson, 1994).

Chapter 4 discusses those theories that have subsequently come to prominence with the revival of the rational actor tradition. First, modern deterrence theories have addressed the principles of certainty, severity and promptness in terms of the administration of criminal justice (Zimring and Hawkins, 1973; Gibbs, 1975; Wright, 1993). Second, contemporary rational choice theories have proposed that people make decisions to act based on the extent to which they expect that choice to maximise their profits or benefits and minimise the costs or losses. Hence, decisions to offend are based on expected effort and reward compared to the likelihood and severity of punishment and other costs of crime (Becker, 1968; Cornish and Clarke, 1986). Routine activities theorists have developed a more sophisticated variant of this argument to propose that the likelihood of a crime increases when there are one or more motivated persons present, a suitable target or potential victim available, and an absence of capable guardians to deter the offender (Cohen and Felson, 1979).

Part Two introduces the predestined actor model. Proponents of this perspective fundamentally reject the rational actor emphasis on free will and replace it with the doctrine of determinism. From this *positivist* standpoint, criminal behaviour is explained in terms of factors, either internal or external to the human being that cause – or *determine* – people to act in ways over which they have little or no control. The individual is in some way predestined to be a criminal.

There are three basic formulations of the predestined actor model: biological, psychological and sociological. All three variants, however, incorporate the same fundamental assumptions, and although each is discussed separately, it will become increasingly apparent to the reader that they are not mutually exclusive. For example, biologists came to embrace sociological factors, while at times it is often difficult to differentiate between biological and psychological explanations.

Three factors were central to the emergence of the predestined actor model. First, there was the replacement of theology as the central explanation of the essence of humanity with science. In particular, the theory of evolution proposed that human beings were now subject to the same natural laws as all other animals (Darwin, 1871). Second, there was development of *social* evolutionism and the view that human beings develop as part of a process of interaction with the world they inhabit (Spencer, 1971 originally 1862–96). Third, there was the philosophical doctrine of positivism and the proposition that we may only obtain knowledge of human nature and society by using the methods of the natural sciences (Comte, 1976 originally 1830–42).

Chapter 5 considers biological variants of the predestined actor model. First, there is an examination of the early biological theories of the 'Italian School' where the central focus is on the notion that the criminal is a physical type distinct from the non-criminal (Lombroso, 1875; Ferri, 1877; Garofalo, 1914). There follows consideration of increasingly sophisticated variants on that theme. First, there is an examination of those theories that consider criminal behaviour to be inherited in the same way as physical characteristics. Evidence to support that supposition has been obtained from three sources: studies of criminal families (Dugdale, 1877; Goddard, 1925; Goring, 1913) twins (Lange, 1930; Christiansen 1968, 1974; Dalgard and Kringlen, 1976; Cloninger and Gottesman, 1987; Rowe and Rogers, 1989; Rowe, 1990) and adopted children (Hutchings and Mednick, 1977; Mednick, 1984). Second, consideration is given to those theories that link criminal behaviour to abnormalities in the genetic structure of the individual (Klinefelter, 1942; Price and Whatmore, 1967; Ellis, 1990; Jones, 1993) and, third, later versions of the body type thesis (Hooton, 1939; Sheldon, 1949; Glueck and Glueck, 1950; Gibbons, 1970; Cortes and Gatti, 1972). Fourth, neurological and brain injuries (Mark and Ervin, 1970; Mednick and Volavka, 1980; Volavka, 1987) and, fifth, different categories of biochemical explanation are scrutinised (Schlapp and Smith 1928; Dalton, 1961, 1964; Schachter, 1962, 1964, 1971; Rose, Bernstein, Gorden and

Catlin, 1974; Keverne, Meller and Eberhart, 1982; Olwens, 1987; Schalling, 1987; Virkkunen, 1987; Ellis and Crontz, 1990; Baldwin, 1990; Fagan, 1990; Fishbein and Pease, 1990; Pihl and Peterson, 1993).

Biological positivists propose that offenders should receive some form of treatment rather than punishment. There thus follows an examination of the treatment options of surgical intervention, chemo-therapy and electro-control.

Chapter 6 considers psychological variants of the predestined actor model. These all have in common the proposition that there are patterns of reasoning and behaviour specific to offenders that remain constant regardless of the different environmental experiences of individuals. There is therefore a criminal mind. Three different psychological perspectives are identified.

First, the psychodynamic approach has its roots in the notion of psychosexual development and the idea of a number of complex stages of psychic development (Freud, 1920; 1927). This approach was later developed through latent delinquency theory, which proposed that the absence of an intimate attachment with parents could lead to later criminality (Aichhorn, 1925; Healy and Bronner, 1936). Maternal deprivation theory later suggested that a lack of a close mother/child relationship in the early years could lead to criminal behaviour (Bowlby, 1952). Other researchers have proposed that the nature of child-rearing practices be closely linked to later behavioural patterns (Glueck and Glueck, 1950; McCord, 1959; Bandura and Walters, 1959; Hoffman and Saltzstein, 1967). Moreover, there are theories that propose criminality to be a product of 'broken families' (Burt, 1945; Mannheim, 1948; Wootton, 1959; West, 1969; Pitts, 1986; Kolvin, Miller, Scott, Gatzanis and Fleeting, 1990; Farringdon, 1992).

Second, behavioural and personality theories have their origins in the notion that behaviour is learned (Skinner, 1938). Criminals thus develop abnormal, inadequate, or specifically criminal personalities or personality traits that differentiate them from non-criminals. These theories – based on the concept of conditioned learning – propose that there are dimensions of personality that can be isolated and measured and thus criminal behaviour predicted (Eysenck, 1970, 1977; Smith and Smith, 1977; McEwan, 1983; McGurk and McDougall, 1981; Farrington, 1984). Antisocial personality disorder proposes that similar techniques can be used to detect individuals who are 'psychopaths' (Cleckley, 1976; Hare, 1980; Feldman, 1977; Hare and Jutari, 1983, 1986; Hollin, 1989) and predict future dangerousness (Kozol, Boucher and Garofalo, 1972; Monahan, 1981; Loeber and Dishion, 1983; Holmes and De Burger, 1989; Omerod, 1996).

Third, cognitive theories are explicitly critical of the determinist nature of the previous two psychological traditions (Tolman, 1932; Piaget, 1952; Skinner, 1981). Social learning theory thus proposes that behaviour is learned through watching what happens to other people and then making *choices* to behave in a particular way (Sutherland, 1947; Akers, 1979, 1985, 1992). In this way psychology can be seen to have moved away from its roots in the predestined model to incorporate notions from the rational actor model.

Chapter 7 considers sociological variants of the predestined actor model. These provided a direct challenge to those variants of the tradition that had focused on the characteristics – whether biological or psychological – of the deviant individual. Thus, in contrast, crime is explained as being a product of the social environment, which provides cultural values and definitions that govern the behaviour of those who live within them. Deviant or criminal behaviour is said to occur when an individual – or a group of individuals – behave in accordance with definitions that conflict with those of the dominant culture. Moreover, such behaviour is transmitted to others – and later generations – by frequent contact with criminal traditions that have developed over time in disorganised areas of the city (Durkheim, 1964 originally 1895; Shaw and McKay, 1972 originally 1931).

Later anomie or strain theories developed the positivist sociological tradition to propose that most members of society share a common value system that teaches us both the things we should strive for in life and the approved way in which we can achieve them. However, without reasonable access to the socially approved means, people will attempt to find some alternative way – including criminal behaviour – to resolve the pressure to achieve (Merton, 1938). Deviant subculture theories develop that argument further by observing that lower-class values serve to create young male behaviours that are delinquent by middle-class standards but which are both normal and useful in lower-class life. Thus, crime committed by groups of young people – or gangs – that seriously victimises the larger community is in part a by-product of efforts of lower-class youth to attain goals valued within their own subcultural social world (Cohen, 1955; Miller, 1958; Cloward and Ohlin, 1960; Spergel 1964; Matza, 1964; Mays, 1954; Morris, 1957; Downes, 1956; Wilmott, 1966; Parker, 1974; Pryce, 1979).

The sociological variant of the predestined actor model has somewhat inevitably been criticised for being overly determinist. In other words, people are seen to engage in criminal behaviour because of environmental conditions that *cause* them to act in ways over which they have little control. Nonetheless, a revised and restricted variant of this approach, that is, a recognition that social factors external to the human being place constraints on the person's choice of action, has been particularly influential and, indeed, would be considered by many today to be an almost common-sense, if partial, explanation of criminal behaviour.

Part Three introduces the victimised actor model. This is a tradition that proposes – with increasingly radical variants – that the criminal is in some way the victim of an unjust and unequal society. Thus it is the behaviour and activities of the poor and powerless sections of society that are targeted and criminalised while the dubious activities of the rich and powerful are simply ignored or not even defined as criminal.

There are two factors central to the emergence of the victimised actor model. First, there emerged during the mid-twentieth century within the social sciences an influential critique of the predestined actor model of human behaviour. Symbolic interactionism (Mead, 1934), phenomenology (Schutz, 1962) and ethnomethodology (Garfinkel, 1967) all questioned the positivist insistence on identifying and analysing the compelling *causes* that drive individuals towards criminal behaviour while at the same being unable to describe the social world in a way that is meaningful to its participants. Positivists were observed to have a restricted notion of criminality that was based on a tendency to accept the conventional morality of rules and criminal laws as self-evident truths. Thus, from this perspective, a particular action is defined as a crime because the state has decreed it to be so. Second, there developed a critique of the orthodox predestined actor model notion that society is fundamentally characterised by consensus. Pluralist conflict theorists alternatively suggest that society consists of numerous interest groups all involved in an essential struggle for resources and attention with other groups (Dahrendorf, 1958). More radical theories – informed by various interpretations of Marxist social and economic theory – view social conflict as having its roots in fundamental discord between social classes struggling for control of material resources (Taylor *et al*, 1973).

Chapter 8 considers social reaction – or labelling – theories (Lemert, 1951; Kitsuse, 1962; Becker, 1963; Piliavin and Briar, 1964; Cicourel, 1968). These propose that no behaviour is inherently deviant or criminal, but only comes to be considered so when others confer this label upon the act. Thus it is not the intrinsic nature of an act, but the nature of the social reaction that determines whether a 'crime' has taken place. Central to this perspective is the notion that being found out and stigmatised, as a consequence of rule-breaking conduct, may cause an individual to become committed to further deviance, often as part of a deviant subculture.

The labelling perspective has also been applied at a group level. The concept of 'deviancy amplification' suggests that the less tolerance there is to an initial act of group deviance, the more acts will be defined as deviant (Wilkins, 1964). This can lead to a media campaign that whips up a frenzy of popular societal indignation – or a 'moral panic' – about a particular activity that is seen to threaten the very fabric of civilisation. For example, 'lager louts', 'football hooligans', 'new age travellers', 'ravers' and even 'dangerous dogs', have all been the subjects of moral panics in recent years. Once labelled as such, those engaged in the particular activity, become ostracised and targeted as 'folk devils' by the criminal justice system reacting to popular pressure (Young, 1971; Cohen, 1973).

Among the critics of the labelling perspective are those who argue that they simply do not go far enough. By concentrating their attention on the labelling powers of front-line agents of the state working in the criminal justice system, the capacity for powerful groups in society to make laws to their advantage and to the disadvantage of the poor and dispossessed, is ignored. These issues are addressed in *Chapter 9*, which considers conflict and radical theories. For both these sets of theorists, laws are formulated to express the values and interests of the most powerful group in society and to restrict behaviour common to less powerful groups, thus disproportionately 'criminalising' the members of these groups. The more radical variants propose that it is the very conditions generated by capitalist political economy that generate crime (Vold, 1958; Turk, 1969; Quinney, 1970; Chambliss, 1987). These latter ideas were further developed in the UK in the late 1960s and early 1970s by 'the new deviancy conference' and the 'new criminology' that sought an explanation of criminal behaviour based on a theoretical synthesis of Marxism and labelling perspectives (Taylor *et al*, 1973; Hall, Critcher, Jefferson, Clarke and Roberts, 1978).

Criticisms of radical criminology have originated from three primary sources. First, traditional Marxists have questioned the manipulation of this theoretical tradition to address the issue of crime (Hirst, 1980). Second, there was the important recognition of the populist con-servatives (or the 'new' right) that most predatory crime is committed by members of the poorer sections of society against their own kind – thus, changing the whole nature of political debate on the crime problem. Third, there was the increasing recognition of this latter reality by sections of the political left and the consequent development of a populist socialist response which is the focus of the final chapter of the fourth part of this book.

Chapter 10 considers the gendered criminal. Feminists propose that it is men who are the dominant group in society and it is privileged males who make and enforce the rules to the detriment of women. Feminism is nonetheless not a unitary body of thought and thus this chapter commences with a brief introduction to different contemporary manifestations of feminism. There follows a discussion of the way in which traditional 'malestream' criminological explanations of female criminality had their roots located firmly in rather unsophisticated biological variants of the predestined actor model long after these had ceased having credible explanatory power for the criminal actions of men (Lombroso and Ferrero, 1885; Thomas, 1907; Pollak, 1961 originally 1950). The feminist critique of those traditional explanations is then explored (Smart, 1977; Heidensohn, 1985). There is then an examination of the impact of feminist critiques in four critical areas: the female emancipation leads to crime debate (Adler, 1975; Simon, 1975), the invalidation of the leniency hypothesis (Pollak, 1950), the emergence of gender-based theories (Heidensohn, 1985) and the recognition and redefinition of previously non-problematic activities such as domestic violence and intra-familial child molestation as serious crimes that need to be taken seriously (Hamner and Saunders, 1984; Dobash and Dobash, 1992). The chapter concludes with an examination of the notion of masculinity and the way in which feminist discourse has encouraged a small but growing group of male writers to take this concept seriously (Connell 1987, 1995; Messerschmidt 1993; Jefferson, 1997).

Chapter 11 considers critical theory that is one of two contemporary variants of the radical tradition in criminology. There are a number of different versions but in general critical criminologists define crime in terms of oppression. Members of the working class, women and ethnic minority groups are the most likely to suffer the weight of oppressive social relations based upon class division, sexism and racism (Cohen, 1980; Box, 1983; Scraton, 1985; Sim, Scraton and Gordon, 1987; Scraton and Chadwick, 1996 originally 1992). The contemporary notion of relative deprivation has been developed – with its roots in anomie theory – and its proposition that crime is committed by members of the poorer sections of society who are excluded from the material good things in life enjoyed by those with economic advantage. They have also importantly drawn our attention to the crimes of the powerful which – as we observed above – have been inadequately addressed by traditional explanations of crime and criminal behaviour.

Critical criminologists have nonetheless been criticised by the other contemporary wing of the radical tradition – the populist socialists or 'left realists' – who consider them to be 'left idealists' with romantic notions of criminals as revolutionaries or latter-day 'Robin Hoods', stealing from the rich to give to the poor, while failing adequately to address the reality that much crime is committed by the poor on their own kind.

Part Four introduces various attempts at integrating different theories both within one of the theoretical traditions outlined in the first three parts of this book and across model boundaries. It is observed that there are three ways by which theories can be developed and evaluated. First, each theory can be considered on its own. Second, there can be a process of theory competition where there is a logical and comprehensive examination of two different perspectives and a consideration of which one most successfully fits the data at hand (Liska, 1987). The third way to construct theory is by theoretical integration where the intention here is to identify commonalties in two or more theories in order to produce a synthesis that is superior to any one individual theory (Farnsworth, 1989).

Chapter 12 considers those socio-biological theories that have attempted a synthesis of biological and sociological explanations. Biosocial theorists argue that the biological characteristics of an individual are only part of the explanation of criminal behaviour; factors in the physical and social environment of the offender are also influential. It is proposed that all individuals must learn to control natural urges toward antisocial and criminal behaviour (Mednick and Christiansen 1977; Mednick, Moffit and Stack, 1987). Environmentally-influenced behaviour explanations address those incidents where outside stimuli such as drug and alcohol use has instigated or enhanced a propensity towards certain forms of behaviour (Fishbein and Pease, 1996).

The socio-biological perspective has been developed by the 'right realist' criminological theorists, Wilson and Herrnstein (1985), who have developed a theory combining gender, age, intelligence, body type and personality factors and have considered these in the context of the wider social environment of the offender. They propose that the interplay between these factors provides an explanation of why it is that crime rates have increased in both periods of economic boom and recession observing that the relationship between the environment and the individual is a complex one.

Chapter 13 discusses recent environmental theories. These are part of a long-established tradition with their foundations firmly located in the sociological version of the predestined actor model. Later British area studies were to incorporate into this tradition notions from the victimised actor model, primarily a consideration of the effects of labelling individuals and groups of residents as different or bad (Damer, 1974;

Gill, 1977). Later North American studies sought to incorporate the discipline of geography to provide a more sophisticated analysis of the distribution of crime and criminals (Brantingham and Brantingham, 1981). However, this was not simply a geographical determinist account. For, in adopting the recognition that crime happens when the four elements of a law, an offender, a target and a place concur, the perspective is brought into contact with those contemporary opportunity theories that characterise recent developments within the rational actor model (Cohen and Felson, 1979). Environmental management theories certainly presuppose the existence of a rational calculating individual whose activities can be restricted or curtailed by changing his or her surroundings (Wilson and Kelling, 1982).

Chapter 14 examines social control theories. Again, these have a long and distinguished pedigree with their origins in both the rational actor and predestined actor models (Hobbes, 1968 originally 1651; Durkheim, 1951 originally 1897; Freud, 1927). Moreover, both social and psychological factors have been employed in order to explain conformity and deviance. Early social theory had proposed that inadequate forms of social control were more likely during periods of rapid modernisation and social change because new forms of regulation could not evolve quickly enough to replace declining forms of social integration (Durkheim, 1951 originally 1897). Early social control theorists – such as the Chicago School – had taken this argument further and proposed that social disorganisation causes a weakening of social control, making crime and deviance more *possible.* Other control theorists nonetheless attached more importance to psychological factors in their analysis of deviance and conformity (Nye, 1958; Matza, 1967; Reckless, 1967). Contemporary control theories are fundamentally based on the assumption that criminal acts occur when an individual has weakened or broken bonds with society (Hirschi, 1969).

In an attempt to remedy identified defects in control theory, different writers have sought to integrate control theory with other perspectives. First, a model expanding and synthesising strain, social learning and control theories begins with the assumption that individuals have different early socialisation experiences and that these lead to variable degrees of commitment to – and integration into – the conventional social order (Elliot, Ageton and Canter, 1979). Second, an integration of control theory with a labelling/conflict perspective – from the victimised actor tradition – seeks to show how 'primary' deviants become 'secondary' deviants. This it is argued is an outcome of the selective targeting of the least advantaged groups in society – by the criminal justice system – acting in the interests of powerful groups (Box 1981,

1987). Third, a further highly influential approach builds upon and integrates elements of control, labelling, anomie and subcultural theory and proposes that criminal subcultures provide emotional support for those who have been stigmatised and rejected by conventional society (Braithwaite, 1989).

More recently there has been an attempt within this tradition to produce a 'general theory of crime' that combines rational actor notions of crime with a predestined actor model (control) theory of criminality (Gottfredson and Hirschi, 1990). In line with the rational actor tradition, crime is defined as acts of force or fraud undertaken in pursuit of self-interest. However, it is the predestined actor notion of (lack of) social control that provides the answer as to exactly who will make the choice to offend when appropriate circumstances arise.

Chapter 15 concludes the fourth part of the book with a consideration of 'left realism', a perspective that had originated as a direct response to two closely related factors. First, there was a reaction among some key radical criminologists on the political left to the perceived idealism of critical criminology and its inherent apology for criminals and criminal behaviour. Second, that reaction had been heightened by the rise of the populist conservatives and their 'realist' approach to dealing with crime. Thus, 'left realists' came to acknowledge that crime is a real problem that seriously impinges on the quality of life of many poor people and must therefore be addressed. From this perspective, a comprehensive solution to the crime problem – a 'balance of intervention' – is proposed (Young, 1994). On the one hand, crime must be tackled and criminals must take responsibility for their actions; on the other hand, the social conditions that encourage crime must also be tackled.

Left realism is not really an integrated theory of crime. It is rather an approach that recognises that there is something to be said for most theories of crime and for most forms of crime prevention. There is a distinct suggestion that insights can be incorporated from each of the three models of crime and criminal behaviour introduced in this book. It is a strategy which has been very influential with the 'New Labour' government elected in the UK in 1997. This was demonstrated by the oft-quoted phrase of Prime Minister Tony Blair first made while previously the shadow Home Secretary: 'tough on crime, tough on the causes of crime'.

The chapter concludes with a case study that considers the issue of social exclusion, criminality and the underclass from different theoretical standpoints introduced in the book. First, the behavioural perspective – normally associated with the populist conservatives – argues that state welfare erodes individual responsibility by giving people incentives not to work and provide for themselves and their family. Moreover, it is observed that those 'controls' that stop individuals and communities from behaving badly – such as stable family backgrounds and in particular positive male role models – have ceased to exist for many members of this identified 'underclass' (Murray, 1990, 1994). Second, structural explanations – normally associated with sociological variants of the predestined actor model, critical criminologists and left idealists – observe the collapse of manufacturing industry, traditional working-class employment and the subsequent retreat of welfare provision in modernist societies as providing the structural pre-conditions for the creation of a socially excluded class (Dahrendorf, 1985; Campbell, 1993; Jordan, 1996; Crowther, 1998). Third, a process model, which has a resonance with left realism, suggests that we identify and address the structural preconditions for the emergence of a socially excluded underclass while at the same time considering and responding to the behavioural subcultural strategies developed by those finding themselves located in that socio-economic position (Hopkins Burke, 1999a).

Chapter 16 concludes by returning to the earlier populist socialist recognition that there is something to be said for most theories of crime and criminal behaviour. This, it is argued, is a stance somewhat alien to the traditional modernist thinking that has underpinned the criminological theorising outlined and discussed in the body of this book. For modernity has been characterised by the development of all-encompassing theories that have sought to provide *exclusive* solutions to all crime while ignoring or being hostile to alternative models or approaches. More sophisticated modernists discussed in the fourth part of the book attempted to develop integrated theoretical perspectives that seek to incorporate elements from different models. These have nonetheless usually fallen into the essential modernist trap of almost arrogantly seeking to explain all criminal behaviour. This, it is proposed, is a flawed project ultimately doomed to failure.

In contrast it is proposed that the basis of a comprehensive programme to address the problem of crime lies in the recognition of the increasing fragmentation and complexity of society. It is a situation that some social scientists have come to term the postmodern condition (Lyotard, 1984): a situation where it is recognised that each model of crime and criminal behaviour – each of the constituent explanations or theories contained in these models – has something to tell us about some crimes, some people who commit crimes, in some situations, sometimes, but not all crimes, always. This it is considered is the future of criminological explanation.

Suggested further reading

For some contrasting accounts from very different perspectives of pre-modern criminal justice and attempts to explain the causes of crime see Foucault *Discipline and Punish – the Birth of the Prison* (1977), Hay 'Property, Authority and the Criminal Law' (1981) and Thompson, *Whigs and Hunters* (1975). Garland 'The Development of British Criminology' (1997) provides something of a pragmatic antidote to those who seek to identify distinct ruptures between pre-modern and modern thinking. For an introduction to the notion of modern society and modernity albeit in the context of his discussion of postmodernity, see Harvey, *The Condition of Postmodernity* (1989). Croall, *Crime and Society in Brtain* (1998) provides an excellent introduction to the different forms of crime in existence and the extent of criminality with a particular emphasis on business and corporate crime.

Part One

The rational actor model of crime and criminal behaviour

The average citizen hardly needs to be persuaded of the view that crime will be more frequently committed if, other things being equal, crime becomes more profitable compared to other ways of spending one's time. Accordingly, the average citizen thinks it obvious that one major reason why crime has gone up is that people have discovered it is easier to get away with it; by the same token, the average citizen thinks a good way to reduce crime is to make the consequences of crime to the would-be offender more costly (by making penalties swifter, more certain, or more severe), or to make the value of alternatives to crime more attractive (by increasing the availability and pay of legitimate jobs), or both. … These citizens may be surprised to learn that social scientists who study crime are deeply divided over the correctness of such views.

(Wilson, 1975: 117)

The first identifiable tradition of explaining crime and criminal behaviour in modern society is the rational actor model. It has its origins in
a range of philosophical, political, economic and social ideas that were
developed and articulated during the seventeenth and eighteenth
centuries and which were fundamentally critical of the established order
and its religious interpretations of the natural world. Two major sets of
ideas provide the intellectual foundations of a major period of social
change: social contract theories and utilitarianism.

The essence of social contract theories is the notion that legitimate
government is the outcome of the voluntary agreement of free moral
agents who are able to exercise their *will* freely. It was the key writers
in this tradition – Thomas Hobbes, John Locke and John-Jacques
Rousseau – and their criticisms of the exercise of arbitrary powers by
monarchs, established churches and aristocratic interests that created the
preconditions for the specific attacks on pre-modern legal systems and
practices later mounted by writers such as Bentham and Beccaria.

Thomas Hobbes (1588–1678) emphasised that it is the exercise of
human free will that is the essence of a social contract. Compliance can
be enforced by the fear of punishment, but only if entry into the contract
and the promise to comply with it has been freely willed, given and
subsequently broken. Hobbes held a somewhat negative view of human
potential and proposed a need for social institutions to support social
contracts and the laws to enforce them. He claimed that in a 'state of
nature' people would be engaged in a 'war of all against all' and life
would tend to be 'nasty, brutish and short'. He proposed therefore that
people should freely subject themselves to the power of an absolute ruler

or institution – a 'Leviathan' – which, as a result of a political-social contract would be legitimately empowered to enforce the contracts that subjects make between themselves (Hobbes, 1968 originally 1651).

John Locke (1632–1704) had a more complex conception of what people are like 'in the state of nature'. He argued that natural law constitutes and protects rights of life, liberty and property: assumptions that, subsequently, significantly shaped the constitutional arrangements of the USA. Locke proposes that the Christian God has presented all men with common access to the 'fruits of the earth', but at the same time individual property rights can be legitimately created when men mix labour with the fruits of the earth, for example by cultivating crops or extracting minerals. He did note however that men have a natural duty not to accumulate more land or goods than they can use and hence, create waste.

Locke proposes that if this natural law is obeyed, a rough equality of the distribution of natural resources can be achieved. Unfortunately, this natural potential towards egalitarianism had been compromised by the invention of a durable medium of exchange – money – that made it possible for men to obtain control over more goods and land than they could use as individuals.

Locke saw the transition from a state of nature to the development of a political society as a response to desires, conflict and ethical un-certainty brought about by the growth of the use of money and con-sequent material inequalities. He saw the expansion of political institutions as a process of achieving a social contract to alleviate the problems of inequality generated by the distortion of natural law arrangements by man. These social contracts developed through three stages. First, people must agree unanimously to come together as a community, and to pool their natural powers, so as to act together to secure and uphold the natural rights of each other. Second, the members of this community must agree, by a majority vote, to set up legislative and other institutions. Third, the owners of property in society must agree, either personally or through political representatives, to whatever taxes that are imposed on them.

Locke disagreed with Hobbes' view that people can legitimately surrender themselves to the absolute rule of a Leviathan. He argued that people gain their natural rights to life and liberty from the Christian God and hold them effectively in trust. These rights are not therefore theirs to transfer to the arbitrary power of another. Further, he argued that government is established to protect rights to property and not to undermine them. The government cannot therefore take or redistribute property without consent. The task of human legislation is not to replace natural law and rights but to give them the precision, clarity and impartial enforceability that are unattainable in the state of nature.

Locke had a relatively optimistic view of human potential in the state of nature. He observed however the inevitable potential for conflict and corruption that arises with the increasing complexity of human endeavour and the 'invention' of money, which permits the accumulation of wealth and the creation of inequalities and conflict. If natural rights are to be preserved, what is required is the consensual development of institutions to clarify, codify and maintain these rights to life, liberty and property. In short, these institutions should constrain all equally in the interests of social harmony (Locke, 1970 originally 1686).

Jean-Jacques Rousseau (1712–1778) was a severe critic of some of the major aspects of the emerging modern world arguing that the spread of scientific and literary activity was morally corrupting. He asserted that human beings had evolved from an animal-like state of nature in which isolated, somewhat stupid individuals lived peacefully as 'noble savages'. Rousseau (1964 originally 1762) claimed originally that humans were naturally free and equal, animated by the principles of self-preservation and pity. As humans developed groups and societies, and engaged in communal activities that gave rise to rules and regulations, the 'natural man' evolved into a competitive and selfish 'social man', capable of rational calculation and of intentionally inflicting harm on others. Rousseau moreover had a pessimistic view of social change and was unconvinced by the idea that the human species was progressing. Civilisation was not a boon to humanity; it was 'unnatural' and would always be accompanied by costs that outweighed the benefits.

With his later work, Rousseau (1978 originally 1775) appeared to be a little more optimistic about the future of humanity. He still asserted that at the beginning of history people were admirable, fundamentally equal, free individuals and that moral corruption and injustice arose as people came to develop more complex forms of society and depend on one another, thus risking exploitation and disappointment. Rousseau was however now prepared to propose political solutions to the moral corruption of society. It is necessary to establish human laws that consider all individuals equally and give all individuals a free vote on the enactment of legislation, he argued.

Rousseau developed the concept of the *general will*, observing that in addition to individual self-interest, citizens have a collective interest in the well-being of the community. He traced the foundations of the law and political society to this idea of the general will – a citizen body, acting as a whole, and freely choosing to adopt laws that will apply equally to all citizens.

Rousseau's work presented a radical democratic challenge to the French monarchical *ancien regime*. In contrast to kings being seen as 'the sovereign', the 'citizen body' were considered to be the rightful holder of that title. The government should represent the popular will of the citizen body. Rousseau argued that only in this way could individuals freely vote for, and obey, the law as an expression of the common good, without contradicting their own interests and needs. This is the basis of Rousseau's version of social contract theory.

Rousseau considered that he had resolved the dilemma of human selfishness and collective interests posed by Hobbes. He had done this without denying the potential existence of a positive and active form of civic freedom, based on self-sacrifice for a legitimate political community.

Social contract theories provide an overwhelming critique of pre-modern forms of government and are also highly relevant to the development of the rational actor model of crime and criminal behaviour. First, there is the claim that human beings once lived in a state of 'innocence', 'grace' or 'nature'. Second, there is the recognition that the emergence of humanity from its primitive state involved the application of *reason* – an appreciation of the meaning and consequences of actions – by responsible individuals. Third, the human 'will' is recognised as a psychological reality, a faculty of the individual that regulates and controls behaviour, and is generally free. Fourth, society has a 'right' to inflict punishment although this right has been transferred to the political state, and a system of punishments for forbidden acts, or a 'code of criminal law', has evolved.

Thus, human beings are viewed as 'rational actors', freely choosing to enter into contracts with others to perform interpersonal or civic duties. Laws can legitimately be used to ensure compliance if they have been properly approved by citizens who are party to the social contract.

A further major intellectual contribution to the development of the rational actor model was the philosophical tradition termed *utilitarianism*. Essentially this assesses the rightness of acts, policies, decisions and choices by their tendency to promote the 'happiness' of those affected by them. The two most closely associated adherents and developers of the approach are the political philosophers Jeremy Bentham and John Stuart Mill.

Jeremy Bentham (1748–1832) proposed that actions of human beings are acceptable if they promote happiness, and they are unacceptable if they produce the reverse of happiness. This is the basis of morality. His most famous axiom is the call for society to produce 'the greatest happiness of the greatest number'. 'Happiness' is understood to be pleasure and unhappiness is pain, or the absence of pleasure. The moral principle arising from this perspective is that if individuals use their reason to pursue their own pleasure then a state of positive social equilibrium will naturally emerge.

For Bentham, pleasures and pains were to be assessed, or 'weighed', on the basis of their intensity, duration and proximity. Moreover, such a calculus was considered to be person-neutral – that is, capable of being applied to the different pleasures of different people. The extent of the pleasure – or the total number of people experiencing it – was also a part of the calculation of the rightness of the outcome of an act. The overall aim was to provide a calculation whereby the net balance of pleasure over pain could be determined as a measure of the rightness of an act or policy.

John Stuart Mill (1806–1873) generally accepted Bentham's position including his emphasis on hedonism as the basic human trait that governs and motivates the actions of every individual. Mill nonetheless wanted to distinguish qualities as well as quantities of pleasures and this posed problems. For it is unclear whether a distinction between qualities of pleasures can be sustained and whether such a distinction can ever be measurable. Mill emphasised, first, that pure self-interest was an inadequate basis for utilitarianism, and suggested that we should take as the real criterion of good, the social consequences of the act. Second, he proposed that some pleasures rank higher than others, with those of the intellect superior to those of the senses. Importantly, Mill recognised both social factors and the quality of the act in seeking an explanation for human behaviour.

Mill has proved to be a formidable and influential philosophical force. It is Bentham, however, who has had the greatest impact on the development of the rational actor model of crime and criminal behaviour. Essentially he provided two central additions to social contract theory. First, there is his notion that the principal control over the unfettered exercise of free will is that of fear, especially the fear of pain; second, the axiom that punishment is the main way of creating fear in order to influence the will and thus control behaviour.

Chapter 2

Classical criminology

It was the Classical School theorists writing in the late eighteenth century who established the essential components of the rational actor model of crime and criminal behaviour. The two key writers were Cesare Beccaria in Italy and Jeremy Bentham in Britain

The Classical theorists

Cesare Beccaria (1738–1794) was an Italian mathematician and the author of *Dei delitti e delle pene (On Crimes and Punishment)* (1963, originally 1764). This book was translated into 22 languages and had an enormous impact on European and US legal thought. It was essentially the first attempt at presenting a systematic, consistent and logical penal system.

Beccaria's major contribution to criminological thought was the concept that the punishment should fit the crime. Criminals are seen to owe a 'debt' to society and punishments should be fixed strictly in proportion to the seriousness of the crime. Torture was considered a useless method of criminal investigation, as well as being barbaric. Moreover, capital punishment was not necessary. A life sentence of hard labour was preferable, both as a punishment and deterrent. Essentially, the use of imprisonment should be greatly extended, the conditions of prisons improved, with better physical care provided and inmates should be segregated on the basis of gender, age and degree of criminality.

Beccaria was a very strong supporter of 'social contract' theory with its emphasis on the notion that individuals can only be legitimately bound to society if they have given their consent to the societal arrangements. It is the law that provides the necessary conditions for the social contract. Punishments exist only to defend people's liberties against those who would interfere with them.

Beccaria's theory of criminal behaviour provides the foundations of the rational actor model and is based on the concepts of free will and hedonism. It is proposed that human behaviour is essentially purposive and based on the pleasure–pain principle. Thus, punishment should reflect that principle. Fixed punishments for all offences must consequently be written into the law and not be open to the interpretation, or the discretion, of judges. Moreover, the law must apply equally to all citizens while the sole function of the court is to determine guilt. No mitigation of guilt should be considered and all who are guilty of a particular offence should suffer the same prescribed penalty.

It is important to recognise that Beccaria's ideas have had a profound effect on modern criminal law and, while they may not be expressed in quite the same way, it is easy to detect resonances of his views in any popular discussion on crime. The doctrine of free will is built into many legal codes and strongly influences popular conceptions of justice.

Jeremy Bentham was a leading disciple of Beccaria. As a philosopher, as we saw above, he is classed as a utilitarian, or a *hedonistic utilitarian*, due to his emphasis on the pursuit of pleasure. He was very much influenced by the philosophical materialism of John Locke which denied the existence of innate ideas and traditional, established religious notions of original sin. He therefore ascribed criminal behaviour to incorrect upbringing or socialisation rather than innate propensities to offend. For Bentham, criminals were not incorrigible monsters but 'forward children', 'persons of unsound mind', who lacked the self-discipline to control their passions, according to the dictates of reason.

Bentham's ideas were very similar to those of Beccaria. His greatest principle, the fundamental axiom of all utilitarian philosophy, is 'the greatest happiness for the greatest number'. People are rational creatures who will seek pleasure and avoid pain. Thus, punishment must outweigh any pleasure derived from criminal behaviour, but the law must not be so harsh and severe as to reduce the greatest happiness. Moreover, the law should not be used to regulate morality, only to control acts harmful to society, which reduce the happiness of the majority. He agreed with Beccaria about capital punishment, that it was barbaric and unnecessary, but disagreed about torture, allowing that on occasion it might be 'necessary'. Furthermore, although Bentham believed in the doctrine of free will, there is a strong hint in his work that suggests criminality might be learned behaviour.

Bentham spent a considerable amount of time and energy designing a prison, an institution to reflect and operationalise his ideas on criminal justice. Prisons were not much used as a form of punishment in pre-modern times, being reserved for holding people awaiting trial, transportation or some other punishment. They were usually privately administered, chronically short of money, undisciplined and insanitary places.

In 1791 Bentham published his design for a new model prison called a Panopticon. The physical structure of this edifice was a circular tiered honeycomb of cells, ranged round a central inspection tower from which each could be seen by the gaolers. He proposed that the constant surveillance would make chains and other restraints superfluous. The prisoners would work 16 hours a day in their cells, the profits of their labour going to the owner of the Panopticon. Bentham described the prison as a 'mill for grinding rogues honest'. It was to be placed near the centre of the city so that it would be a visible reminder to all of the 'fruits of crime'. Furthermore, said Bentham, such an institution should act as a model for schools, asylums, workhouses, factories and hospitals that could all be run on the 'inspection principle' to ensure internal regulation, discipline and efficiency.

Underpinning all of these institutions of social control was a shared regime and common view of discipline and regimentation as mechanisms for changing the behaviour of the inmates. The rigorous regime proposed as the basis of these institutions was itself part of a more general discipline imposed on the working class in the factories. Michel Foucault (1977) and Michael Ignatieff (1978) have both traced the development of the prison as a concept and as a physical institution. Both noted that it was one of many 'carceral' institutions developed around the time to rationalise and discipline human activity along the lines of early modern thought.

The imposing new penal institutions soon competed for domination of the new urban skylines of modernity with the great palaces, cathedrals and churches that had long provided the symbols of the concerns of pre-modernity. While the Panopticon idea was not widely implemented, a variation on the theme was developed and built from the early nineteenth century and still forms a substantial part of the prison estate in many countries.

The limitations of Classicism

The philosophy of the Classical theorists was reflected in the *Declaration of the Rights of Man* in 1789 and the *French Penal Code* of 1791, the body of criminal law introduced in the aftermath of the French Revolution. The authors of these documents had themselves been inspired by the writings of the major Enlightenment philosophers, notably Rousseau. It was nonetheless attempts such as these to put these ideas of the Classical School into practice that exposed the inherent problems of its philosophy of criminal justice.

The Classical theorists had deliberately and completely ignored differences between individuals. First offenders and recidivists were treated exactly alike, solely on the basis of the particular act that had been committed. Children, 'idiots' and the insane were all treated as if they were fully rational and competent.

This appearance in court of people who were unable to comprehend the proceedings against them did little to legitimise the new French post-revolutionary criminal code. Consequently, the code was revised in 1810, and again in 1819, to allow judges some latitude in deciding sentences. In this way the strict, formal, philosophical elegance of the Classical model was breached. It became increasingly recognised that people were not equally responsible for their actions and a whole range of experts gradually came to be invited into the courts to pass opinion on the degree of reason that could be expected of the accused. Judges were now able to vary sentences in accordance with the degree of individual culpability argued by these expert witnesses. It was this theoretical compromise that led to the emergence of a modified criminological perspective that came to be termed the *neo-Classical School*.

The neo-Classical compromise

Neo-Classicists such as Rossi (1787–1848), Garraud (1849–1930) and Joly (1839–1925) modified the rigorous doctrines of pure Classical theory by revising the doctrine of free will. In this modified form of the rational actor model, ordinary sane adults were still considered fully responsible for their actions, and all equally capable of either criminal or non-criminal behaviour. It was now recognised, however, that children – and in some circumstances, the elderly – were less capable of exercising free choice and were therefore less responsible for their actions. The insane and 'feeble-minded' might be even less responsible. There were here the beginnings of a recognition that various innate predisposing factors may actually determine human behaviour: a perception that was to be the fundamental foundation of the predestined actor model that is the focus of Part Two of this book.

It was these revisions to the penal code that admitted into the courts for the first time, non-legal 'experts' including doctors, psychiatrists and, later, social workers. They were gradually introduced into the criminal justice system in order to identify the impact of individual biological, psychological and social differences. The purpose of this intervention was to determine the extent to which offenders were responsible for their actions. The outcome of this encroachment was that sentences became more individualised, dependent on the perceived degree of responsibility of the offender and on mitigating circumstances.

Moreover, it was now recognised that a particular punishment would have a differential effect on different people. Consequently, punishment came increasingly to be expressed in terms of punishment appropriate to rehabilitation. Though, as those eminent proponents of the more radical variant of the victimised actor model, Taylor, Walton and Young (1973: 10) were later to observe:

There was, however, no radical departure from the free will model of man involved in the earlier Classical premises. The criminal had to be punished in an environment conducive to his making the correct moral decisions. Choice was (and still is) seen to be a characteristic of the individual actor – but there is now recognition that certain structures are more conducive to free choice than others.

The neo-Classicists thus retained the central rational choice actor model notion of free will, but with the amendment that certain circumstances may be less conducive to the unfettered exercise of free choice than others. Indeed, it can be convincingly argued that most modern criminal justice systems are founded on this somewhat awkward theoretical compromise between the rational actor model of criminal behaviour and the predestined actor model. This debate between free will and determinism is perhaps one of the most enduring in the human and social sciences.

In summary, it is possible to identify the following central attributes of the Classical and neo-Classical schools that laid down the central foundations of the rational actor model. First, there is a fundamental concentration on the criminal law and the simple adoption of a legal definition of crime. This leaves the perspective crucially exposed to the criticism that legal definitions of crime change over time and space. Second, there is the central concept that the punishment should fit the crime rather than the criminal. This leaves it exposed to the criticism that it fails to appreciate the impact of individual differences in terms of culpability and prospects for rehabilitation. Third, there is the doctrine of free will according to which all people are free to choose their actions. This notion is often allied to the hedonistic utilitarian philosophy that all people will seek to optimise pleasure but avoid pain. From this perspective, it is assumed that there is nothing 'different' or 'special' about a criminal that differentiates them from other people. It is a doctrine thus exposed to the criticism that it fails to appreciate that the exercise of free will may be constrained by biological, psychological or social circumstances. Fourth, there is the use of non-scientific 'armchair' methodology based on anecdote and imaginary illustrations in place of empirical research. It was therefore an administrative and legal criminology, concerned more with the uniformity of laws and punishment rather than really trying to explain criminal behaviour.

The rational actor model went out of fashion as an explanatory model of criminal behaviour at the end of the nineteenth century. It was to be replaced by the new orthodoxy of the predestined actor model in its various guises. However, it continued to inform criminal justice systems throughout the world.

The enduring influence of Classicism

The enduring influence of the Classical school is evident in legal doctrine that emphasises conscious intent or choice, for example, the notion of *mens rea* or the guilty mind; in sentencing principles, for example, the idea of culpability or responsibility; and in the structure of punishment, for example, the progression of penalties according to the seriousness of the offence or what is more commonly known as the 'sentencing tariff'.

Philosophically, the ideas of the Classical school are reflected in the contemporary 'just deserts' approach to sentencing. This involves four basic principles. First, only a person found guilty by a court of law can be punished for a crime. Second, anyone found to be guilty of a crime must be punished. Third, punishment *must not be more* than a degree commensurate to or proportional to the nature or gravity of the offence and culpability of the offender. Fourth, punishment *must not be less* than a degree commensurate to or proportional to the nature or gravity of the offence and culpability of the criminal (von Hirsch, 1976).

Such principles are clearly founded on the theoretical tradition established by Beccaria and Bentham. There is an emphasis on notions of free will and rationality, as well as proportionality and equality, with an emphasis on criminal behaviour that focuses on the offence not the offender, in accordance with the pleasure–pain principle, and to ensure that justice is served by equal punishment for the same crime. 'Just deserts' philosophy eschews individual discretion and rehabilitation as legitimate aims of the justice system. Justice must be both done and seen to be done. It is an approach closely linked with the traditional Classical school notion of 'due process'.

Packer (1968) observes that whole contemporary criminal justice system is founded on a balance between the competing value systems of *due process* and *crime control*. Due process maintains that it is the purpose of the criminal justice system to prove the guilt of a defendant beyond a reasonable doubt in a public trial as a condition for the imposition of a sentence. It is based on an idealised form of the rule of law where the state has a duty to seek out and punish the guilty but must prove the guilt of the accused (King, 1981). Central to this idea is the presumption of innocence until guilt is proved.

A due process model requires and enforces rules governing the powers of the police and the admissibility and utility of evidence. There is recognition of the power of the state in the application of the criminal law but there is a requirement for checks and balances to be in place to protect the interests of suspects and defendants. The use of informal or discretionary powers is seen to be contrary to this tradition.

A strict due process system acknowledges that some guilty people will go free and unpunished. This is considered acceptable however in order to prevent wrongful conviction and punishment. The arbitrary or excessive use of state power is seen to be a worse evil. Problematically, a high acquittal rate gives the impression that the criminal justice agencies are performing inadequately and the outcome could be a failure to deter others from indulging in criminal behaviour.

A crime control model, in contrast, prioritises efficiency and getting results. The emphasis is on catching, convicting and punishing the offender. There is almost inherent in this model a 'presumption of guilt' (King, 1981) and less respect for legal controls that exist to protect the individual defendant. These are seen as practical obstacles that need to be overcome in order to get on with the control of crime and punishment. If occasionally some innocent individuals are sacrificed to the ultimate aim of crime control then so be it. Such errors should however be kept to a minimum. Agents of the law should ensure through their professionalism that they apprehend the guilty and allow the innocent to go free.

In the crime control model the interests of victims and society are given priority over those of the accused. The justification is that swifter processing makes the system appear more efficient and that it is this that will deter greater criminality. In other words, if you offend you are likely to be caught and punished. It is therefore not worth it. The primary aim of crime control is to punish the guilty and deter criminals as a means of reducing crime and creating a safer society.

It was observed that the rational actor model had gone out of fashion as an explanatory model of criminal behaviour with the rise of the predestined actor tradition at the end of the nineteenth century. It was to return very much to favour with the rise of the 'new' political right – or populist conservatism – during the last quarter of the twentieth century. However, it was to be a revival where the purist Classical tradition of 'due process' promoted in particular by Beccaria was to be very much superseded by the interests of the proponents of the crime control model of criminal justice.

Suggested further reading

The best exposition and introduction of the core ideas of the Classical School and the fundamental concepts of the rational actor model is still provided by the most accessible original account by Beccaria, *On Crimes and Punishments* (1986). King, *The Framework of Criminal Justice* (1981), Packer, *The Limits of the Criminal Sanction* (1968) and von Hirsch, *Doing Justice* (1976) provide essential demonstrations of the enduring and revitalised influence of the Classical School and rational actor thinking on the contemporary legal system and jurisprudence.

Chapter 3

Populist conservative criminology

It was with the emergence of the 'new political right' – or populist conservatives – during the 1970s and 1980s both in the USA and the UK that there was to be a substantial revival of interest in the rational actor model as a means of explaining crime and criminal behaviour.

The rise of the political new right

At that time conservative writers in both countries were mounting a vigorous moral campaign against various forms of 'deviance'. In 1979, Margaret Thatcher made crime a major election issue for the first time in the post-war period in Britain. Her general concern was to re-establish 'Victorian values' and to this end targeted the supposed permissive society of the 1960s and its perceived legitimisation in 'soft' social science.

In criminology this perceived liberal indulgence was epitomised by the other two explanatory models discussed in this book. First, there was the dominant orthodoxy of the twentieth century – the 'predestined actor' model – with its focus on discovering the causes of crime and, having once located them offering treatment and rehabilitation to the miscreant. Second, there were the more radical variants of the 'victimised actor' model with their critique of an unfair and unequal society, and their policy assumptions of understanding, forgiveness and non-intervention, which were gaining increasing popularity with the idealistic but at that time still electorally viable political left.

Right-wing intellectuals observed that it was not merely that left-wing and liberal thought had simply failed to *see* problems inherent in 'soft' approaches to crime, discipline, education, and so forth. This so-called progressive theorising had itself provided a basis for the *acceleration* of the permissive syndromes in question. The 'new right' argued that in such a spiralling, de-moralising culture, it was clear that crime and violence would inevitably increase. Thus, real problems and sociological apologies alike had to be confronted, and an attempt made to reassert the virtue and necessity of authority, order and discipline (Scruton, 1980, 1985).

In social policy in general (Morgan, 1978) and in the area of crime and deviance in particular (Dale, 1984) an assault was mounted on liberal and radical left trends. Consequently, we were to see the enthusiastic reintroduction of the idea of retributive punishment – serious crimes are simply evil, after all – and arguments for the protection of society from danger. From this populist conservative perspective, punishment is essentially about devising penalties to fit the crime and ensuring that they are carried out, thus reinforcing social values.

In short, this concern to treat the miscreant as an offender against social morality and not as a candidate for reform can be seen as a contemporary form of the rational actor model – but one with a distinctly retributive edge.

James Q. Wilson and 'right realism'

James Q. Wilson first published *Thinking About Crime* in the USA in 1975. This was well after the election of a Republican president with a mandate to 'get tough' on offenders by strengthening the criminal justice system, installing a tough Attorney-General and giving the police more powers. Wilson nonetheless rejects much of the traditional conservative approach to crime control as well as that offered by the political left. Moreover, he accepted the arguments of the liberals that increased police patrols, longer prison sentences for offenders and changes of personnel in central government posts could have little effect on crime levels. He was however scornful of those arguments that denied the existence of crime as a real problem. On the contrary, crime is quite simply an evil that requires a concerted and rigorous response.

Wilson is suspicious of those proponents of the predestined actor model of criminal behaviour who call for treatment not punishment. Instead of looking for causes which are difficult to discern and which in any case we may not be able to alter, action is advocated to increase the 'costs' of offending. In short, the benefits of leading an honest and considerate existence should be made more attractive to those who would otherwise take the wrong direction in life.

Right realism emphasises the findings of victim surveys that show that the burden of crime falls disproportionately on the poor, the disadvantaged and those least able to defend themselves. However, they deny absolutely the notion – proposed by the radical variants of the victimised actor model – of a struggle of an oppressed class against an unjust society. They stress the point that both perpetrators and victims of predatory crime tend to come from the same community. Wilson (1975: 21) observes the individualistic nature of offending and adopts a utilitarian explanation for human action:

> If the supply and value of legitimate opportunities (i.e. jobs) was declining at the very time that the cost of illegitimate opportunities (i.e. fines and jail terms) was also declining, a rational teenager might well have concluded that it made more sense to steal cars than to wash them.

The implication of this utilitarian argument would seem to support both increasing the benefits of 'non-crime' (by providing more and better jobs) and increasing the costs of crime (by the use of imprisonment). Wilson nonetheless concentrates on the latter half of the equation. In short, populist conservative crime control strategies tend to place far more emphasis on the stick than the carrot.

Right realists also differ from previous conservatives in the way they believe that punishment should be applied. Recognising that the USA imprisons a very large proportion of its population for longer periods than other countries who have far lower crime rates, Wilson stresses the certainty of punishment more than its severity. Thus, it is proposed that one of the reasons increased police activity does not itself reduce crime is that the value of an arrest depends on whether a conviction results and on the subsequent actions of the criminal justice system. Wilson observes that, once the chances of being caught, convicted and imprisoned are accounted for, a given robbery is four times more likely to result in imprisonment in the UK than in California and six times more likely in Japan.

It is argued that offenders do not decide to transgress on the basis of the length of sentence, but first of all on the probability of the sentence being applied: 'consequences gradually lose their ability to control behaviour in proportion to how delayed or improbable they are' (Wilson and Herrnstein, 1985: 49). Felson (1994: 9), another criminologist widely associated with right realism and whose work is discussed in more detail in the following chapter, provides a neat and often quoted analogy:

> What happens when you touch a hot stove: you receive a quick, certain, but minor pain. After being burned once, you will not touch a hot stove again. Now think of an imaginary hot stove that burns you only once every 500 times you touch it, with the burn not hurting until five months later. Psychological research and common sense alike tell us that the imaginary stove will not be as effective in punishing us as the real stove.

The answer, according to Wilson, involves catching more offenders – by increasing police effectiveness – and improving the consistency of the criminal justice system. A poor police/public relationship in the very areas where crime is most prevalent compromises the effectiveness of the police. Poor relations lead to a blockage of information and co-operation flow, from the public to the police, together with hostility, mistrust and even protection for offenders by their victims.

The US criminal justice system, although it passes longer prison sentences, convicts fewer of those it tries for predatory crime than do other countries. Wilson and Herrnstein (1985) consequently argue *against* long sentences, observing that undue severity might persuade the prisoner that he has been treated inequitably, and prompt him to exact revenge by further offending. Moreover, the longer the available sentence, the less likely judges are to impose them, thus the certainty principle is flouted further.

On the issue of the deterrent value of sentencing, Wilson and Herrnstein adopt a traditional rational actor model stance. They lament the irrationality of the criminal justice system, which they argue, reflects the view of judges that prison does not act as a deterrent. In support of their argument, they cite the low proportion of recidivists who are sent to prison. They thus call for fixed-term sentences for offences, regardless of the age of the offender and other attributes, such as the scope for rehabilitation.

It is observed that differential sentences for the same crime reflect a wish to change the behaviour of the offender; if the aim is to deter others, the sentence must be fixed and certain. Moreover, differential sentencing causes a moral dilemma. Those who are perceived less likely to re-offend receive shorter sentences, which in practice means that young, poor black offenders from unstable family backgrounds are sent to prison for longer than older, white middle-class offenders from stable family backgrounds who have committed the same offence.

Right realists do, however, argue for the use of imprisonment as an incapacitator. Recidivists, they note, commit most known crime. Therefore, if offenders in particular categories are certain to be locked up, even for a short period, then the rate of offending in those categories must fall. However, this loss of liberty need not necessarily take the form of conventional imprisonment. Incarceration overnight, or at weekends only, would have the same effect, just so long as it is certain to be applied and rigorously imposed. Wilson's neo-Classical approach to deterrence, sentencing and incapacitation are neatly encapsulated in the conclusion of *Thinking About Crime* thus:

> Wicked people exist. Nothing avails except to keep them apart from innocent people. And many people, neither wicked nor innocent, but watchful, dissembling, and calculating of their opportunities, ponder our reaction to wickedness as a cue to what they might profitably do.
>
> (Wilson, 1975: 235-6)

The right realist approach stresses the importance of upholding public order and public morality to assist with the fight against crime. Wilson devotes much of his writing to evaluating the effects of drugs and alcohol on offenders. He argues that the brutalising of residential areas by public disorder and incivilities – such as vandalism – can lead to crime that drives away 'decent' people. The area is then left to the law-breakers who are free to commit further offences unchecked by the 'normal' influence of social control (Wilson and Kelling, 1982). This idea provided the impetus to attempts to control crime by a process of 'environmental management' that included cleaning up graffiti and litter, removing drunks and beggars from streets and repairing the damage caused by vandals. This notion is revisited in Chapter 13 of this book.

Suggested further reading

For a discussion of the failings of the then dominant predestined actor model and the – at the time – quite influential victimised actor model as a precursor the rise of the popular conservatism and right realism see Dale, 'The Politics of Crime' (1984), Morgan, *Delinquent Fantasies* (1978) and Scruton, *The Meaning of Conservatism* (1980). Wilson, *Thinking about Crime* (1975), Wilson and Herrnstein, *Crime and Human Nature* (1985) and Wilson and Kelling, 'Broken Windows' (1982) are essential key texts associated with right realism.

Chapter 4

Contemporary rational actor theories

It was seen in the previous chapter that interest in the rational actor model of crime and criminal behaviour was revived both in the UK and the USA during rise of the political new right – or populist conservatives – during the 1970s and 1980s. This chapter considers three groups of contemporary rational choice theories that have come very much to prominence with that revival: (i) contemporary deterrence theories (ii) rational choice theory and (iii) routine activities theory.

Contemporary deterrence theories

At the core of contemporary deterrence theories are the principles of certainty, severity and celerity of punishment, proportionality, specific and general deterrence (Zimring and Hawkins, 1973; Gibbs, 1975; Wright, 1993). The deterrence doctrine proposes that in order to deter, punishment must be both swift and certain. The notion of celerity concerns the swiftness with which sanctions are applied after the commission of a crime. Certainty refers to the probability of apprehension and punishment. If the latter is severe, certain and swift, people will, it is proposed, rationally calculate there is more to be lost than gained from committing crime. Moreover, it is argued that certainty is more effective in deterring crime than severity of punishment. The more severe the available punishment, the less likely it is to be applied; while on the other hand, the less certain the punishment, the more severe it will need to be to deter crime (Akers, 1997).

Deterrence is said to operate in one of two ways. First, in the case of 'specific deterrence', the apprehended and punished offender will refrain from repeat offending if they are certain to be caught and severely punished. Second, in the case of 'general deterrence' the punishment of offenders by the state is seen to serve as an example to the general population who will thus refrain from criminal behaviour (Zimring and Hawkins, 1973). The research evidence on the deterrent effectiveness of sentencing has, however, remained ambiguous.

Among the earliest studies of deterrence were examinations of murder rates in various constituencies before and after the abolition of capital punishment. Ehrlich (1975) used a subsequently much criticised econometric version of rational choice theory to propose that every execution carried out in the USA deterred seven or eight other murders. His findings were however at odds with studies previously conducted in that country that had found that the availability of the death penalty in state legislation had no effect on the murder rate (Sellin, 1959; Bedau, 1964). Moreover, following the abolition of capital punishment for murder in England and Wales in 1965, research has suggested there has been no identifiable impact on the rate of homicide (Beyleveld, 1979; Morris and Blom Cooper, 1979).

It has often been suggested that murder, particularly in a domestic context, is a crime where the offender is highly unlikely to make a rational choice before committing the act. If that is the case, the potential consequences will be irrelevant and deterrence unlikely. In this context Walker (1985) argues that capital punishment is no more effective a deterrent than a sentence of life imprisonment.

We have seen that proponents of the rational actor model assume that potential offenders calculate the rewards and risks associated with crime. Research supports the suppositions of the right realists discussed in the previous chapter and suggests that the likelihood of detection is a more important part of that calculus than the potential level of punishment (Beyleveld 1978, 1979). Certainly the chances of being caught in the commission of an offence by a passing police patrol are extremely low in the UK (Bottomley and Coleman, 1981), while the detection rates for burglary vary between 9 per cent and 46 per cent depending on the locality. The extent to which people believe that they might be caught is therefore probably a more important variable.

Even if punishment does deter effectively, a number of objections can be raised to the use of sentences for this purpose. Beyleveld (1978) suggests that the types of punishment needed to deter a potential offender will vary substantially between different people, different crimes and different circumstances. Therefore, in order to deter crime, it might well be necessary to set sentences at a level totally out of proportion to the seriousness of the offence (Wright, 1982). This is rather at odds with the central rational choice actor model concept that the punishment should fit the crime. Moreover, when a particular offender has not been deterred then he or she must receive the threatened punishment. The consequences of such punishment may be simply counterproductive (Wright, 1982).

Martin and Webster (1971) have argued that conviction and punishment may simply push an individual into a situation where they have little to lose from further offending. The opportunity to live by legitimate means may be reduced and the individual with previous convictions is pushed towards further illegitimate activity regardless of the consequences. This is an argument similar to that proposed by the labelling theorists working in the victimised actor model tradition which is the focus of the third part of this book. Central to that perspective is the notion that being caught and stigmatised may lead to an offender becoming committed to further offending behaviour.

Wright (1982) suggests that the possibility of severe punishment encourages offenders to try harder to avoid detection and conviction. This can lead to violent escapes and to time being wasted by not guilty pleas that have no realistic chance of success. Moreover, child sex offenders who could benefit from help might be deterred from seeking it.

The use of punishment as a deterrent is based on the core rational choice actor model assumption that people choose to commit crime. Imposing deterrent sentences on those individuals who have little or no control over their impulses, or who break the law unwittingly, would appear to be morally indefensible. It can, however, be legitimately argued that deterrence remains a valid option in the case of intentional calculating offenders (Walker, 1980).

Rational choice theory

The considerable revival of interest in the rational actor model has been clearly demonstrated by the considerable government enthusiasm for situational crime prevention measures. These have been energetically promoted as governments essentially lost patience with the failure of criminologists to solve the apparently never-ending explosion in the crime figures. Certainly, spending in the UK since the late 1970s has been devoted more to finding and evaluating pragmatic solutions to particular offences rather than to developing criminological theory. At the same time most professional crime prevention practitioners who enjoy government patronage have come to accept the central nostrum that crime is an outcome of the opportunity to offend. Regardless of offender motivation, removal of that opportunity, it is argued, will reduce the incidence of crime. Consequently whole ranges of measures have been introduced in order to remove or reduce the opportunity to offend.

Target hardening in its simplest form can amount to no more than closing a door after leaving a room or building unoccupied. At a more sophisticated level, it can take the form of toughened glass 'anti-bandit' screens, specially designed security fencing and armoured safes. If a target can be removed completely instead of simply being protected even more impressive results are possible. Such strategies include the centralisation of cash transactions and the issue of tokens for use with gas and electricity meters. Where valuable targets cannot actually be removed, an alternative strategy lies in reducing their attraction to thieves. For example, chequebooks were much more attractive to thieves before the growth in the use of guarantee cards.

Proponents of the effectiveness of formal surveillance argue that potential offenders will be deterred by the threat of being seen, and agencies – such as the police and private security companies – that engage in such activities will deter offenders (Mayhew, 1984). On the other hand, the concept of natural surveillance is founded on the notion that by observing their environment as they go about their everyday business, people can provide themselves with some protection against crime. Moreover, commercial organisations can seek to protect themselves by the careful positioning of their employees.

These pragmatic strategies for reducing the opportunity to offend are theoretically informed by more recent variants of the rational actor model. Earlier and less sophisticated variants of rational choice theory had tended to compare the decision-making process adopted by offenders with straightforward economic choice. Thus, Gary Becker (1968) proposed that the potential offender calculates the legitimate opportunities of earning income available, the amount of reward they offer, the amounts offered by illegal methods, the probability of arrest, and the likely punishment. The person chooses the activity, legal or illegal, that offers the best return. Suggested preventive strategies, such as those proposed by the right realists, would involve reform of the law and its administration in order to alter the equation and make crime appear less attractive.

It is perhaps not surprising that these early theories have been accused of implying too high a degree of rationality by comparing criminal choices too closely with market-place decisions, and, at the same time, failing to explain expressive non-economically motivated criminal activity such as vandalism (Trasler, 1986). In the first instance, however, it has been argued that the amateurish criminal who makes wildly inaccurate estimates is no less a rational being than a consumer who runs up huge debts (Sullivan, 1973). In the second case, Clarke (1987) observes that while the motivation behind some expressive crimes may be pathological, their planning and execution may be highly rational.

A more sophisticated and highly influential variant of rational choice theory has been developed notably through the work of Clarke and Cornish. From their perspective crime is defined as 'the outcome of the offender's choices or decisions, however hasty or ill-considered these might be' (Clarke, 1987: 118). In other words, offenders invariably act in terms of a *limited* or *bounded* form of rationality. They will not always obtain all the facts needed to make a wise decision and the information available will not necessarily be weighed carefully. It is an approach that avoids the inherent tendency within the predestined actor model to treat criminals as a category of humanity apart from law-abiding citizens. From the rational choice perspective, crime is simply rational action performed by fairly ordinary people in response to particular pressure, opportunities and situational inducements (Hough, Clarke and Mayhew, 1980; Trasler, 1986).

Clarke (1987) is nonetheless not entirely dismissive of the predestined actor model suggesting that most of the factors seen as predisposing an individual to commit crime can be interpreted in terms of their influence on offender cognitive decision-making. This suggestion that individuals respond to situations in different ways because they bring with them a different history of psychological conditioning is examined further in the final section of Chapter 6.

Bennett (1986) observes that an offence rarely happens because of a single decision. In fact, a series of decisions will probably be made, starting with the original choice to offend, somewhere at some time, and ending with the final decision to act against a particular target. Therefore, both dispositional *and* situational factors are involved. Others note the operation of a conscious selection process at the scene of burglaries (Brantingham and Brantingham, 1984; Mayhew, 1984), while situational factors would clearly be expected to exert more influence nearer the criminal event (Bennett, 1986; Heal and Laycock, 1986). If these suppositions are correct, there are clear implications for crime prevention practitioners in deciding when and where to intervene in the potential offender's sequence of decisions.

Routine activities theory

Elements of rational choice theory can also be found in routine activities theory. This perspective observes that for a personal or property crime to occur, there must be at the same time and place a perpetrator, a victim, and/or an object of property. The crime event can take place if there are other persons or circumstances in the locality that encourage it to happen. On the other hand, the crime can be prevented if the potential victim or another person is present who can take action to deter it.

Cohen and Felson (1979) have taken these basic elements of time, place, objects, and persons to develop a 'routine activities' of crime events. These elements are placed into three categories of variables that increase or decrease the likelihood that persons will be victims of 'direct contact' predatory – personal or property – crime. These categories are *motivated offenders*, *suitable targets* of criminal victimisation, and *capable guardians* of persons or property. The likelihood of crime increases when there is one or more persons present who are motivated to commit a crime, a suitable target or potential victim that is available, and the absence of formal or informal guardians who could deter the potential offender. In short, 'the risk of criminal victimisation varies dramatically among the circumstances and locations in which people place themselves and their property' (Cohen and Felson, 1979: 595).

Cohen and Felson argue that fundamental changes in daily activities related to work, school, and leisure since World War II have placed more people in particular places at particular times. This has both increased their accessibility as targets of crime and at the same time keeps them away from home as guardians of their own possessions and property.

In his more recent work, Felson (1994) has come to place less emphasis on the significance of formal guardians – such as the police – because he has reached the conclusion that crime is a private phenomenon largely unaffected by state intervention. He now emphasises the natural crime prevention and deterrence that occurs in the informal control system, the 'quiet and natural method by which people prevent crime in the course of daily life' (Felson, 1994: xii–xiii). Ordinary people, oneself, friends, family, or even strangers are the most likely capable guardians.

Cohen and Felson (1979) relate crime rates to a 'household activity ratio', that is, the percentage of all households that are not husband–wife families or where the wife is employed outside the home. Such households are considered more vulnerable to crime victimisation because their members are away from home more and less able to function as guardians of their property. Moreover, they are more likely to possess more desirable goods to be stolen, while at the same time they are more exposed to personal crime away from home. Controlling for age composition and unemployment, Cohen and Felson found that the changes in household activity were correlated with changes in the rates of all major predatory violent and property crimes.

Cohen, Kluegel and Land (1981) have developed a more formalised version of routine activities theory and renamed it 'opportunity' theory. This considers elements of exposure, proximity, guardianship and target attractiveness as variables that increase the risk of criminal victimisation. But these are not measured directly. These are assumed from variations in age, race, income, household consumption, labour force participation, and residence in different areas of the city obtained from US crime victimisation surveys. Their findings nonetheless support most of their propositions.

Cromwell, Durham, Akers and Lanza-Kaduce (1995) studied the responses of the formal and informal control systems to the devastation of hurricane Andrew that occurred in Florida in 1982. They found that the natural disaster temporarily increased the vulnerability of persons and property as crime targets. For a short time, there was nearly a complete loss of police protection in some of the neighbourhoods. Motivated offenders with previous records were attracted to the areas in the aftermath of the storm while at the same time some local people took criminal advantage of the situation. There was however little looting and crime rates actually went down during the time when the community was most vulnerable only to increase again after the initial impact period. Cromwell *et al* explain these findings as being most likely the result of neighbours watching out for neighbours, citizens guarding their own and other property (sometimes with firearms) citizens' patrols, and other steps taken to aid one another in the absence of government and formal control.

The fact that some people may be motivated to commit crime when targets are made vulnerable by such events as natural disasters raises important questions about the concept of motivated – or potential – offender that purist versions of the rational actor model are ill-equipped to answer. Quite simply does the concept of motivated offender in routine activities theory refer only to someone who has an inherent predisposition to offend? Or does it include anyone who is enticed by the opportunity for quick gain itself, even though they may not have previously existing criminal intentions?

Akers (1997) observes that routine activities theory is simply a way of explaining why people become victims of crime. It fails categorically to explain why it is that some people engage in criminal behaviour and others do not. There is a taken-for-granted assumption that such people exist and that they commit crimes in certain places and at times when the opportunities and potential victims are available. It tells us absolutely nothing about these people and their motivations. It is the predestined actor model discussed in the following part of this book that offers numerous suggestions.

The rational actor revisited

The Classical theorists had emphasised the rationally calculating, reasoning human being who could be deterred from choosing to commit criminal behaviour by the threat of a fair and proportionate punishment. Moreover, they had proposed that all citizens should be treated equally in terms of a codified and rationalised legal system. In terms of the influential social contract theories of the time – epitomised and institutionalised by the initial aftermath of the French and US revolutions at the end of the eighteenth century – human beings were (mostly) all seen to be *equal* citizens. In this purist initial version of the rational actor model of crime and criminal behaviour the implicit emphasis was very much on a due process criminal justice model epitomised by such notions as the 'rights of man' and the 'rule of law'.

This purist version was both amended and fell into decline for three closely interlinked reasons. First, it became clear that not all are equally rational calculating human beings: a recognition that was to herald the end of what in practice had been a rather short-lived notion that all are human beings are equal. Second, there was an increasing awareness that a rational due process criminal justice intervention was having little effect on the crime statistics. There was a growing group of recidivists who were apparently not deterred by this strategy. Third, the latter discovery neatly coincided with the rise of the predestined actor model – the focus of the following part of this book – and its central supposition that criminals are a separate entity from law-abiding citizens.

Thus, the revised version of the rational actor model, which came to the fore with the rise of the political 'new right' in the last quarter of the twentieth century, *implicitly* accepted the predestined actor notion that there are different categories of human beings while denying the central notion of that model which proposed treatment or rehabilitation in preference to punishment. The implication of this revised theoretical schema when interpreted by contemporary conservative politicians seeking the support of the electorate seems to be to accept the notion proposed by James Q. Wilson that there are simply evil people – or perhaps more accurately a class or underclass of evil people – who need to be targeted by the agencies of the criminal justice system. Thus, with this revised formulation of the rational actor model there has been an emphasis on a crime control model criminal justice intervention that promotes the detection and punishment of offenders as the main priority.

Suggested further reading

For a comprehensive introduction to the notion of 'deterrence' in contemporary criminal justice and jurisprudence observed from a US perspective, see Gibbs, *Crime, Punishment and Deterrence* (1975) and Zimring and Hawkins, *Deterrence* (1973). Walker, *Punishment, Danger and Stigma: the Morality of Criminal Justice* (1980), *Sentencing: Theory, Law and Practice* (1985) provides the equivalent from a UK perspective. For further discussion of contemporary rational choice theory and situational crime prevention see Clarke, ' "Situational" Crime Prevention' (1980), Clarke and Mayhew (eds), *Designing Out Crime* (1980), Cornish and Clarke, *The Reasoning Criminal* (1986) and Mayhew *et al*, *Crime and Opportunity* (1976). Cohen and Felson, 'Social Inequality and Predatory Criminal Victimization' (1979) and Felson, *Crime and Everyday Life* (1994) are key routine activities theory texts.

Part Two

The predestined actor model of crime and criminal behaviour

The method which we … have inaugurated is the following. Before we study crime from the point of view of a juristic phenomenon, we must study the causes to which the annual recurrence of crimes in all countries is due. These are natural causes, which I have classified under the three heads of anthropological, telluric and social. Every crime, from the smallest to the most atrocious, is the result of the interaction of these three causes, the anthropological condition of the criminal, the telluric environment in which he is living, and the social environment in which he is born, living and operating. It is a vain beginning to separate the meshes of this net of criminality.

(Ferri, 1968: 71–2, originally 1901)

It was shown in Part One of this book that the rational actor model of crime and criminal behaviour proposes that human beings possess free will. This enables them to make rational decisions about what actions they should take whether these are legal or illegal. It is also proposed that as rational calculating human beings they should be held fully accountable for their actions. These ideas, as we have seen, had been highly influential in changing criminal justice policies during the late eighteenth and early nineteenth centuries particularly in France. However, it was with the publication of the first national crime statistics in that country in 1827 that it became clear that these data were astonishingly regular. Some places, furthermore, had higher rates while others had lower and these differences remained relatively constant from year to year. Rational actor model proponents had expected random changes in the number of crimes. The regularity of the new crime statistics, however, suggested that rather than being entirely the product of free will, criminal behaviour must be influenced by other factors.

It was also clear that crime rates were increasing rather than decreasing and so was the rate of recidivism or repeat offending. People who had received the prompt proportionate punishment administered by the new French code were committing more offences rather than less. This suggested that the Classical rational actor notion that changes in punishment policies alone could reduce crime was simply wrong.

These recognitions were to be highly influential in the rise of the predestined actor model of crime and criminal behaviour: a tradition with its origins in a very different view of society and human nature than that proposed by the Classical school. It emerged in the nineteenth century during a period of rapid industrialisation and the consolidation of capitalism as the dominant mode of production in Europe. At this time there was a major concentration of peasants into large cities, the creation and expansion of the factory system and the introduction of new productive technologies. These changes saw the flow of labour into employment in the industrial sphere and the emergence of a new social class – the working class, or the proletariat.

The rise of the urban working class was accompanied by major industrial, social and political conflict. Life was hard for these people. Child labour was common and there was a thin dividing line between conditions experienced by those working for a living and those condemned to the poorhouse. Living and working conditions were harsh, dirty and crowded. At the same time, the capitalist class was amassing huge fortunes and adopting opulent lifestyles. The contrast in circumstances and opportunities between the two classes was immense.

It was at this time that the working class began to organise itself industrially and politically. Although banned by law, workers began to combine into trade unions and there was a growing sympathy for fledgling socialist notions of a 'classless society'. This was reflected in the proliferation of alternative working-class publications, pamphlets and daily press, and in the formation of socialist parties. It was also a time of new thinking about the nature of human beings and of society in general.

Proponents of the predestined actor model – or positivist school of criminology – rejected the rational actor model emphasis on free will and replaced it with the doctrine of determinism. They were to argue that criminal behaviour could be explained in terms of factors, either internal or external to the human being, which cause people to act in a way over which they have little or no control. In some way, it is the destiny of the individual to become a criminal.

There are three basic formulations of the predestined actor model: biological positivism (the focus of Chapter 5), psychological positivism (Chapter 6) and sociological positivism (Chapter 7). All three versions are, however, founded on the same fundamental assumptions, and although each is discussed separately, it will become increasingly apparent to the reader that they are not mutually exclusive.

Three sets of ideas were to provide the intellectual foundations of the predestined actor model. First, there was the notion of evolution and science. Before the latter half of the nineteenth century, explanations of the essence of humanity had been provided by theology. From that time onwards such fundamental questions became increasingly the preserve of science, in particular, biology.

The biggest influence on the development of biology was the work of the English naturalist Charles Darwin (1809–82). His major works, *The Origin of Species* (1968, originally 1859), *The Descent of Man* (1871) and *Expression of Emotion in Man and Animals* (1872), are widely held to mark the end of 'pre-scientific' thinking about the causes of human behaviour. Previously it had been assumed that human beings were a species distinct from the rest of the animal world. Humans were assumed, as we observed in the first part of this book, to have free will, and therefore the ability to choose a course of action based on their assessment of the pleasures and pains that various alternatives are likely to provide. It was Darwin's theory of evolution that first seriously challenged such views.

According to evolutionary biology, humans are animals subject to the laws of nature like all other animals. It is these laws rather than free will or choice that must therefore govern human behaviour. The task of scientists interested in criminal behaviour is therefore to isolate and identify those causal forces that determine that conduct. Inevitably, the first place they looked for such forces was in the biological constitution of the offender.

The second set of ideas was provided by social evolutionism of which Herbert Spencer (1820–1903) was the major theorist. In the 1850s he had produced a series of essays, especially 'The Development Hypothesis' and 'Progress: Its Law and Cause', which drew from biology the elements of a general evolutionary *Naturphilosophie*. This was to be the basis of his multi-volume *System of Synthetic Philosophy* (1862–96), which first expounded a set of general evolutionary principles that he then applied to biology, psychology, sociology and ethics. In sociology in particular, Spencer broke new ground in comparative data collection and synthesis.

Spencer had been an evolutionist before Darwin and he had always held the view that human characteristics are inherited. And it was this aspect of his work that was to be the biggest influence on the development of the predestined actor model. Spencer, however, went much further than Darwin had done. He explained evolution as the product of the progressive adaptation of the individual character to the 'social state' or society. In this respect his sociology rests on definite psychological foundations. His major contribution to the development of sociology, however, is his recognition that human beings develop as part of a process of interaction with the social world they inhabit. This significant thesis that environmental factors influence the development of the human being was, as we shall see, to be increasingly important and latterly fundamental to the development of the predestined actor model.

The third set of ideas focused on the positivist method devised by the philosopher and social visionary Auguste Comte (1798–1857) who perhaps is best known for giving a name to the subject he outlined rather than practised, sociology. The foundation of his thought was his search in chaotic times – exemplified by the major transition from pre-dominantly agrarian to urban societies throughout Western Europe – for principles of cultural and political order that were consistent with this apparently forward march of society. In his later writings, especially the *Discours sur L'esprit Positif* ('Discourse on the Positive Spirit'), the *Systeme de la Politique Positif* ('System of Positive Polity') and the *Catechism of Positive Religion*, Comte provided the design for a new social order. This work provides the theoretical foundations of the social positivism that is the focus of Chapter 7.

For Comte (1976), positivism is the doctrine that the methods of the natural sciences provide the only means of obtaining knowledge of human nature and society. This knowledge has to be constructed out of evidence obtained from the senses – from empirical data – although there is to be a role for theoretical conceptualisation in order to make sense of this data. From the positive standpoint, therefore, truth can never be attained through abstract speculation or pure intellectual philosophising. On the contrary, the laws that govern all events in the world – for all are caused in regular discoverable ways – are available to the rigorous observer. Having obtained their empirical data, the scientists can then formulate these laws in order to subject then to test and verification.

None of this was new – British empirical philosophers, such as, Hume, had said as much for two hundred years – but what *was* radical was the application of the positivist faith in discoverable laws to *social* laws. The implications were colossal, for positivist knowledge could offer the means for peaceful reconstructions of social order by the elite of enlightened scientists and intellectuals. It was this aspect of his work that undoubtedly influenced the early biological criminologists discussed in the following chapter.

Chapter 5

Biological theories

The foundations of the biological variant of the predestined actor model of crime and criminal behaviour can be located primarily in the work of Cesare Lombroso, Enrico Ferri and Raffaele Garofalo. These early and highly influential biological criminologists – or the Italian School as they are usually known – argued that criminology should focus primarily on the scientific study of criminals and criminal behaviour.

Early biological theories

Cesare Lombroso (1836–1909) was both a psychiatrist at the University of Turin and a physician employed in the Italian penal system. In 1875 he published his most famous work *L'Uomo Delinquente* (*On Criminal Man*). The primary theme in this early work is that criminals represent a physical type distinct from non-criminals. Said to represent a form of degeneracy apparent in physical characteristics suggestive of earlier forms of evolution, they are *atavistic*, throwbacks to earlier forms of evolutionary life. Ears of unusual size, sloping foreheads, excessively long arms, receding chins and twisted noses are indicative signs of criminality. Although essentially a biological positivist, we should note that in the later editions of his work, Lombroso came increasingly to pay attention to environmental factors such as climate, poverty, immigration and urbanisation.

Lombroso now classified criminals in four main categories. First, *born criminals* are simply those who can be distinguished by their physical atavistic characteristics. Second, the category *insane criminals* includes idiots, imbeciles, paranoiacs, epileptics and alcoholics. Third, *occasional criminals* or *criminaloids* are those who commit crimes in response to available opportunities, though they too have innate traits that predispose them to criminal behaviour. Fourth, *criminals of passion* are those motivated to commit crime because of anger, love or honour.

Lombroso made little reference to female offenders. He considered female criminality to be restricted to prostitution and abortion, and a man was invariably responsible for instigating these crimes. This stereotypical view – that women engage in prostitution because of their sexual nature – totally disregarded the obvious motivation of economic necessity, and was to remain an influential explanation of female criminal behaviour until very recently and is revisited in Chapter 10.

Lombroso undoubtedly used primitive methodology; it was based on very limited data and a very simplistic use of statistics. Furthermore, he did not have a general theory of crime that would enable him to organise his data in any meaningful way (Taylor, Walton and Young, 1973). Criminals were simply those who had broken the law. Thus the problem appeared deceptively straightforward. All one needed to do was locate the differences between people that produce variances in their tendencies to violate the law.

Early biological proponents of the predestined actor model fundamentally assumed that offenders differ in some way from non-offenders. They then problematically observed that offenders appeared to differ among themselves and committed different types of crime. Moreover, offenders who committed the same type of crime appeared alike in terms of important characteristics. The solution to this problem was to subdivide the criminal population into types, each of which would be internally comparable with respect to the causes of crime, and different from other types on the same dimensions.

Most today consider the approach of Lombroso to have been simplistic and naïve. He nonetheless made three important contributions to the development of modern explanations of crime and criminal behaviour. First, he directed the study of crime away from the armchair theorising that had characterised the early proponents of the rational actor model towards the scientific study of the criminal. Second, although his methodology was rather primitive, he demonstrated the importance of examining clinical and historical records. Third, and most significantly, he recognised the need for multi-factor explanations of crime that include not only hereditary, but social, cultural and economic factors. These latter important factors were also emphasised by both Enrico Ferri and Raffaele Garofalo.

Enrico Ferri (1856–1929) was not simply a biological positivist.

Significantly, he argued that criminal behaviour could be explained by studying the interaction of a range of factors. First, there are *physical factors* such as race, geography and temperature. Second, there are *individual factors* such as age, sex and psychological variables. Thirdly, there are *social factors* such as population, religion and culture (Ferri, 1895).

Ferri proposed that improving the social conditions of the poor could control crime and to that end advocated the provision of subsidised housing, birth control and public recreation facilities. It was a vision that fitted well with the socialist views of Ferri. In the 1920s he was invited to write a new penal code for Mussolini's Fascist state, but his positivistic approach was rejected for being too much of a departure from rational actor model legal reasoning. Sellin (1973) argues that Ferri was attracted to Fascism because it offered a reaffirmation of the authority of the state over the excessive individualism that he had always rejected.

Raffaele Garofalo (1852–1934) was both an academic and a practising lawyer remembered for his doctrine of 'natural crimes'. He argued that because society is a 'natural body', crimes are offences 'against the law of nature'. Criminal behaviour is therefore unnatural. The 'rules of nature' are the rules of right conduct revealed to human beings through their powers of reasoning. For Garofalo the proper rules of conduct come from thinking about what such rules should be allowed or prohibited. He nonetheless identified acts that he argued no society could refuse to recognise as criminal and, consequently, repress by punishment.

Garofalo argued that these *natural crimes* violated two basic human sentiments found among people of all ages, namely the sentiments of *probity* and *pity*. The latter is the sentiment of revulsion against the voluntary infliction of suffering on others, while the former refers to respect for the property rights of others. Garofalo argued that these sentiments are basic moral sensibilities that appear in the more advanced forms of civilised society. He contended, moreover, that some members of society may have a higher than average sense of morality because they are superior members of the group. True criminals, on the other hand, lack properly developed altruistic sentiments. They have psychic or moral anomalies that can be inherited.

Garofalo identified four criminal classes, each one distinct from the others because of deficiencies in the basic sentiments of pity and probity. The first class, *murderers* are totally lacking in both pity and probity and will kill and steal whenever the opportunity arises. Lesser criminals are, however, more difficult to identify and this category is subdivided on the basis of whether criminals lack sentiments of either pity or probity. Thus, the second class, *violent criminals*, lack pity and can be influenced by environmental factors such as the consumption of alcohol, or the fact that criminality is endemic to the particular population. The third class, *thieves*, suffer from a lack of probity; a condition that might be more the product of social factors than is the case for criminals in the other categories. His final category contains sexual criminals, some of whom will be classified among the violent criminals because they lack pity. Others require a separate category because their actions stem from a low level of moral energy rather than a lack of pity.

The penological implications of the respective theories of Lombroso and Garofalo are substantially different. The former had wanted to provide treatment for and change deviants so that they could be reintegrated back into society. The latter reasoned that criminal behaviour demonstrated a failure to live by the basic human sentiments necessary for the survival of society. Criminals should therefore be eliminated in order to secure that survival. Life imprisonment or overseas transportation was proposed for lesser criminals.

Vold (1958) notes that both Garofalo and Ferri were prepared to sacrifice basic human rights to the opinion of 'scientific experts' whose decisions would take no account of the opinions of either the person on whom they were passing judgement or the wider general public. He observes that their work was acceptable to Mussolini's regime in Italy, because it provided scientific legitimisation for ideas of racial purity, national strength and authoritarian leadership. It will be seen in the following sections that later biological explanations of crime and criminal behaviour became increasingly more sophisticated. The implications of the tradition established by Garofalo and Ferri taken to their logical conclusion nonetheless remain the same. If an incurable criminal type exists and can be identified then the logical solution is surely to isolate and remove such individuals permanently from society. Some would suggest that this process of isolation take place before the individual has the opportunity to offend. The notion of treatment should not therefore automatically be assumed to be a soft option to the punishment intervention advocated by proponents of the rational actor model; the term treatment can have much more sinister connotations with serious civil rights implications. We should perhaps therefore be grateful that the latter apparently more sophisticated biological variants of the predestined actor model remain inherently problematic.

Inherited criminal characteristics

An idea arose at the end of the nineteenth century that criminality is inherited in the same way as physical characteristics. Evidence to support this supposition has been obtained from three sources: (i) criminal family studies; (ii) twin studies and (iii) adopted children studies. We will consider each in turn.

Criminal family studies

Criminal family studies have their origins in the work of Dugdale (1877) who traced 709 members of the Juke family, finding that the great majority were either criminals or paupers. Goddard (1914) subsequently published his study in which he had traced 480 members of the Kallikak family and found a large number of them to have been criminals. Interestingly, while both researchers had observed social as well as inherited criminal characteristics as causes of crime, both emphasised the link between criminality and feeblemindedness. Indeed, following the invention of intelligence tests (IQ tests) by Alfred Binet in 1905, inherited feeblemindedness was commonly proposed as a principal cause of crime, although it was to go out of fashion for some considerable time from the 1920s onwards.

Goring (1913) reported a fairly sophisticated study of 3,000 prisoners, with a history of long and frequent sentences, and a control group of apparently non-criminals. The prisoners were found to be inferior to the control group in terms of physical size and mental ability, strong associations between the criminality of children and their parents, and between brothers, were found. Furthermore, it was found that children who were separated from their parents at an early age because the latter were imprisoned were as likely – or more likely – to become criminals, compared with other children not separated in this way. Thus, contact with a criminal parent did not seem a significant factor associated with criminal conduct. Goring therefore claimed that the primary source of criminal behaviour is inherited characteristics rather than environmental factors.

The main identified weakness of Goring's study is his failure to properly control for the effects of the environment. Fundamentally, any research that attempts to locate the influence of inherited characteristics will have difficulty in eliminating environmental effects. Attempts to overcome this problem were, however, made by those involved in the study of twins and adopted children.

Twin studies

There are clear genetic differences between identical (monozygotic) twins and fraternal (dizygotic) twins. Identical twins occur when a single fertilised egg produces two embryos. They are genetically identical. Fraternal twins are the outcome of two different eggs being fertilised at the same time. They are as genetically different as children born after separate pregnancies. It is obvious that differences in the behaviour of identical twins cannot be explained by different inherited characteristics. On the other hand, various studies have proposed that similarities in their conduct can be explained by shared heredity.

Lange (1930) examined a group of 30 men, comprising 13 identical twins and 17 fraternal twins, all of who had a prison record. He found that in 77 per cent of cases for the identical twins, the other brother had such a record. However, for the fraternal twins, only 12 per cent of the second twins had a prison record. This percentaged relationship is referred to as a criminal concordance. Two hundred pairs of ordinary brothers, near to each other in age, were also compared. Where one brother had a criminal record, the same applied to the other brother in only 8 per cent of cases. Lange thus concluded that heredity plays a major part in the causation of criminal behaviour.

Christiansen (1968) examined official registers to discover how many of 6,000 pairs of twins born in Denmark between 1881 and 1910 had a criminal record. In the 67 pairs of identical male twins where at least one brother had a criminal record, the criminal concordance was 35.8 per cent. There were 114 pairs of fraternal male twins where at least one brother was a convicted criminal, but the criminal concordance was only 12.3 per cent. The criminal concordance was found to be higher for both categories where more serious offences had been committed.

A problem with twin studies is a lack of clarity about the sort of characteristics that are supposed to be passed on. This is important, as variations might reveal themselves in quite different forms of behaviour (Trasler, 1967). For example, some pairs of twins in Lange's study had committed very different types of offences from each other. It could well be the case, therefore, that a predisposition to offend is inherited but the actual form of offending is determined by other factors.

Christiansen did not, however, claim that inherited characteristics were the only – or for that matter the dominant – factor that led to the higher concordance for identical twins. He was of the opinion that twin studies could increase our understanding of the interaction between the environment and biological traits. In fact, he used variations in concordance rates in urban and rural areas to suggest that environmental factors might play a greater part in an urban setting. It is, nonetheless, a central criticism of such studies that they cannot accurately assess the balance between the effects of inherited characteristics and those of the environment. Twins are more likely than ordinary siblings to share similar experiences in relation to family and peers. It is possible that such similarities will be greater in the cases of identical twins.

Dalgard and Kringlen (1976) studied 139 pairs of male twins where at least one brother had a criminal conviction. Concordances of 25.8 per cent and 14.9 per cent were found for identical and fraternal twins, respectively. However, when the researchers controlled for mutual closeness, no appreciable difference in concordance rates was found between the types of twins. They concluded that hereditary factors were not significant in explaining crime. However, Cloninger and Gottesman (1987) reviewed the same data and reached a very different conclusion. They argued that if Dalgard and Kringlen had been correct, then the environmental effects would cause psychologically close identical twins to act in the same way, and psychologically distant identical twins to act differently. This did not happen.

A more recent twin study supports both inherited characteristics and environmental explanations of criminality. Rowe and Rogers (1989) collected data from self-report questionnaires involving 308 sets of twins in the Ohio State school system in the USA. They concluded that inherited characteristics partly determine the similarity of behaviour of same-sex and identical twins. However, they recognised that interaction between siblings could cause initially discordant siblings to become concordant in their levels of offending. Moreover, as twins are brought up together as a general rule, it becomes virtually impossible to reach any firm conclusion as to the role of inherited characteristics alone (Rowe, 1990). Studies of adopted children have sought to overcome that inherent methodological problem.

Adopted children studies

In the case of adopted children – where contact with a criminal parent has obviously been limited – any association between criminal behaviour can be attributed to inherited characteristics with a greater degree of certainty.

Hutchings and Mednick (1977) carried out a study of male adoptees born in Copenhagen between 1927 and 1941. They found that 48 per cent of young males with a criminal record and 37.7 per cent with a record of minor offences had a birth father with a criminal record. Among young males without a criminal record, 31.1 per cent had a birth father with such a record. The study discovered that an adoptee was more likely to have a record where both the birth and adoptive father had previous convictions.

In a further comparison, 143 of the adoptees with criminal records were matched with a control group containing the same number of adoptees without convictions. Among the sample group, 49 per cent were found to have criminal birth fathers, 18 per cent had criminal birth mothers and 23 per cent had criminal adoptive fathers. Among the control group 28 per cent were found to have criminal birth fathers, 7 per cent had criminal birth mothers and 9.8 per cent had criminal adoptive fathers. On the basis of these findings a very strong link between inherited characteristics and criminal behaviour was proposed.

The research was later replicated in a wider study that encompassed all non-familial adoptions in Denmark between 1924 and 1947 (Mednick, Gabrielli, William and Hutchings, 1984). A similar though slightly less strong correlation between birth parents and their adoptee children was found, again the most significant results being when both birth and adoptive parents were criminal. The researchers concluded that there was an inherited characteristic element that was transmitted from the criminal parents to their children that increased the likelihood of the children becoming involved in criminal behaviour. It is, however, important to note that adoption agencies try to place children in homes situated in similar environments to those from which they came. It therefore remains a possibility that it is upbringing not inherited characteristics that cause criminal behaviour. On the other hand, some people may be genetically endowed with characteristics that render them more likely to 'succumb to crime' (Hutchings and Mednick, 1977: 140).

In more recent years there have been attempts to rehabilitate notions of a link between intelligence and criminal behaviour. This interest in intelligence is based on a controversial position, taken in the late 1960s, that proposed intelligence to be genetically based, and that differences in IQ can be used to explain different criminal propensities between ethnic groups (see Shockley, 1967; Jensen, 1969). Robert Gordon (1986) argued from that perspective that IQ is the best predictor of offending behaviour among various groups.

Hirschi and Hindelang (1977) reviewed studies on IQ and offending behaviour and found that as a predictor of offending behaviour IQ is at least as good as any of the other major social variables. Furthermore, they noted that IQ is also strongly related to social class and ethnic group. Because offending behaviour is viewed as the province of lower-class, young people from ethnic minorities, this relationship implies that such people have lower IQs. This argument has understandably received a great deal of criticism. For example, Menard and Morse (1984) argued that IQ is merely one of the ways in which juveniles are disadvantaged in US society. They saw societal and institutional response to these disadvantages as the real explanation for offending behaviour.

In general, critics of IQ tests have noted that the way in which the tests are constructed provides advantages to those who are middle class and white. Moreover, it is argued that the tests do not measure innate intelligence, but rather some other ability, such as a facility in language or cultural concepts.

Genetic structure

A further category of biological explanations of crime and criminal behaviour considers abnormalities in the genetic structure of the offender. Crucial abnormalities that have been identified are those related to the sex chromosomes. People usually have 23 pairs of chromosomes, 46 in all. The sex of a person is determined by one of these pairs. The normal complement in a female is XX and in a male XY. In some men, however, an extra chromosome has been found to be present.

Klinefelter, Reifenstein and Albright (1942) found that sterile males often display a marked degree of feminisation together, sometimes, with low intelligence and increased stature. It was later found that these men with 'Klinefelter's syndrome' had an extra X chromosome. In 1962, Court Brown conducted a study of Klinefelter males in psychiatric institutions and discovered an abnormally high incidence of criminal behaviour among his subjects. His study suggested that Klinefelter males be over-represented among the population of homosexuals, transvestites and transsexuals. It is important to recognise, however, that such activities are no longer illegal.

Later studies looked at incarcerated criminals and focused on individuals with an XYY complement of sex chromosomes, in order to test the hypothesis that they might be characterised by extra maleness, and therefore be more aggressive. Casey in 1965 and Neilson in 1968 conducted the first major studies at the Rampton and Moss Side secure hospitals, respectively. Men with an extra Y chromosome tend to be very tall, generally of low intelligence and often present EEG abnormalities (EEG is discussed on pp. 65–67). Many of these early examples were found to have histories of criminal and aggressive behaviour with theft and violent assault their characteristic offences.

Price and Whatmore (1967) noted that subjects with an extra Y chromosome tend to be convicted at an earlier age than other offenders. They come from families with no history of criminality, tend to be unstable and immature without displaying remorse and have a marked tendency to commit a succession of apparently motiveless property crimes. Witkin, Mednick, and Schulsinger (1977) nonetheless explain the over-representation of such men in institutions to be the result of their slight mental retardation.

A range of criticisms has been made of these genetic structure theories. First, almost all the research has been concentrated on inmates in special hospitals and has revealed more evidence of psychiatric disorder than criminality. Second, there does not appear to be any fixed and identifiable XYY syndrome, which means the concept is not useful in predicting criminal behaviour. Third, the offending behaviour of some young males with an extra X chromosome may be due to anxiety in adolescence about an apparent lack of masculinity. Fourth, all the young male offenders with an identified extra Y chromosome have come from working-class backgrounds. It is possible that because young males with an extra Y chromosome are usually tall and well built, they may be defined as 'dangerous' by judges and psychiatrists, and thus more likely to be incarcerated than fined. Finally, there are thousands of perfectly, normal and harmless people in the general population who have either an extra X or Y chromosome.

Advances in genetic science in recent years have led to a revival of claims that aspects of criminality can be accounted for by genetic factors. Ellis (1990) looked to processes of natural selection operating on genetic evolution to explain some aspects of criminal behaviour. He has argued that some criminal activities, especially rape, assault, child abuse and property offences, are linked to powerful genetic forces. Nonetheless, he offers no proof of genetic connections with crime and criminal behaviour, merely presenting a hypothesis based on assumptions of inherent animal-like behaviour.

It has become increasingly apparent, however, that an inclination to contract many diseases is strongly affected by inheritance; and the particular genes related to particular diseases are currently being identified. There have been recent suggestions that insurance companies might wish to examine the genetic characteristics of potential clients. Geneticists have nevertheless been much more cautious in claiming that human behaviour is primarily an inherited characteristic – in short, that it is our genes that determine how we act. The discovery that some traits of personality can be explained by a genetic component (Jones, 1993) does, however, greatly strengthen the possibility that some criminal behaviour can be explained by a genetic susceptibility triggered by environmental factors. This point is revisited in Chapter 12.

Criminal body types

A further category of the biological variant of the predestined actor model has its roots directly in the Lombrosian tradition of concentrating on body type. Kretschmer (1946, originally 1921) identified four criminal body types. First, *asthenics* are lean and narrowly built, flat-chested and skinny with their ribs easily counted. Second, *athletics* have broad shoulders, deep chests, flat stomachs and powerful legs. Third, *pyknics* are of medium build with an inclination to be rotund with rounded shoulders, broad faces and short stubby hands. Fourth, *mixed types* are unclassifiable. Kretschmer argued that the asthenic and athletic builds are associated with schizophrenic personalities, while pyknics are manic-depressives.

Hooton (1939) conducted a detailed analysis of the measurements of more than 17,000 criminals and non-criminals. He concluded that criminals are organically inferior to other people, that low foreheads indicated inferiority, and that 'a depressed physical and social environment determines Negro and Negroid delinquency to a much greater extent than it does in the case of Whites' (Hooton, 1939, Vol. 1: 329). Hooton was widely condemned for the racist overtones of his work and his failure to recognise that the prisoners he studied represented only those who had been caught, convicted or imprisoned. Moreover, his control group appeared to be representative of no known population of humanity.

Sheldon (1949) produced the first modern systematic linking of body traits with criminal behaviour but was highly influenced by earlier work. He shifted attention from adults to offending male youths, studying 200 between 15 and 21 years of age in an attempt to link physique to temperament, intelligence and offending behaviour. Sheldon classified the physiques of the boys by measuring the degree to which they possessed a combination of three different body components. First, *endomorphs* tended to be soft, fat people. Second, *mesomorphs* were of muscular and athletic build. Third, *ectomorphs* had a skinny, flat and fragile physique. Sheldon concluded that most offenders tended towards mesomorphy and, moreover, because the youths came from parents who were offenders, the factors that produce criminal behaviour are inherited.

Glueck and Glueck (1950) conducted a comparative study of offenders and non-offenders and gave considerable support to Sheldon. They found that, as a group, the offenders were found to have narrower faces, wider chests, larger and broader waists and bigger forearms than upper arms than the non-offenders. Approximately 60 per cent of the offenders were found to be predominantly mesomorphic. The researchers, like their predecessors, failed nonetheless to establish whether the mesomorphs were offenders because of their build and disposition, or because their physique and dispositions are socially conceived as being associated with offenders. Or indeed whether a third set of factors associated with poverty and deprivation affected both their body build and offending behaviour.

Body-type theories can be criticised for ignoring different aspects of the interaction between a person's physical characteristics and their social circumstances. People from poorer backgrounds will tend to have a poorer diet and thus be small in stature. Young people in manual occupations are likely to acquire an athletic build. The over-representation of such people among convicted criminals may thus be explained by a variety of socio-cultural, rather than biological, factors.

Gibbons (1970) argues that the high proportion of mesomorphy among offenders is due to a process of social selection. The nature of their activities is such that deviants will be drawn from the more athletic members of that age group. Cortes and Gatti (1972), in contrast, propose that such arguments falsely accuse biological explanations of criminal behaviour of being more determinist than they actually are. They propose that as physical factors are essential to the social selection process, human behaviour has both biological and social causes. This point is revisited in Chapter 12.

Psychoses and brain injuries

This category of the biological variant of the predestined actor model addresses neurological conditions that supposedly *cause* criminal behaviour. There is little evidence, however, that brain injuries actually lead to criminal behaviour. There have been cases reported, but these are very rare, and studies suggest that the original personality and social background of the person are of greater significance. A brain injury might accentuate an underlying trend to aggression, however, if it occurs in a specific area of the brain.

There is some evidence of association between criminality and 'minimal brain dysfunction' (MPD). This is a condition that can lead to learning disabilities in school and thus – by various routes – to offending behaviour. There is little evidence, however, of neurological malfunction in these cases. The usual personality changes associated with brain injury are forgetfulness, impaired concentration and diminished spontaneity in thought.

There are some organic psychoses that are associated with brain lesions or malfunctions. First, *epidemic encephalitis* is a condition that was widespread among children in the 1920s and was often linked to destructiveness, impulsiveness, arson and abnormal sexual behaviour. Second, *senile dementia* is a general organically based deterioration of the personality that affects some old people and may be accompanied by arson, paranoid delusions and deviant sexual behaviour. Third, *Huntingdon's chorea* is an inherited disease involving brain decay – characterised by involuntary and disorganised movements, apathy and depression – that may result in vicious assaults in a fit of uncontrollable temper. Fourth, *brain tumours* – especially in the temporal lobe region – can activate the neural systems linked to aggressive behaviour that can result in outbursts of rage, violence and even murder. The surgical removal of the tumour reverses the condition. Fifth, much attention has been devoted in the criminological literature, from Lombroso onwards, towards *epilepsy,* particularly temporal lobe epilepsy. Some, but by no means all, victims of this illness do sometimes make violent assaults on people during and occasionally between seizures (Mark and Ervin, 1970).

There appears to be a relationship between violent and aggressive behaviour and malfunctions of the limbic system. The part of the brain that is concerned with mediating the expression of a broad range of emotional and vegetative behaviour such as hunger, pleasure, fear, sex and anger. Various studies have shown that it is possible by electrical stimulation of the brain, to induce aggressive behaviour in otherwise placid subjects (see Shah and Roth, 1974). Removing or burning out that part of the brain that appears to be responsible for aggression can also control aggression. It is also possible to electrically stimulate other parts of the brain to produce docility.

Stafford Clark and Taylor (1949 cited in Shah and Roth, 1974), in a study of unprovoked 'abnormal' killers found that 73 per cent had abnormal EEG readings and among 'clearly insane' murderers, the incidence was 86 per cent. EEG (electroencephalogram) is a record of the rhythmical waves of electrical potential occurring in the vertebrate brain, mainly in the central cortex. Other studies have also shown that EEG abnormalities are highest among aggressive psychopathic criminals and lowest among emotionally stable groups (see Mednick and Volavka, 1980; Volavka, 1987).

EEG abnormality is often associated with chromosomal abnormality. Thus, the majority of people who have an extra X or Y chromosome also have EEG abnormalities. Epileptics always have EEG abnormalities and so too, very frequently, do those with a psychiatric condition known as psychopathy. This condition is discussed more fully in the following chapter in addressing psychological explanations of crime and criminal behaviour. There are, however, three possible explanations of the link between EEG abnormality and psychopathy. First, psychopaths do not have the same levels of sensory perception as other people. Second, the condition may be associated with the malfunction of specific brain mechanisms, particularly those concerned with emotion. Third, the pattern of brainwaves is different in children and adults; thus what is normal for the child is abnormal for the adult.

It is this last possible explanation that has led to the development of the concept of EEG motivation, and it seems probable that this proceeds in parallel with psychological motivation. Much of the psychiatric abnormality shown in the behaviour disorders of early adult life can be related to emotional immaturity. Much of this tends to disappear as an individual passes into his or her 30s and 40s. It is among persons of this type that EEG abnormality is most commonly found.

There is undoubtedly a *correlation* between psychopathy and abnormal EEG. On the other hand, criminals diagnosed as psychopathic but with normal EEG patterns are quite common. At the same time there are many non-criminal people with bizarre EEG patterns. Moreover, anti-convulsant drugs that stabilise brain rhythms have no effect on psychopaths. EEG patterns are extremely difficult to interpret and quite often 'experts' disagree totally. It has not been possible therefore to produce the foundations of a general explanation of crime and criminal behaviour from studies of the brain and central nervous system. Hans Eysenck has attempted to develop a general theory based on the automatic nervous system. His work is nonetheless psychological and is discussed in the following chapter.

Biochemistry

There are five identifiable categories of biochemical explanations of crime and criminal behaviour: (i) sexual hormones; (ii) blood sugar levels; (iii) adrenaline sensitivity; (iv) allergies and diet; (v) substance abuse. We will consider each in turn.

(i) Sexual hormones

Glands such as the pituitary, adrenals, gonads, pancreas and thyroid produce hormones. They control, and are themselves controlled by, certain anatomical features that affect the thresholds for various types of responses and have extensive feedback loops with the central nervous system. Schlapp and Smith (1928) first suggested a causal relationship between hormones and criminal behaviour. They argued that either an excess or underproduction of hormones by the ductless glands could lead to emotional disturbance followed by criminal behaviour.

It has long been recognised that male animals – of most species – are more aggressive than females and this has been linked to the male sex hormone, testosterone (Rose, Bernstein, Gorden and Catlin, 1974; Keverne, Meller and Eberhart, 1982). The relationship between sex hormones and human behaviour appears more complex even though testosterone has been linked with aggressive crime such as murder and rape. In most men testosterone levels nonetheless probably do not significantly affect levels of aggression (Persky, Smith and Basu, 1971; Scarmella and Brown, 1978). Studies of violent male prisoners suggest that testosterone levels have had an effect on aggressive behaviour. However, these results were not as strong as expected from the studies of animals (Kreuz and Rose, 1972; Ehrenkranz, Bliss and Sheard, 1974).

Problematically, these studies of humans have not differentiated between different forms of aggression. Other studies have however sought to address these problems. Olwens (1987) conducted a study of young men with no marked criminal record and found a clear link between testosterone and both verbal and physical aggression. He further noticed a distinction between provoked and unprovoked aggressive behaviour. The former tended to be more verbal than physical and was in response to unfair or threatening behaviour by another person. The latter was violent, destructive and involved activities such as starting fights and making provocative comments. The relationship between testosterone and unprovoked violence was nevertheless found to be indirect and would depend on other factors such as how irritable the particular individual was. Schalling (1987) discovered that high testosterone levels in young males were associated with verbal aggression but not with actual physical aggression. This suggests a concern to protect their status by threats. Low-testosterone-level boys would tend not to protect their position, preferring to remain silent. Neither study suggests a direct link between testosterone and aggression, but in a provocative situation those with the highest levels of testosterone are more likely to resort to violence.

Ellis and Coontz (1990) note that the testosterone level peaks during puberty and the early 20s and this correlates with the highest crime rates. It is a finding that they claim provides persuasive evidence for a biological explanation of criminal behaviour and observe that it explains both aggressive and property crime. Sociological researchers, they argue, have failed to explain why it is that this distribution exists across all societies and cultures. There is, however, no evidence of a causal relationship between criminal behaviour and the level of testosterone. The link may be more tenuous with testosterone merely providing the environment necessary for aggressive behaviour to take place.

(ii) Blood sugar levels

Hypoglycaemia or low blood sugar levels – sometimes related to diabetes mellitus – may result in irritable, aggressive reactions, and may culminate in sexual offences, assaults and motiveless murder (see Shah and Roth, 1974). Shoenthaler (1982) conducted experiments where it was discovered that by lowering the daily sucrose intake of young offenders held in detention it was possible to reduce the level of their antisocial behaviour. A discussion of the effects of under-nutrition on the central nervous system and thus on aggression can be found in Smart (1981). Virkkunen (1987) has linked hypoglycaemia with other activities often defined as antisocial such as truancy, low verbal IQ, tattooing and stealing from home during childhood. Moreover, hypoglycaemia has been linked with alcohol abuse. If alcohol is drunk regularly and in large quantities, the ethanol produced can induce hypoglycaemia and increase aggression (Clapham, 1989).

(iii) Adrenaline sensitivity

The relationship between adrenaline and aggressive behaviour is a similar area of study to that involving testosterone. Each involves the relationship between a hormonal level and aggressive antisocial behaviour. Schachter (cited in Shah and Roth, 1974) found that injections of adrenaline made no difference to the behaviour of normal prisoners but a great difference to psychopaths. Hare (1982) found that when threatened with pain, criminals exhibit fewer signs of stress than other people. Mednick, Pollock, Volavka and Gabrielli (1982) discovered that not only do certain – particularly violent – criminals take stronger stimuli to arouse them, but also once they are in a stressed state they recover more slowly to their normal levels than do non-criminals. Eysenck (1959) had offered a logical explanation for this relationship some years previously. An individual with low stress levels is easily bored, it was argued, becomes quickly disinterested in things, and craves exciting experiences. Thus, for such individuals normal stressful situations are not disturbing. They are exciting and enjoyable, something to be savoured and sought after.

Baldwin (1990) suggests that the link between age and crime rates can be partially explained by considering arousal rates. He observes firstly that children quickly become used to stimuli that had previously excited them and thus seek ever more thrilling inputs. The stimulus received from criminal-type activities nonetheless declines with age, as does the level of physical fitness, strength and agility required performing many such activities. Baldwin interestingly explains both the learning of criminal behaviour and its subsequent decline in terms of stimuli in the environment. The question is then posed as to whether the production of adrenaline is biologically or socially dictated.

(iv) Allergies and diet

There have been suggested links between irritability and aggression that may lead individuals in some circumstances to commit criminal assault, and allergic reactions to such things as pollen, inhalants, drugs and food. Research on the criminological implications of allergies continues but studies indicate two main reactions in these patients. First, *emotional immaturity* is characterised by temper tantrums, screaming episodes, whining and impatience, while, second, *antisocial behaviour* is characterised by sulkiness and cruelty.

More recent research has attempted to bring together earlier work on blood sugar levels, allergies and other biochemical imbalances. The basic premise of the theory of 'biochemical individuality' is that each person has an absolutely unique internal biochemistry. We all vary in our daily need for each of the 40-odd nutrients – minerals, vitamins, carbohydrates, etc – required to stay alive and healthy. From this idea flows the concept of 'orthomolecular medicine' that proposes that many diseases are preventable and treatable by the proper diagnosis, vitamin supplementation and avoidance of substances that would bring on an illness or preclude a cure. Prinz, Roberts and Hantman (1980) have proposed that some foods, and in particular certain additives, have effects that may lead to hyperactivity and even criminality; while a low level of cholesterol has often been linked with hypoglycaemia, particularly when alcohol use has been involved (see Virkkunen, 1987).

At first sight, it might appear absurd to link criminal behaviour with vitamin deficiency. The evidence for an active role for biochemical disturbance in some offences of violence is, however, too great to be ignored. Indeed, some quite impressive results have been obtained in the orthomolecular treatment of some mental disorders. For example, Vitamin B3 (niacin) has been used successfully to treat some forms of schizophrenia (see Lesser, 1980; Pihl, 1982; Raloff, 1983). Moreover, there is some evidence that addiction to both drugs and alcohol may be related to unmet biochemical individual needs.

(v) Substance abuse

Substance abuse is usually brought about by the intake of drugs in the widest sense. Some of these drugs are legal and freely available such as alcohol, which is drunk and glues and lighter fluids which are inhaled. The medical profession prescribes some such as barbiturates, while others – such as cannabis, amphetamines, LSD, MDA or 'Ecstasy', opiates (usually cocaine or heroin) – are only available illegally. Alcohol is more significant for criminality than other drugs, partly because it is legal and its extremely common usage makes it readily available. It has long been associated with antisocial activity, crimes and criminality. Saunders (1984) calculated that alcohol was a significant factor in about 1,000 arrests per day or over 350,000 a year. Flanzer (1981) estimated that 80 per cent of all cases of family violence in the USA involved the consumption of alcohol, while De Luca (1981) estimated that almost a third of the cases of violence against children in the home were alcohol-related. More general studies have discovered a strong link between alcohol and general levels of violence (Collins, 1988; Fagan, 1990).

Drug taking does not have as long an association with criminal behaviour as alcohol consumption. It was only at the beginning of the twentieth century that drugs were labelled as a major social problem and came to be regulated. Drugs are chemicals and once taken alter the chemical balance of the body and brain. This can affect behaviour. The way that behaviour is altered varies according to the type and quantity of the drug taken (see Fishbein and Pease, 1990; Pihl and Peterson, 1993). The biological effects of cannabis and opiates such as heroin tend to reduce aggressive hostile tendencies, while cocaine and its derivative crack are more closely associated with violence. Interestingly, some see both alcohol and drug misuse as intrinsically wrong and thus in need of punishment. Others see them as social and personal problems requiring understanding and treatment. The first solution has generally been applied in the case of (illegal) drugs, while the second has tended to be more acceptable in the case of (legal) alcohol.

Treating the offender

Central to the biological variant of the predestined actor model is the notion that criminality arises from some physical disorder within the individual offender. It is therefore argued that by following a course of treatment, individuals can be cured of the predisposing condition that causes their criminality. We will now briefly consider three forms of individualised treatment: surgical intervention, chemotherapy and electro-control.

Surgical intervention

Surgical intervention often means pre-frontal leucotomy, a technique that severs the connection between the frontal lobes and the thalamus. It causes some degree of character change – mainly a reduced anxiety level – and has been used with some success to treat the paranoid and paraphrenic types of schizophrenia, but has now been largely replaced by neuroleptic drugs. It has also been used on 'sexually motivated' and 'spontaneously violent' criminals. Castration has been used on sex offenders in Denmark and the USA with indecisive results. Stürup in Denmark claimed 'acceptable' results with sex offenders, but Mueller (1972 cited in Menard and Morse, 1984) tells of a rapist in California who – following castration – turned from rape to child molesting and murder.

Chemotherapy

Chemotherapy involves the use of drugs in treatment programmes and also for control purposes. Some drugs are used for the treatment of specific behaviour patterns; for example antabuse has been used in the treatment of alcoholics, cyclozocine for heroin addicts (both are blocking agents), benperidol (cyproterone acetate), an anti-libidinal drug, and stilboestrol (a female hormone) for sex offenders.

Benperidol and stilboestrol constitute 'chemical castration' and their use on prisoners in the UK and USA instigated widespread intense debate. Proponents insist that these only be used on people who freely offer their services as volunteers. There are, however, considerable reservations as to whether one can ever find 'free volunteers' in prison. These drugs have unpleasant side effects. For example, stilboestrol causes atrophy of the genitals, female breast development, nausea, feminisation, obesity and serious psychiatric disorders.

Some drugs are used exclusively for control purposes. Mace and CS gas are routinely used for riot control. Sedatives and tranquillisers are frequently used to keep potentially troublesome prisoners calm. In nineteenth-century prisons opium was used for this purpose and in the contemporary UK, valium, librium and largactil are generally used. In the USA a heavy tranquilliser (prolixin) is used. This reduces hostility, anxiety, agitation and hyperactivity, often producing a zombie-like effect. It has some other unpleasant side effects; according to the manufacturers these include automatic reactions, blurred vision, bladder paralysis, glaucoma, faecal impaction, techychardia, liver damage, skin disorders and death. It is extensively used in prisons for the sole purpose of keeping troublemakers quiet.

Electro-control

Electro-control is still a little futuristic since the research programme is still under way in the USA. The idea is to plant a telemetric device on, or in, the prisoner. This will transmit data about the physical state of the subject to a central computer programmed to assess from the information the mental state of the subject. If the indications are that he or she is about to commit an offence an impulse is sent to a receiver planted in the brain that has the potential to cause pain, paralysis or even death. These devices could enable a dangerous offender to be safely released from prison. The two main obstacles to the implementation of such schemes have been the limited range of the equipment and ethical concerns raised by civil liberty groups.

Conclusions

Each of the attempts to explain crime and criminal behaviour discussed in this chapter follows directly in the biological predestined actor model tradition established by Lombroso. Each theory has sought explanations in the measurable, organic part of individuals, their bodies and their brains. It is certainly impossible to deny that some of these studies really do explain the criminality of a very small minority of offenders. Closer investigation of individual cases, however, demonstrates that social and environmental factors have been equally important. Indeed, it is important to note that most of the researchers, from Lombroso onwards, came to increasingly recognise that reality.

The early biological positivists had proposed that discoveries about the natural world – and natural laws – would find a counterpart within human behaviour. The criminological emphasis of this approach has thus been on the scientist as the detached objective neutral observer who has the task of identifying natural laws that regulate criminal behaviour. Once these natural laws have been discovered, a reduction in offending behaviour is seen as possible by the use of treatment programmes aimed at ameliorating or eliminating the causes of that behaviour. It has also been proposed that investigations should be extended into the lives of individuals who are deemed to be 'at risk' of offending in order that treatment might be instigated and many offences be prevented before they occur. In short, criminal behaviour is perceived to be a sickness – an inherently problematic analysis – that has led to treatments that are intrusive, in some cases unethical, and on occasion with horrendous wider implications.

The early biological positivists had replaced the rational calculating individual of the rational actor model with an organism subject to the forces of biological heredity and impulsive behaviour beyond conscious control. From this same source, however, came Social Darwinism, a mode of thought based on the notion that *The Origin of the Species* offered a new evolutionary and scientific basis for the social sciences as well as for biology. It was an idea highly compatible with interests in the wider world and was soon used to give 'scientific' legitimacy to an old idea, namely that the capacity for rational judgement, moral behaviour and, above all, business success was not equally distributed among the various races and divisions of humanity.

Quite prominent figures of late-nineteenth-century social science began to argue that African, Indians, the 'negroes' of North American, paupers, criminals and even women had inherited smaller brains and a reduced capacity for rational thought and moral conduct than everyone else. Such ideas were particularly appealing in the USA, which was experiencing an influx of immigrants of diverse ethnic background and where people were particularly ready to equate the biological processes of natural selection with the competition of an unrestricted market. In both Britain and the USA programmes of selective breeding were proposed to encourage progress or to prevent civilisation from de-generating (Jones, 1980). It was a view that was to remain popular into the early decades of the twentieth century and was to obtain support from the 'science' of *eugenics* and its supporters who were concerned with 'improving' the genetic selection of the human race. The biological variant of the predestined actor model of crime and criminal behaviour was highly compatible with this viewpoint. Goring (1913) was convinced that criminality was passed down through inherited genes and in order to reduce crime, recommended that people with such characteristics should not be allowed to reproduce. The more recent and rigorous research in search of the 'criminal gene' has rather similar implications.

In 1994 a new Centre for Social, Genetic and Development Psychiatry was opened at the Maudsley Hospital in south London to examine what role genetic structure plays in determining patterns of behaviour, including crime (Muncie, 1999). The following year a major conference was held behind closed doors to discuss the possibility of isolating a criminal gene – the basis of which rested on the study of twins and adoptees (Ciba Foundation, 1996). Moreover, one of the best-selling social science books of the 1990s, *The Bell Curve* (Herrnstein and Murray, 1994) claimed that black people and Latinos are over-represented among the ranks of the poor in the USA because they are less intelligent. The suggestion is that inherited genes mainly determine IQ and that people with low IQ are more likely to commit crime because they lack foresight and are unable to distinguish right from wrong. Muncie (1999) observes that such theories continue to be attractive, at least to some, because they seem to provide scientific evidence that clearly differentiates us from 'them', an out-group which we feel legitimately entitled to target, outlaw and in the final instance, eradicate. It is an argument that Einstadter and Henry (1995) note to be characteristic of totalitarian regimes whether they are Nazi Germany, the former USSR, and by extension to the more recent forced therapy programmes in the USA.

Morrison (1995) observes that the Holocaust – the systematic extermination of over six million people by Nazi Germany during the Second World War – was undoubtedly the crime of the twentieth century, yet it had provided such a great problem for criminology that it had never been mentioned in any textbook. For he observes the essential question to be whether the Holocaust is at odds with modernity or simply the logical consequence of a project of which we might note the biological variant of the predestined actor model of crime and criminal behaviour to simply be a component. There is certainly strong available evidence to support the latter proposition. The Jewish social theorist Hannah Arendt argues that the Holocaust destroyed the semblance of any belief that evil must be motivated by evil and conducted by evil people. She observes that, 'the sad truth of the matter is that most evil is done by people who never made up their mind to be either good or bad' (Arendt, 197: 438). Morrison (1995: 203) observes that this horrendous and unsurpassable crime can only be explained by 'the weakness of individual judgement in the face of reason, in the face of the claims of organisation, in the face of claims of the normal, in the face of claims for progress... '.

The outcome was to destroy our belief in the right of experts – whether they are scientists, social engineers or managerial politicians – to think for us unquestioned. It was no longer possible to take the notion of modernist civilisation for granted or to accept a unilinear image of social progress in human affairs. The biological variant of the predestined actor model of crime and criminal behaviour had led to the plausibility of ideas such as sterilisation, genetic selection and even death for the biologically untreatable. Such work was now unpalatable for many in the context of the mid-twentieth century experience of mass systematic extermination in death camps of outsider groups whether based on their ethnicity (in the case of the Jews, Slavs and Gypsies), their sexuality (in the case of homosexuals), their health (in the case of the disabled and seriously ill) or their behaviour (in the case of whole categories of criminals).

In more recent years there has been a sustained campaign to rehabilitate biological theories with the recognition that physical and social environment factors are more closely linked. There remain however serious ethical implications surrounding possible treatment regimes. These issues are revisited in Chapter 12.

Suggested further reading

Biological positivism is an extremely wide subject area and there are thus many relevant texts. Students are therefore advised to use the references in the text as a guide to specific interests. Ferri, *Three Lectures by Enrico Ferri* (1968) is nonetheless a timeless original still worth considering as a general introduction to early criminological positivism *per se*, while Shah and Roth, 'Biological and Psychophysiological Factors in Criminality' (1974) provide an overview of some of the crucial earlier research in this tradition. For some more recent and very different examples of biological positivism see Herrnstein and Murray, *The Bell Curve* (1994) from a right realist perspective, and Jones, *The Language of the Genes* (1993) from an eminent contemporary geneticist. For a discussion of the wider implications of biological positivism in modern society see Bauman, *Modernity and the Holocaust* (1989), Morrison, *Theoretical Criminology* (1995) and Taylor *et al*, *The New Criminology* (1973) who provide very different but essential accounts.

Chapter 6

Psychological theories

We saw in the previous chapter that proponents of the biological variants of the predestined actor model argue that criminal behaviour is the outcome of factors internal to the physical body of the individual human being that predisposes that person to criminality. For psychological positivists, the search for the causes of crime is directed to the mind and thus we encounter the notion of the 'criminal mind'. For proponents of this perspective, there are patterns of reasoning and behaviour that are specific to offenders and these remain constant regardless of their different social experiences.

There are three broad categories of psychological theories of crimes and we will examine each in turn. It will be seen that the first two groupings – psychodynamic and behavioural learning theories – are firmly rooted in the predestined actor tradition. The third group – cognitive learning theories – reject much of that tradition by incorporating notions of creative thinking and thus choice, in many ways more akin to the rational actor model.

Psychodynamic theories

Psychodynamic explanations of crime and criminal behaviour have their origins in the extremely influential work of Sigmund Freud (1856–1939). His assertion that sexuality is present from birth and has a subsequent course of development is the fundamental basis of psychoanalysis and one that has aroused a great deal of controversy. Freud originally proposed that experiences of sexual seduction in childhood are the basis of all neurosis. Subsequently, he changed his mind. The seductions had not actually taken place but were fantasies. It is this notion of the repressed fantasy that is the core tenet of the psycho-analytic tradition.

Within, the psychoanalytical model, developed by Freud, the human personality has three sets of interacting forces. First, there is the *id*, which are the primitive biological drives. Secondly, there is the superego – or conscience – that operates in the unconsciousness but is comprised of values that are internalised through a person's early interactions, in particular with their parents. Third, there is the ego or the conscious personality. This has the task of balancing the demands of the id against the inhibitions imposed by the superego, as a person responds to external influences (Freud, 1927).

Freud himself proposed two different models of criminal behaviour. The first views certain forms of criminal activity – for example arson, shoplifting and some sexual offences – essentially to reflect a state of mental disturbance or illness. His theory of psychosexual development proposes a number of complex stages of psychic development that may easily be disrupted, leading to neuroses or severe difficulties in adults. Crucially, a disturbance at one or more of these stages in childhood can lead to criminal behaviour in later life.

Of essential importance to the psychosexual development of the child is the influence of the parents. And importantly many of these influences are unconscious. Neither parents nor children are in fact aware of how they are influencing each other. This is an important recognition. For, in a sense, it reduces the responsibility of the parents for producing children that offend.

The second model of criminal behaviour proposes that offenders possess a 'weak conscience'. Hence, for Freud, the development of the conscience is of fundamental importance in the upbringing of the child. A sense of morality is closely linked to guilt, and those possessing the greatest degree of unconscious 'guilt' are likely to be those with the strictest consciences. Such people are therefore the most unlikely to engage in criminal behaviour.

Guilt is something that results *not* from committing crimes, but rather from a deeply embedded feeling that develops in childhood, the out-come of the way in which the parents respond to the child's trans-gressions. It is an approach that led to a proliferation of tests attempting to measure conscience or levels of guilt, with the belief that this would allow a prediction of whether the child would later become a criminal.

The Freudian approach is firmly embedded in the predestined actor model of crime and criminal behaviour. Unconscious conflicts or tensions *determine* all actions. The purpose of the conscious (ego) is to resolve these tensions by finding ways of satisfying the basic inner urges by engaging in activities sanctioned by society. The later Freudian tradition was more concerned with elaborating the development of the ego more specifically.

Aichhorn (1925) argued that at birth a child has certain instinctive drives that demand satisfaction. The child is unaware of, and obviously unaffected by, the norms of society around it. It is thus in an 'asocial state' and the task is to bring it into a social state. When the child's development is ineffective he or she remains asocial. If the instinctive drives are not acted out they become suppressed and the child is in a state of 'latent delinquency'. Given outside provocation, this latent delinquency could be translated into actual offending behaviour.

Aichhorn concluded that many of the offenders with whom he had worked had underdeveloped consciences. This was the result of the absence of an intimate attachment with their parents while children. The proposed solution was to locate such children and place them in a happy environment where they could identify with adults in a way they had previously not experienced. The aim of such identification was to develop the child's superego.

Aichhorn identified two further categories of criminal. First, there were those with fully developed consciences but who had identified with parents who were criminals themselves. Second, there were those who had been allowed to do whatever they liked by over-indulgent parents.

Healy and Bronner (1935) conducted a study of 105 pairs of brothers where one was a persistent offender and the other a non-offender. It was found that only 19 of the offenders and 30 of the non-offenders had experienced good quality family conditions. These findings suggest that circumstances within a household may be favourable for one child but not the sibling. It was proposed that the latter had not made an emotional attachment to a 'good parent', hence impeding the development of a superego.

Healy and Bronner also found that siblings exposed to similar unfavourable circumstances might react differently. One may become an offender while others do not. The proposed explanation was that offenders are more emotionally disturbed and express their frustrated needs through deviant activities. The non-offender's thwarted needs were, on the other hand, channelled into other socially accepted activities. Healy and Bronner emphasised that the growth and effect of conscience are complicated matters that vary between individuals, Thus, one might condemn stealing but condone lying, or vice versa.

Friedlander (1949) argued that some children develop antisocial behaviour or a faulty character that leave them prone to deviant behaviour. Redl and Wineman (1951) similarly argued that some children develop a delinquent ego. The outcome is a hostile attitude towards authority because the child has not developed a good ego and superego.

✳ John Bowlby (1952) influentially argued that offending behaviour takes place when a child has not enjoyed a close and continuous relationship with its mother during its formative years. He studied 44 juveniles convicted of stealing and referred to the child guidance clinic where he worked. Bowlby compared them with a control group of children – matched for age and intelligence – which had been referred to the same clinic, but not in connection with offending behaviour. However, no attempt was made to check for the presence of criminal elements, therefore exposing the study to criticism on methodological grounds (Morgan, 1975).

Bowlby found that 17 of those with convictions for stealing had been separated from their mothers for extended periods before the age of five, in contrast to only two of the control group. Fourteen of the convicted group were found to be 'affectionless characters', persons deemed to have difficulty in forming close personal relationships – while none of the controls were thus labelled.

Maternal deprivation theory was to have a major and lasting influence on the training of social workers (Morgan, 1975), while other researchers have sought to test it empirically. Their findings have tended to suggest that the separation of a child from its mother is not, in itself, significant in predicting criminal behaviour. Andry (1957) and Grygier (1969) both indicated a need to take account of the roles of both parents. Naess (1959, 1962) found that offenders were no more likely to have been separated from their mothers than were non-offenders. Little (1965) found that 80 per cent of a sample of boys who had received custodial sentences had been separated from at least one parent for varying periods. In fact, separations from the father were found to be more common. Wootton (1959, 1962) argues that there is no evidence that any effects of separation of its child from its mother will be irreversible. She notes that while only a small proportion of offenders may be affected in this way, there is also a lack of information about the extent of maternal deprivation among non-offenders in general. Rutter (1981), in one of the most comprehensive examinations of the maternal deprivation thesis, considers the stability of the child/mother relationship to be more important than the absence of breaks. He proposes that a small number of substitutes can carry out mothering functions, without adverse effect, provided that such care is of good quality. The crucial issue is considered to be the quality of child-rearing practices.

Glueck and Glueck (1950) found that the fathers of offenders provided discipline that was generally lax and inconsistent. The use of physical punishment by both parents was found to be common and the giving of praise rare. Parents of non-offenders were, however, found to use physical punishment more sparingly and were more consistent in their use of discipline. McCord, McCord and Zola (1959) agreed with the Gluecks that the consistency of discipline was more important than the degree of strictness. Bandura and Walters (1959) found that the fathers of aggressive boys are more likely to punish such behaviour in the home while approving of it outside. They also used physical punishments more than the fathers of their control group.

Hoffman and Saltzstein (1967) identified and categorised three types of child-rearing techniques. First, *power assertion* was found to involve the parental use of – or threats to use – physical punishment and/or the withdrawal of material privileges. Second, *love withdrawal* is where the parent withdraws – or threatens to withdraw – affection from the child, for example, by paying no attention to it. Third, *induction* entails letting the child know how its actions have affected the parent, thus encouraging a sympathetic or empathetic response. Essentially, the first technique primarily relies on the instillation of fear, while the other two depend on the fostering of guilt feelings in the child.

Hoffman and Saltzstein offer five explanations for the association to be found between moral development and the use of child-rearing techniques. First, an open display of anger and aggression by a parent when disciplining a child increases the dependence of the latter on external control. Punishment connected with power assertion dissolves both the anger of the parent and the guilt of the child more rapidly. Second, love withdrawal and induction, and the anxiety associated with them, has a longer-lasting effect so that the development of internal controls are more likely. Third, where love withdrawal is used, the punishment ends when the child confesses or makes reparation. This is referred to as engaging in a corrective act. In the case of physical punishment, however, there is likely to be a lapse of time between it being carried out and the child performing a corrective act. Fourth, withholding love intensifies the resolve of the child to behave in an approved manner in order to retain love. Fifth, the use of induction is particularly effective in enabling the child to examine and correct the behaviour that has been disapproved of.

Hoffman and Saltzstein propose that it is people who have been raised through the use of love withdrawal or induction techniques that are less likely to engage in offending behaviour. This is because of the greater effect of internalised controls. People raised on the power assertion method depend on the threat of external punishment to control their behaviour and thus will only remain controlled as long as that risk is present, certain and sufficiently intense. It is only internal controls that are likely to be ever-present.

A number of studies have gone beyond child-rearing practices to assess the relevance of more general features of the family unit in the causation of criminal behaviour. Some of these conducted in both the USA and the UK have suggested that a 'broken home', where one of the birth parents is not present, may be a factor in the development of offending behaviour.

Glueck and Glueck (1950) measured the frequency of broken homes among their samples and found that 60 per cent of the offenders came from such a home, compared with only 34 per cent of the controls. In Britain, Burt (1945) and Mannheim (1948) also found a high proportion of offenders came from such a home. Others point to the reality that the 'broken home' cannot be considered a homogenous category (Bowlby, 1952; Mannheim, 1955; Tappan, 1960). A range of different factors needs to be considered. Nye (1958) and Gibbens (1963) note that offending behaviour is more likely to occur among children from intact but unhappy homes.

While West (1969) echoed the observations of Wootton (1959) about the difficulties of defining a broken home, his study with Farrington (1973) found that about twice as many offenders – compared with controls – came from homes broken by parental separation before the child was ten years old. Comparing children from a home broken by separation with those homes broken by the death of a parent, more children from the former were found to be offenders. Moreover, 20 per cent of the former group became recidivists, whereas none of those from the second group did.

Monahan (1957) suggested that broken homes were found far more among black than white offenders. Pitts (1986) claimed a link between criminality and homelessness and found that African Caribbean youths tend to become homeless more than their white counterparts. Chilton and Markle (1972) had previously observed, however, that the rate of family breakdown is in general much higher in the case of black than white families, and this may explain why it is that more black young offenders come from broken homes.

Two more recent studies conducted in the UK have reported that broken homes and early separation predicted convictions up to age 33 where the separation occurred before age five (Kolvin, Miller, Scott,

Gatzanis and Fleeting, 1990), and that it predicted convictions and self-reported offending behaviour (Farringdon, 1992). Morash and Rucker (1989) nonetheless found that although it was single-parent families who had children with the highest rates of deviancy, these were also the lowest-income families. Thus, the nature of the problem – broken home, parental supervision, low income – was unclear. These possible explanations of crime and criminal behaviour are revisited in more detail in later chapters.

Behavioural learning theories

The second category of psychological explanations of crime and criminal behaviour – behavioural learning theories – have their origins in the work of Ivan Petrovich Pavlov and B.F. Skinner. Pavlov had famously studied the processes involved in very simple, automatic animal behaviours, for example, salivation in the presence of food. He found that these responses that occur spontaneously to the natural (or *unconditioned*) stimulus, could be made to happen (*conditioned*) to a stimulus that was previously neutral, for example, a light. If you consistently turn the light on just before feeding the animal, then eventually the animal will salivate when the light comes on, even though no food is present. This conditioning can of course be undone: if you continue to present the light without the food, eventually the animal will stop salivating to it. This contrary process is called *extinction*.

To some extent the conditioning process is specific to the exact stimulus presented but it can also generalise to other similar stimuli. If the animal has been conditioned to salivate to a red light, for example, it would salivate slightly if a blue light is turned on. However, you could train it to salivate *only* to the red light, by never rewarding it with food when presented with the blue light. For behaviourists, the notion of differential conditioning is a key one for understanding how learning works.

Pavlov's work was carried out on automatic behaviours occurring in response to stimuli. B.F. Skinner extended the same principle to active learning, where the animal has to *do* something in order to obtain a reward or avoid punishment. Much the same principle applies. The occurrence of the desired behaviour is increased by positive reinforcement and eventually extinguished by non-reinforcement.

Learned behaviours are much more resistant to extinction if the reinforcement has only occasionally been used during learning. This makes sense. If you put money in a ticket machine and no ticket comes out, you stop using the machine. On the other hand, many people put money in gaming machines even though they pay out prizes infrequently.

The behaviour can be differentially conditioned so that it occurs in response to one stimulus and not another. Indeed, in a sense all *operant conditioning* – as this type of learning is called – is differential conditioning. The animal learns to produce certain behaviours and not others, by the fact that only these receive reinforcement.

One further process has to be considered in order to explain the behaviour of the animals in conditioning experiments. If learning really happened as described, then the excitation produced by reinforcement would continue to build up over repeated trials, and a rat, for example, would continually press a bar for food, more and more frequently, until it died of exhaustion. What actually happens is that responses to the stimulus become *less* frequent as it is repeated, eventually stopping altogether, but start again at their old level if there is a break between presentations. To explain this phenomenon, behavioural learning theorists have presumed a 'quantity' of inhibition that builds up as the response is repeated, until it exceeds the level of excitation and stops the responses occurring. It dies down when the animal is not responding, leaving the level of excitation unchanged and so the response recommences.

It is Hans Eysenck who has sought to build a *general* theory that explains all crime and criminal behaviour based on the psychological concept of conditioning. Central to his theory is the notion of the human conscience which he considers to be a conditioned reflex. We have seen above that the Freudians have been interested in the notion of conscience but Eysenck viewed the concept very differently.

Eysenck's theory is not easy to compartmentalise. He argues from the biological predestined actor perspective that individuals are genetically endowed with certain learning abilities that are conditioned by stimuli in the environment. At the same time, he accepts the rational actor model premise that crime can be a natural and rational choice activity where individuals maximise pleasure and minimise pain. People are said to learn the rules and norms of society through the development of a conscience. This is acquired through learning what happens when you take part in certain activities. In short, the virtuous receive rewards while the deviant is punished.

Eysenck describes three dimensions of personality: *extroversion*, which has two different components, impulsiveness and sociability and which are partly independent of each other; *neuroticism*, and *psychoticism*. Each dimension takes the form of a continuum that runs from high to low. Low extroversion is sometimes termed introversion. In the case of neuroticism, a person with a high score would be regarded as neurotic and someone with a low score, stable. Scores are usually obtained by the administration of a personality questionnaire of which there are several versions. It is usual to abbreviate the descriptions of a person's score, for example, high N (neuroticism), high E (extroversion), and high P (psychoticism).

Each of these personality dimensions has distinct characteristics. Someone with a high E score would be outgoing and sociable, optimistic and impulsive. A high N person is anxious, moody and highly sensitive, while those with low scores on these continuums present the very opposite of these traits. Insensitivity to others, a liking for solitude, sensation seeking and lack of regard for danger have been linked with psychoticism (Eysenck, 1970). Feldman (1977) observes a similarity between this description of psychoticism and antisocial personality disorder or psychopathy discussed later in this section.

Eysenck (1977) argues that various combinations of the different personality dimensions within an individual affects their ability to learn not to offend, and consequently the level of offending. Someone with a high E and a high N score – a neurotic extrovert – will not condition well. A low E and N score – a stable introvert – is the most effectively conditioned. Stable extroverts and neurotic introverts come somewhere between the two extremes in terms of conditioning.

Various researchers have sought to test Eysenck's theory. Little (1963) compared the scores for convicted young offenders on the extroversion and neuroticism dimensions with those for non-offenders. He found no difference in relation to extroversion but the offenders scored higher on the neuroticism scale. Neither dimension appeared to be related to repeat offending. Hoghughi and Forrest (1970) compared scores for neuroticism and extroversion between a sample of convicted youths and a control group of supposedly non-offenders, or at least those with no convictions. The offenders were rated higher on the neuroticism scale but were found to be less extroverted than their controls. A finding that of course could be explained by the very real possibility that it is the very experience of detention that could make a young person neurotic.

Hans and Sybil Eysenck (1970) tested 178 incarcerated young offenders on all three personality dimensions and followed up this research on their release. They found that 122 had been reconvicted and all of these scored significantly higher in relation to extroversion than the others. Allsopp and Feldman (1975) conducted a self-report study and found a significant and positive association between scores for E, N and P levels of antisocial behaviour among girls between 11 and 15 years of age. The strongest association was found in relation to psychoticism. Their study of schoolboys conducted the following year reached similar conclusions (Allsop and Feldman, 1976).

Less research has been conducted in relation to adult criminals. However, where E and N scores for prisoners have been compared with those for non-prisoners, the former receive higher scores for neuroticism, and repeat offenders have been found to be more neurotic than first offenders. Little evidence has been found, however, to suggest that adult criminals are more extrovert than non-criminals (Feldman, 1977). Eysenck nevertheless responds to his critics by pointing out that extroversion has two components, sociability and impulsiveness. He proposes that it is impulsiveness that is associated with criminal behaviour; sociability is of less significance (Eysenck, 1970). Many personality tests simply provide a score for extroversion that combines those for the two components. Thus, a person who is highly impulsive but very unsociable will receive an E score midway on the personality continuum.

The association between psychoticism and criminal behaviour has been the subject of very little research. Smith and Smith (1977) and McEwan (1983) found a positive relationship between psychoticism and repeat offending. However, the work of Allsop and Feldman (1975, 1976) and McGurk and McDougall (1981) suggests that combinations or clusters of scores for the three dimensions are more important than scores for individual dimensions.

Research has been conducted in order to test for a relationship between personality types and offence type. Hindelang and Weis (1972) found that with minor offences, such as vandalism and traffic offences, the descending order of offending was as they had predicted. Thus, high E plus high N, high E and low N or low E and high N, then low E and low N. However, this was found to be not true of offences involving theft or aggression. Eysenck, Rust and Eysenck 1977) found that thieves or violent offenders had lower N scores than other groups, conmen had lower P scores, and there was no variation for E scores. McEwan and Knowles (1984) simply found no association between offence type and personality cluster.

There seems to be considerable uncertainty and ambiguity about the validity and veracity of Eysenck's theory. Farrington (1994) nonetheless suggests that this approach seems to at least identify a distinct link between offending and impulsiveness, but he found no significant links with personality.

Antisocial personality disorder appears to be a relatively recent term, and interchangeable with that of psychopathy. There are various and not always consistent definitions of this condition but in general these emphasise such traits as an incapacity for loyalty, selfishness, irresponsibility, impulsiveness, inability to feel guilt and failure to learn from experience. One feature common to all descriptions is a lack of empathy or affection (Blackburn and Maybury, 1985). The American Psychiatric Association (1968) had proposed that a person should be diagnosed as having 'antisocial personality disorder' when the above characteristics are 'inflexible, maladaptive, and persistent, and cause significant functional impairment or subjective distress'. Explanations are nonetheless many and varied.

McCord and McCord (1964) had suggested a lack of parental affection to be one of the key contributory factors. Robins (1966) found that children who behaved in a psychopathic manner were more likely to have fathers who were psychopathic or alcoholics themselves. On the other hand, Cleckley (1964) found that many of his psychopathic patients came from a happy and supportive family background. Indeed, Hare (1970) observes that most people from a disturbed background do not develop antisocial personality disorder.

Some researchers have studied the functioning of the central nervous system by using the electroencephalogram (EEG) that tests for abnormalities in the electrical activity of the brain in psychopaths. Syndulko (1978) suggested that irregularities are frequently shown in EEG testing of those with antisocial personality disorder. Hare and Jutari (1986) found, however, that the EEGs of psychopaths were normal while they were active, but abnormal while they were resting.

Other studies have examined the functioning of the automatic nervous system (ANS) in those diagnosed as having antisocial personality disorder. The level of activity in the ANS is assessed by measuring the conductivity of the skin (electrodermal reactivity) and the level of cardiac reactivity. Hare and Jutari (1983) found that when psychopaths are resting their level of electrodermal reactivity is exceptionally low. Hollin (1989) suggests that fast heart rate may be a sign that the psychopath is lowering the level of cortical arousal by 'gating out' the sensory input related to unpleasant situational stimuli.

Eysenck (1963) had found that those diagnosed with antisocial personality disorder are mostly extroverted. This suggests the possible relevance of the personality characteristics of psychopaths in explaining their antisocial behaviour. Extroverts are said to be more difficult to socialise because of difficulties in learning. This might therefore apply to psychopaths and their difficulties may have a physiological foundation. If this is the case, then we might assume that psychopaths will be very poor at learning to avoid the unpleasant stimuli associated with particular acts. Hollin (1989) observes that the findings from such studies vary according to the type of unpleasant stimulus used. When poor performance was met with physical pain or by disapproval, psychopaths obtained worse results than controls. Psychopaths were none-theless better learners when the consequences were a financial penalty.

Some studies have examined the responsiveness of psychopaths to reward learning where correct responses are rewarded by social approval. The findings are mixed but there is no evidence that psychopaths are less amenable than other people to reward learning (Feldman, 1977).

Feldman (1977) observes that the subjects of antisocial personality disorder research may be unrepresentative, merely being those who have been brought to the attention of the authorities. Psychopathic behaviours may be extremely widespread and psychopaths might well be found in legitimate occupations such as business, medicine and psychiatry (Cleckley, 1976). It is only when they engage in proscribed activities that the individuals will come to the attention of the authorities. Nevertheless, considering the findings of the different types of learning studies, there is some evidence that psychopaths may be undersocialised because of the way they learn. It is also possible that these difficulties arise from physiological factors.

Vold, Bernard and Snipes (1998) suggest that the term 'psychopath' is simply a useful term employed by psychiatrists who wish to describe a certain type of person who exhibits particular types of behaviour and attitudes. They argue that when it is applied to criminals, the term seems to be merely a label attached to particularly serious offenders. It does nothing to help recognise such offenders in advance, to explain their behaviour or prescribe suitable treatment.

Some psychiatrists who have argued that they are able to identify future dangerous offenders have disputed this notion. Vold *et al* (1998: 101) have responded by noting that 'if that is their claim, then their track record so far has been poor'. Kozol, Boucher and Garofalo (1972) sought to predict the future dangerousness of a group of high-risk offenders prior to their release from prison and failed to predict two-thirds of the violent crime that subsequently occurred. Monahan (1981) com-prehensively reviewed the clinical techniques used for predicting violent behaviour and concluded that it can only be done within very restricted circumstances. He stated that it is not possible to predict violence over an extended period or when a person is moving from one situation to another, for example, being released from prison.

Vold *et al* (1998) note that researchers have subsequently moved away from trying to predict future violent behaviour towards the more general possibility that the person might engage in any form of offending behaviour. Most of this research has focused on juveniles rather than adults. Loeber and Dishion (1983) show that the strongest predictor of later offending behaviour is early childhood problem behaviours such as disruptive classroom conduct, aggressiveness, lying and dishonesty. The stability of these behavioural problems over time suggest that these people may have certain personality characteristics – even if they do not show up on personality tests – that are associated with antisocial behaviour.

In recent years personality typing – or offender profiling – has been used, particularly in the USA, to help detect particular types of criminals. It is a method found to have been most useful in the detection of serial murders. Serial murder is a repetitive event. The murderer kills at a number of different times, frequently spanning a matter of months or years, and they are often committed at different locations. The murders are often brutal and sadistic and the victims are strangers. Most people consider such killers to be simply mad. Holmes and De Burger (1989) argue, however, that such murderers are not suffering from any psychological illness, for in this type of case there is characteristically a motive.

Four main types of serial killer are described. First, there is the *visionary motive type* – where the killer commits crimes because they hear voices or see visions. The act itself is usually spontaneous and disorganised and committed only in response to the voices. Second, there is the *mission-oriented motive type* – where the killer has a goal, usually to rid the world of a particular type of person. These people are not psychotic but have a strong wish to solve a particular problem. The victims are usually strangers, chosen because they fit into a certain category; the act is usually well planned and efficiently carried out. Third, there is the *hedonistic type* who kills basically for pleasure.

There are however two sub-categories. The thrill-orientated killer enjoys the excitement of killing and so kills for pleasure. The victims chosen are random strangers with no specific characteristics. The killing is spontaneous and disorganised. The lust killer, on the other hand, kills for a sexual motive, obtaining gratification by abusing others. The victim is usually a stranger who possesses the required characteristics.

Fourth, there is the *power/control-oriented type* who is very difficult to distinguish from the lust or thrill-seeking types. In order to prove control, the killer may well carry out sexual acts, but the sex is only a form of power over the victim. The latter will be a stranger who has specific characteristics and the crime will be organised and planned. The killing is often very sadistic.

The psychological profile is, however, only one of many ways of finding a solution to a murder. The science on which it is based is not an exact one and this fact is often overlooked. Omerod (1996) notes the limitations of the methodology and argues that offender profiling is only useful in a few cases such as rape, killing or arson. The profile only describes a type of person and does not identify an individual. Thus, the profile can only usefully supplement other investigative methods.

Cognitive learning theories

Both psychodynamic and behavioural learning theories have clear foundations in the predestined actor model. Later more sophisticated variants of those traditions became more readily accepting of rational actor model notions of albeit limited choice. They nonetheless both remained committed to the central notion of psychological positivism that proposes that there are patterns of reasoning and behaviour specific to offenders that remain constant regardless of their different social experiences. The third psychological tradition has its foundations in a fundamental critique of the predestined actor model.

The behavioural learning theorists had emphasised the role of environmental stimuli and overt behavioural response. This perspective did not, however, satisfactorily explain why people attempt to organise, make sense of and often alter the information they learn. There emerged a growing recognition that mental events – or cognition – could no longer be ignored (Kendler, 1985). Cognitive psychologists were to propose that by observing the responses that individuals make to different stimulus conditions it is possible to draw inferences about the nature of the internal cognitive processes that produce those responses.

Many of the ideas and assumptions of cognitivism have their origins in the work of the Gestalt psychologists of Germany, Edward Tolman of the USA and Jean Piaget of Switzerland. Gestalt psychologists emphasised the importance of organisational processes in perception, learning, and problem-solving and proposed that individuals were predisposed to organise information in particular ways (Henle, 1985). Tolman (1959) had been a prominent learning theorist at the time of the behavioural movement but subsequently developed a distinctively cognitive perspective. He was influenced by the Gestalt theorists and included internal mental phenomena in his perspective of how learning occurs. Piaget (1980) was a Swiss biologist and psychologist renowned for constructing a highly influential model of child development and learning. This theory is founded on the idea that the developing child builds cognitive structures – mental 'maps', schema or networked concepts – for understanding and responding to physical experiences within his or her environment. Piaget further asserted that a child's cognitive structure increases in sophistication with development, moving from a few innate reflexes such as crying and sucking to highly complex mental activities. His theory identifies four developmental stages of cognitive development, each influenced by physiological maturation and interaction with the environment and characterised by qualitatively different forms of thought.

B.F. Skinner (1968) had, as we have seen above, argued from an operant conditioning perspective that the person must actively respond if they are to learn. Cognitivists share that view with Skinner; however, they place the emphasis on mental rather than physical activity. This social learning theory emphasises that behaviour may be reinforced not only through actual rewards and punishments, but also through expectations that are learned by watching what happens to other people. Ultimately the person will make a choice as to what they will learn and how.

An early proponent of the notion that crime is simply a normal learned behaviour was Gabriel Tarde (1843–1904). He had argued that criminals are primarily normal people who by accident of birth are brought up in an atmosphere in which they learn crime as a way of life. His 'laws of imitation' were essentially a cognitive theory in which the individual was said to learn ideas through the association with other ideas, and behaviour was said to follow from those ideas. The first law proposes that people imitate one another in proportion to how much contact they have with each another. Thus imitation is most frequent and changes most rapidly in urban areas. His second law proposes that the inferior usually imitates the superior. Tarde argued that such offences as drunkenness and murder had originated as crimes committed by royalty but had been subsequently imitated by other social classes. Moreover, those in rural areas later imitated crimes originating in the city. His third law suggests that newer fashions replace older ones, for example, murder by shooting has come to replace that by knifing. Vold *et al* (1998) observe the theory to be important because it was the first attempt to describe criminal behaviour in terms of normal learned behaviour rather than in terms of biological or psychological defects. Ultimately, the model of learning on which the theory is based was relatively simple. Tarde did, however, heavily influence Edwin H. Sutherland's later differential association theory and the latter continues to have a huge impact on criminology, particularly in the USA.

Sutherland had originally embarked on this line of enquiry with his research reported in *The Professional Thief* (1937). This had consisted of a description of major elements of the criminal profession of theft as related to him by a thief with the alias 'Chic Conwell'. Sutherland discovered that thieving has its own techniques, codes, status, organisation and traditions that were imitated in other groups considered non-criminal.

The term 'differential association' was first used to explain interaction patterns by which thieves were restricted in their physical and social contacts to association with other thieves. It was, at this stage of its development, more or less a synonym for a criminal subculture. In 1939 the concept was used to develop a theory of criminal behaviour that proposed that crime be learned much like any other activity. It was argued that the frequency and consistency of their contacts with patterns of criminality determined the chance that a person would participate in systematic criminal behaviour. The basic cause of such behaviour was that the existence of different cultural groups with different normative structures within the same society had produced a situation of *differential social organisation*.

Certain shortcomings were identified with this early version of differential association theory. Fundamentally, it said little about the processes through which this 'contamination through exposure' could be resisted through a variety of personal or social differences. It was a rather narrow and deterministic version of learning theory particularly as it tended to rule out such psychological factors as conscience and moral understanding.

Sutherland (1947) consequently revised his theory to now argue that criminal behaviour occurs when individuals acquire sufficient sentiments in favour of law violation to outweigh their association with non-criminal tendencies. Those associations or contacts that have the greatest impact are those that are frequent, early in point of origin or the most intense. He argued that at this level of explanation it was not necessary to explain why a person has particular associations; this involved a complex set of social interactions and relationships. But he maintained that it was the existence of differential social organisation that exposed people to varied associational ties. The theory also remains in contrast to other psychological explanations, in that it retains a dominant sociological argument that the primary groups to which people belong exert the strongest influence on them. This formulation won wide acceptance because it was held to be sufficient to explain the occurrence of all criminal conduct.

Some key questions nonetheless remained unanswered. What kind of associations are intense ones? What if criminal attitudes are more compelling than others and thus are able to overcome a primary affiliation to convention, even though criminal association ties are fewer? It can be argued that the theory neglects personality traits, provides no place for variations in opportunities to engage in law-breaking and cannot explain spontaneous crimes of passion. It will be seen in the following chapter that sociological delinquent subcultural theories have their roots in Sutherland's arguments about the content of what is learned.

Sutherland is particularly remembered for his attempts to apply his differential association theory to white-collar crime or crimes of the powerful. He noted that the vast majority of criminological data compiled had been in relation to offenders from the lower classes, but he also observed that businessmen committed enormous amounts of crime (Sutherland, 1940). He therefore considered traditional explanations of criminality to be based on a false premise and misleading. Indeed there is some empirical support for this position. Geis (1967) examined evidence given to hearings into the illegal price-fixing activities of some companies in the USA. He found that people taking up new posts tended to find price-fixing to be an established practice and routinely they became involved as part of learning their new job. Baumhart (1961) had previously found unethical behaviour on the part of businessmen to be influenced by superiors and peers, with both him and Geis suggesting that the learning process is reinforced by 'rewards' and 'punishments'. Clinard (1952) argued, however, that differential association does not explain why it is that some individuals exposed to the same processes do not deviate, and proposed that the theory should be adapted to take personality traits into account.

Others have maintained the view that crime is normal learned behaviour and have sought to explain that this learning does not have to take place in intimate personal groups. These theories argue that learning can take place through direct interactions with the environment, independent of associations with other people, through the principles of operant learning. Burgess and Akers (1968) were to later rewrite the principles of differential association in the language of operant conditioning. They proposed that criminal behaviour could be learned both in non-social situations that are reinforcing and through social interaction in which the behaviour of other persons helps to reinforce that behaviour.

Akers (1985) later revised the theory and it now focused on four central concepts. First, *differential association* is considered the most important source of social learning. It refers to the patterns of interactions with others that are the source of social learning either favourable or unfavourable to offending behaviour. However, the indirect influence of more distant reference groups, such as the media, are also now recognised. Second, *definitions* reflect the meanings that a person applies to their own behaviour. For example, the wider reference group might not define recreational drug use as deviant. Third, *differential reinforcement* refers to the actual or anticipated consequences of a particular behaviour. Thus, it is proposed that people will do things that they think will result in rewards and avoid activities that they think will result in punishment. Fourth, *imitation* involves observing what others do. Whether they actually choose to imitate that behaviour, however, will depend on the characteristics of the person being observed, the behaviour the person engages in and the observed consequences of that behaviour for others.

Akers, Krohn, Lanza-Kaduce and Radosevich (1979) propose that the learning of criminal behaviour takes place through a specific sequence of events. It starts with the differential association of the individual with other individuals who have favourable definitions of criminal behaviour; they provide a model of criminal behaviour to be imitated and social reinforcements for that behaviour. Thus, primarily differential association, definitions, imitation and social reinforcements explain the initial participation of the individual in criminal behaviour. After the individual has commenced offending behaviour, differential reinforcements determine whether the person will continue with that behaviour.

Akers (1992) argues that the social learning process explains the link between social structural conditions and individual behaviours. For example, the modernisation process and social disorganisation, strain conditions and economic inequality that have all been linked with criminal behaviour affect the individual's differential associations, definitions, models and reinforcements. These issues are further discussed in the following chapter and the third part of this book.

Conclusions

Psychological explanations of crime and criminal behaviour have firm foundations in the predestined actor model of crime and criminal behaviour. It is the implication of both the psychodynamic and behaviourist learning traditions that there is such a thing as the criminal mind or personality. In some way this determines the behaviour of the individual. The causes are dysfunctional, abnormal emotional adjustment or deviant personality traits formed in early socialisation and childhood development. The individual is as a result of these factors destined to become a criminal. The only way to avoid that destiny is to identify the predisposing condition and provide some form of psychiatrist intervention that will in some way ameliorate or preferably remove those factors and enable the individual to become a normal law-abiding citizen.

The more recent cognitive learning approach involves a retreat from the purist predestined actor model approach. First, there is recognition of the links between the psychology of the individual and important predisposing influences or stimuli available in the social environment, but the behavioural learning theorists accept that point. It is the second recognition that is the important one. For criminals are now seen to have some degree of choice. They can choose to imitate the behaviours of others or they can choose not to. There may be a substantial range of factors influencing their decision and these may suggest to the individual that in the particular circumstances – when the opportunity arises – criminal behaviour is a rational choice to make. Thus we can see the links between recent cognitive learning theories and contemporary variants of the rational actor model. In short, the active criminal can in favourable circumstances make the choice to change their behaviour and cease offending or on the other hand the individual living in circumstances where criminal behaviour is the norm can choose not to take that course of action in the first place. From this perspective, crime is not inevitably destiny.

Suggested further reading

Psychological positivism is again an extremely wide subject area and there are thus many relevant texts. Students are therefore advised to use the references in the text as a guide to specific interests. However, for a general but comprehensive psychological account of criminal behaviour see Feldman, *Criminal Behaviour* (1977) and Hollin, *Psychology and Crime* (1989). Freud, *A General Introduction to Psychoanalysis* (1920) still provides an excellent introduction to the main tenets of psychoanalysis; while for a discussion and critique of the psychoanalytic tradition of explaining criminal behaviour see Farrington, 'Juvenile Delinquency' (1992), *Crime* (Introduction) (1994). For a comprehensive discussion of the research on maternal deprivation theory see Rutter, *Maternal Deprivation Reassessed* (1981). Eysenck, *Crime and Personality* (1977) gives a comprehensive introduction to his notion of the criminal personality. The cognitive psychology perspective is well represented by Sutherland, *Principles of Criminology* (1947) for the original and highly influential differential association theory and Akers, *Deviant Behaviour* (1985) for more contemporary social learning theory. Holmes and De Burger, *Serial Murder* (1989) is essential reading for those interested in serial killers, while Omerod, 'The Evidential Implications of Psychological Profiling' (1996) and Ainsworth, *Offender Profiling and Crime Analysis* (2001), is worthy of consultation on offender profiling.

Chapter 7

Sociological theories

We saw in the previous two chapters that both the biological and psychological variants of the predestined actor model of crime and criminal behaviour locate the primary impulse for criminal behaviour in the individual. The sociological version essentially rejects these individualist explanations and proposes that those behaviours defined as criminal behaviour are simply those that deviate from the norms acceptable to the consensus of opinion in society. This perspective should not be confused with that of the victimised actor model – the focus of the third part of this book – which proposes that it is the weak and powerless who are defined as criminal and targeted by the rich and powerful in an inherently unequal and unfair society. Sociological positivists recognise that crime is a socially constructed entity but at the same time acknowledge that it poses a real threat to the continuance of that society and thus needs to be controlled in some way.

The sociological variant of the predestined actor model involves the 'scientific' measurement of indicators of 'social disorganisation', such as rates of crime, drunkenness and suicide, in specified urban areas. Proponents of this perspective recommend that once the whereabouts of existing and potential 'trouble spots' in society are identified, these must be 'treated', controlled or, in future, prevented, if serious social disorder is to be avoided. It is a long-established tradition with its roots in the work of the nineteenth-century 'moral statisticians', Quételet (in Belgium) and Guerry (in France) and their social campaigning counterparts in England – Mayhew, Colquhoun, Fletcher and others – who used early empirical methods to investigate the urban slums where crime and deviance flourished. It is an enduring tradition that owes much to the important contribution to sociology established by Emile Durkheim.

Emile Durkheim and social disorganisation theory

Emile Durkheim was the founding father of academic sociology in France and a major social theorist working at the turn of the twentieth century. It was because of the strength and rigour of his large and complex sociological theory that he was able to assert powerfully the merits of social factors in explaining individual and group action. For Durkheim it was not just the psychological and biological versions of the predestined actor model that were unable to provide an adequate explanation of social action. He was also strongly opposed to those theoretical ideas – social contract theory and utilitarianism – that had provided the foundations of the rational actor model. In short, a society divided into different interest groups on an unequal basis is not one in which 'just contracts between individuals and society could be made' (Durkheim, 1933 originally 1893: 202).

At this point a few words of caution should be indicated. Durkheim is often misrepresented as a conservative indistinguishable from his French predecessor Auguste Comte. Taylor, Walton and Young (1973) – the eminent radical criminologists discussed fully in the third part of this book – and the present author (Hopkins Burke, 1998b, 1999b) consider this orthodox interpretation to be a gross simplification of a significant, radical, social and criminological theorist. Indeed, much of what has been said about Durkheim is more appropriate to the work of Comte.

Comte argued that the process whereby with the development of industrialised society people have become increasingly separated into different places of residence and employment has subverted the moral authority of a previously united society. Thus, from this perspective, people are seen to commit criminal acts not because it is in their material interests to do so, but because there is no strong moral authority influencing them to do otherwise. For Comte, it is the purpose of positivist social science to create this higher authority.

The essential difference between Comte and Durkheim lies in their differing views of human nature. For Comte, the human being has a natural and inherent desire to reach perfection. It is the creation of a moral authority by social scientists which can create the ordered society that will bring about that state of being. Durkheim simply rejects this view. It is utopian and idealistic to argue that a higher moral authority could restrain human desires at all times in history. Durkheim, in contrast to Comte, proposes a 'dualistic' view of human nature: a duality between the needs of the body and the soul. Human instincts are biologically given, while it is the task of the social world to develop through the human 'soul' an adherence to a *moral consensus* that is the basis of social order and control. With the changing nature of complex modern society that consensus is a shifting and adaptable entity.

It is possible to observe a similarity between Durkheim and Freud, for both argue that an increased repression of the individual conscience is the basis of the development of a civilised society. There are, however, substantial differences in their positions. For Durkheim, individual desires have to be regulated not simply because they have certain biological needs and predispositions, but because the failure to control this aspect of the person can lead to a situation of disharmony and despair, culminating in what he terms egoism and anomie. Durkheim did agree with Freud that individuals were not really human until they had been socialised. Freud, however, saw socialisation and the development of a conscience as necessary for individual well-being. For Durkheim, the lack of socialisation and a conscience leads to conflict between the individual and society.

Durkheim was also opposed to the utilitarians because he considered them to be idealists rather than social scientists. He recognised that moral authority can only be acceptable to men and women if it is relevant to their particular position in a changing society. If people are caught up in occupations that are unsuitable to their talents – and they recognise this underachievement – they can have little enthusiasm for moral authority. Central to Durkheim's social theory is his concern with social change and his enthusiasm to eradicate the 'forced division of labour'.

It was in *The Division of Labour in Society*, first published in 1893, that Durkheim described the processes of social change that accompany the industrial development of society. He argued that earlier forms of society had high levels of mechanical solidarity, while the more developed industrial societies are characterised by an advanced stage of 'organic' solidarity. However, a further note of caution needs to be indicated here. No society is entirely mechanical or organic. Any given society is in a state of development between the two extremes. Indeed, there may well be many pockets of intense mechanical solidarity in highly developed organic societies. This is a point well worth remembering.

For Durkheim societies with high levels of mechanical solidarity are characterised by the conformity of the group. There is a likeness and a similarity between individuals and they hold common attitudes and beliefs that bind one person to another. Now this is a form of social solidarity that may at first sight appear attractive – suggesting popular notions of the close-knit community – but at the same time severe restrictions are placed on the ability of an individual to develop a sense of personal identity or uniqueness. Thus, co-operation between individual members of the group is restricted to what can be achieved through the close conformity of each member to a single stereotype.

Durkheim argues that such societies can further be identified by a very intense and rigid collective conscience where members hold very precise shared ideas of what is right and wrong. There are, however, individuals within that group who differ from the uniform ideal and in these cases the law is used as an instrument to maintain that uniformity. Moreover, repressive and summary punishments are used against individuals and minority groups who transgress against the collective conscience of the majority. This punishment of dissenters usefully em-phasises their inferiority while at the same time encouraging com-mitment to the majority viewpoint. In this sense crime is a normal feature of a society with high levels of mechanical solidarity. Punishment performs a necessary function by reinforcing the moral consensus, or worldview, of the group. A reduction in behaviour designated as criminal would as a necessity lead to other previously non-criminal activities becoming criminalised. Indeed, Durkheim takes this argument a step further and claims that a society with no crime would be abnormal. The imposition of tight controls that make crime impossible would seriously restrict the potential for social progress.

Durkheim argues that with greater industrialisation societies develop greater levels of organic solidarity. There is a more developed division of labour and different groups become dependent on each other. Social solidarity now relies less on the maintenance of uniformity between in-dividuals, and more on the management of the diverse functions of different groups. Nevertheless, a certain degree of uniformity remains essential.

Time to indicate a further cautionary note. There has been a tendency, encouraged by some influential introductory sociology textbooks, for students to confuse the arguments presented by Durkheim on the increasing development of organic society, with those put forward by nineteenth-century conservatives, and the German sociologist Ferdinand Tönnies. For those writers, it was precisely this increasing fragmentation of communal beliefs and values that was the problem. Thus, the proposed solution for the proponents of that perspective lies in re-establishing the moral certainties of a society with high levels of mechanical solidarity. This we should note is not the argument presented by Durkheim.

For Durkheim, the division of labour is a progressive phenomenon. Its appearance signals not the inevitable collapse of morality, but the emergence of a new *content* for the collective conscience. The focus is now on the obligation of society to the individual person. Previously, under mechanical solidarity the emphasis had been on the obligation of the individual to society. Now to give the maximum possible encouragement to individual rights does not mean that altruism – that is, self-sacrifice for others – will disappear. On the contrary, moral individualism is *not* unregulated self-interest but the imposition of a set of reciprocal obligations binding individuals together (Durkheim, 1933 originally 1893). Here lies the essential originality of Durkheim's interpretation of the division of labour.

For Adam Smith (1910, originally 1776), the founder of free-market economics and the utilitarians, the specialisation of economic exchange is simply an effect of the growth of wealth and the free play of economic self-interest. For Durkheim, the true significance of the division of labour lies in its *moral* role. It is a source of restraint upon self-interest and thereby renders society cohesive. The idea that unbridled *egoism* – or competitive individualism – could ever become the basis of a civilised order is for Durkheim quite absurd. In short, Durkheim regarded the cohesion of nineteenth-century *laissez-faire* society, with its wholly unregulated markets, its arbitrary inequalities, and its restrictions on social mobility and its 'class' wars, as a dangerous condition. Such imperfect social regulation leads to a variety of different social problems, including crime.

Durkheim put forward two central arguments to explain the growth of crime and criminal behaviour in modern industrial societies. First, such societies encourage a state of unbridled 'egoism' that is contrary to the maintenance of social solidarity and conformity to the law. Second, the likelihood of inefficient regulation is greater at a time of rapid modernisation, because new forms of control have not evolved sufficiently to replace the older, and now less appropriate, means of maintaining solidarity. In such a period, society is in a state of normlessness or 'anomie'; a condition characterised by a breakdown in norms and common understandings.

Durkheim claimed that without external controls, a human being has unlimited needs. Society consequently has a right to regulate these needs by indicating the appropriate rewards that should accrue to the individual. Except in times of crisis, everyone has at least a vague perception of what they can expect to earn for their endeavours. However, at a time of economic upheaval, society cannot exert controls on people's aspirations. During a depression, people are forced to lower their sights, a situation which some will find intolerable. When there is a sudden improvement in economic conditions, social equilibrium will also break down and there is no limit on aspirations.

Although there is controversy about the accuracy of Durkheim's theory taken as a whole, his notion that crime was linked to a breakdown in social controls was a major inspiration to different sociologists in the twentieth century. In particular, his concept of anomie had a marked influence on the later work of Robert Merton discussed below. Moreover, the twin notions of anomie and egoism are extremely useful in helping to explain the nature of crime and criminal behaviour that occurred in the UK during a more recent period of economic and social disruption, the 1980s and the early 1990s. The aftermath of that period is still with us and will be examined in later chapters of this book. In the meantime, we will consider the more readily recognised influence that is apparent in the work of the Chicago school of criminology.

The Chicago school

In the early part of the twentieth century, the USA underwent a major transition from a predominantly rural and agricultural society to one based on industrial and metropolitan centres. Chicago, for example, grew from a town of 10,000 inhabitants in 1860 to a large city with a population of over two million by 1910. Life was nevertheless hard; wages were low; hours were long. Factory conditions were appalling and living in slum tenements created serious health problems (see Lilly, Cullen and Ball, 1986).

Sociologists working at the University of Chicago reached the conclusion that growing up and living in such conditions undoubtedly influenced the outcome of people's lives. Moreover, crime and criminal behaviour in such an environment could not simply be explained in the individualist terms proposed by the biological and psychological versions of the predestined actor model. It made more 'sense' when viewed as a social problem. From this perspective, it was argued that the poor are not simply born into a life of crime but are driven by the conditions of their social environment. By changing that environment it would be possible to reverse the negative effects of the city and transform these people into law-abiding citizens.

Robert Park (1921) contributed two central ideas to the work of the Chicago school. First, he proposed that like any ecological system, the development and organisation of the city is neither random nor idiosyncratic but patterned. Human communities, like plants, live together symbiotically. In other words, different kinds of human beings share the same environment and are mutually dependent on each other. At the same time, patterns of change in the city are comparable to changes in the balance of nature. The human population in US cities was seen to be migratory, rather than fixed. New immigrants moved into the poor areas and replaced the previous inhabitants as they moved out to the suburbs. Second, Park observed that the nature of these social processes had their impact on human behaviours like crime, and these could be ascertained only through careful study of city life. It was a research agenda that several researchers were to embrace.

Ernest Burgess (1928) produced a model of the city that provided a framework for understanding the social roots of crime. He argued that as cities expand in size, the development is patterned socially. They grow radially in a series of concentric zones or rings. Burgess outlined five different zones and proposed that a competitive process decided how people were distributed spatially amongst these. Commercial enterprises were located in the central business district in close proximity to the transport systems. The most expensive residential areas were in the outer zones, away from the bustle of the city centre, the pollution of the factories and the homes of the poor. However, it was the 'zone in transition' that was the particular focus of study.

The zone in transition contained rows of deteriorating tenements, often built in the shadow of ageing factories. The outward expansion of the business district led to the constant displacement of residents. As the least desirable living area, the zone was the focus for the influx of waves of immigrants who were too poor to reside elsewhere. Burgess observed that these social patterns weakened family and communal ties and resulted in 'social disorganisation'. It was this disorganisation thesis that was influentially presented as the primary explanation of criminal behaviour.

It was Clifford Shaw and Henry McKay (1972, originally 1931) who set out to empirically test concentric zone theory. Collating juvenile court statistics in order to map the spatial distribution of juvenile of-fending throughout Chicago did this. Their analysis confirmed that offending behaviour flourished in the zone in transition and was inversely related to the affluence of the area and corresponding distance from the central business district. By studying court records over several decades, they were also able to show that crime levels were highest in slum neighbourhoods regardless of which racial or ethnic group resided there. Moreover, as these groups moved to other zones, their offending rates correspondingly decreased. It was this observation that led Shaw and McKay to conclude that it was the nature of the neighbourhoods – not the nature of the individuals who lived within them – that regulated involvement in crime.

Shaw and McKay emphasised the importance of neighbourhood organisation in allowing or preventing offending behaviour by children and young people. In more affluent communities, parents fulfilled the needs of their offspring and carefully supervised their activities. In the zone in transition families and other conventional institutions – schools, churches, and voluntary associations – were strained, if not destroyed, by rapid urban growth, migration and poverty. Left to their own devices, young people in this zone were not subject to the social constraints placed on their contemporaries in the more affluent areas, and they were more likely to seek excitement and friends in the streets of the city.

Shaw actively promoted appreciative studies of the deviant, using the criminal's 'own story' by means of participant observation in their particular deviant world. This became known as the ethnographic or 'life-history' method and led to the publication of titles like *The Jack Roller: A Delinquent Boy's Own Story, The Natural History of a Delinquent Career* and *Brothers in Crime* (Shaw, 1930, 1931, and 1938). These studies showed that young people were often recruited into offending be-haviour through their association with older siblings or gang members.

Shaw and McKay concluded that disorganised neighbourhoods helped produce and sustain 'criminal traditions' that competed with conventional values and could be 'transmitted down through successive generations of boys, much the same way that language and other social forms are transmitted' (Shaw and McKay, 1972: 174). Thus, young people growing up in socially disorganised inner-city slum areas characterised by the existence of a value system that condoned criminal behaviour could readily learn these values in their daily interactions with older adolescents. On the other hand, youths in organised areas, where the dominance of conventional institutions had precluded the development of criminal traditions, remained insulated from deviant values and peers. Accordingly, for them an offending career was an unlikely option.

Shaw and McKay fundamentally argued that juvenile offending could only be understood by reference to the social context in which young people live. In turn, this context itself was a product of major societal transformations brought about by rapid urbanisation and massive population shifts. Young people born and brought up in the socially disorganised zone in transition were particularly vulnerable to the temptations of crime. As conventional institutions disintegrated around them, they were given little supervision, and were free to roam the streets where they were likely to become the next generation of carriers of the area's criminal tradition. It was this aspect of their work that provided the foundations for Edwin Sutherland's theory of 'differential association' discussed in the previous chapter.

The work of the Chicago school has nonetheless been criticised from a number of standpoints. First, it has been observed that while the deterministic importance of the transmission of a 'criminal culture' is emphasised there is substantially less detail provided on the origins of that culture. Second, there have been criticisms of a tendency to see the spatial distribution of groups in the city as a 'natural' social process. The role that power and class domination can play in the creation and perpetuation of slums and the enormous economic inequality that permeates such areas is ignored. Third, it has been proposed that they provide only a partial explanation of criminality that seems best able to explain involvement in stable criminal roles and in group-based offending behaviour.

The Chicago school criminologists have nevertheless had a substantial influence on the development of sociological explanations of crime and criminal behaviour. Particularly influential has been the recognition that where people grow up – and the people with whom they associate – is closely linked to a propensity for involvement in criminal activity.

The Chicago school has also had a further practical influence. In the 1930s Clifford Shaw established the 'Chicago Area Project' (CAP). The intention was to allow local residents in socially deprived areas the autonomy to organise neighbourhood committees in the fight against crime. The project encompassed several approaches to crime prevention. First, a strong emphasis was placed on the creation of recreational programmes that would divert young people from criminal activity. Second, efforts were made to have residents take pride in their community by improving the physical appearance of the area. Third, CAP staff members would attempt to mediate on behalf on young people in trouble with those in authority, such as schoolteachers. Fourth, local people were employed as 'street credible' workers in an attempt to persuade youths that education and a conventional life-style was in their best interest. Schlossman, Zellman and Shavelson (1984) conducted an evaluation of 50 years of the CAP project and reached the conclusion that it had long been effective in reducing rates of reported juvenile offending.

In summary, social disorganisation theory, as developed by Shaw and McKay, called for efforts to reorganise communities. The emphasis on cultural learning suggested that treatment programmes that attempt to reverse the criminal learning of offenders could counter crime. In general, young offenders should be placed in settings where they will receive pro-social reinforcement, for example, through the use of positive-peer-counselling.

Anomie theory

Anomie – or strain – theory attempts to explain the occurrence of not merely crime but also wider deviance and disorder. In this sense it is a wide-ranging, essentially sociological explanation that promises a comprehensive account of crime and deviance causation, but – while it provides a major contribution to this endeavour – ultimately fails to fulfil this ambition.

Robert Merton borrowed the term anomie from Emile Durkheim in an attempt to explain the social upheaval that accompanied the Great Depression of the 1930s and later the social conflicts that occurred in the USA during the 1960s. His writings are particularly significant because they challenged the orthodoxy of the time that saw the USA as being characterised by the term, 'the American Dream'. It was a vision of a meritocratic society in which hard work and endeavour – in the context of conservative values – would supposedly distribute social and economic rewards equitably.

Merton essentially followed the Chicago school sociologists in rejecting individualistic explanations of crime and criminal behaviour but nonetheless took his sociological argument a step further than Durkheim had done. Whereas his predecessor had considered human aspirations to be natural, Merton argued that they are usually socially learned. Moreover, there are – and this is the central component of his argument – social structural limitations imposed on access to the means to achieve these goals. His work therefore focuses upon the position of the individual within the social system rather than on personality characteristics. In his words, 'our primary aim lies in discovering how some social structures exert a definite pressure upon certain persons in the society to engage in nonconformist conduct' (Merton, 1938: 672).

Merton proposed that this central aim could be achieved by distinguishing between *cultural goals* and *institutionalised means*. The former are those material possessions, symbols of status, accomplishment and esteem that established norms and values encourage us to aspire to, and are, therefore, socially learned. The latter are the distribution of opportunities to achieve these goals in socially acceptable ways. Merton observes that it is possible to overemphasize either the goals or the means to achieve them and that it is this that leads to social strains, or anomie.

Merton was mainly concerned with the application of his theory to the USA and proposed that in that culture there was an overemphasis on the achievement of goals such as monetary success and material goods, without sufficient attention being paid to the institutional means of achievement. It is this cultural imbalance that leads to people being prepared to use any means, regardless of their legality, to achieve that goal (Merton, 1938: 674). The ideal situation would be where there was a balance between goals and means. In such circumstances, individuals who conform would feel that they were justly rewarded.

Deviant, especially criminal, behaviour results when cultural goals are accepted, for example, people would generally like to be financially successful, but access to the means to achieve that goal is limited by the position of a person in the social structure. Merton outlined five possible reactions – or adaptations – that can occur when people are not in a position to legitimately attain internalised social goals.

Conformity

Conformity is a largely self-explanatory adaptation whereby people tend to accept both the cultural goals of society and the means of achieving them. Even if they find their social ascent to be limited, they still tend not to 'deviate'. Merton claimed that in most societies this is the standard form of adaptation, for if this were not the case society would be extremely unstable. He did, however, note that for many people, whose access to the socially dictated 'good things in life' through established institutionalised means was in some way more difficult than conventionally portrayed, the 'strain' to achieve might well become intolerable. People could alleviate the strain in such instances by either changing their cultural goal and/or by withdrawing their allegiance to the institutionalised means. In following either or both courses, people would be deviating from norms prescribing what should be desired (success), or how this should be achieved (legitimate means such as education, approved entrepreneurship or conscientious employment). The following four 'modes of adaptation' describe various ways of alleviating 'strain' generated by social inequalities.

Retreatism

Merton considered retreatism to be the least common adaptation. Retreatists are those who reject both social goals *and* the means of obtaining them. These are true 'aliens'; they are 'in the society but not *of* it' (Merton, 1938: 677). It is a category of social 'drop-outs' which includes among others drug addicts, psychotics, vagrants, tramps and chronic alcoholics.

Ritualism

Merton identifies many similarities between 'ritualists' and 'conformists'. An example of the ritualist is a person who adheres to rules for their own sake. Bureaucrats who accept and observe the rules of their organisations uncritically provide the classic example. Those in rule-bound positions in the armed services, social control institutions or the public service, may be particularly susceptible to this form of adaptation where the emphasis is on the means of achievement rather than the goals. These people, or groups, need not of course be particularly successful in attaining their conventional goals; their overemphasis on the 'means' clouds their judgement on the desirability of appreciating the goals.

Innovation

The innovator is the usual focus for the student of crime and criminal behaviour. The innovator is keen to achieve the standard goals of society – wealth, fame or admiration – but, probably due to blocked opportunities to obtain these by socially approved means, embarks on novel, or innovative, routes. Many 'innovative' routes exist in complex organic societies, so much so that some innovators may be seen to overlap with 'conformists'. For example, the sports, arts and entertainment industries frequently attract, develop and absorb 'innovators', celebrating their novelty in contrast to the conformist or ritualist, and providing opportunities for those whose circumstances may frustrate their social ascent through conventionally prescribed and approved routes.

The innovator may be exceptionally talented, or may develop talents, in a field that is restricted or unusual and conventionally deemed worthy of celebration for its novelty. These innovators are relatively unthreatening to conventional views of the acceptable means of social achievement. There are others, however, who appear to pose a distinctly destabilising influence on conventional definitions of socially acceptable means of achievement. It is one of the strengths of anomie – or strain theories – that they open the potential to appreciate that some of these 'innovations' may be seen as merely 'deviant', and subjectable to informal social controls and censure, while others are proscribed by the criminal law of the relevant jurisdiction.

Some activities are usually seen as 'criminally' censurable in most societies, although they may be excusable in certain circumstances. Robbery is usually seen as an offence when committed against an individual or an institution such as a bank. This might not be the case when committed in wartime against the persons or institutions of an 'enemy' state. Homicide is regarded as a serious offence in most jurisdictions, yet it is acceptable when promoted by socially or politically powerful interests in times of war. Similarly, where does the financial 'entrepreneur' stretch the bounds of legality or previously established 'acceptable' business means to the achievement of previously determined goals? Lilly *et al* (1986) provide the example of stock exchange regulation abusers in the 1980s as an example of innovative business deviants. At a time when business deregulation had generated many fortunes, some people were encouraged by the circumstances to take opportunities to shorten the means to the social goal of wealth through 'insider dealing' and similar practices.

In short, the innovator may be seen to overemphasize the goals of achievement over the means. Conventionally regarded success may be achieved by any means that seem appropriate to the innovator, who strives to overcome barriers to achievement by adopting any available strategies for achieving established goals.

Rebellion

For Merton rebellious people are those who not merely reject but also wish to change the existing social system and its goals. Rebels thus reject both the socially approved means and goals of their society. The emergence of popular images of the potential of both innovative and rebellious modes of adaptation to the standard social and economic patterns of western life in the 1960s did much to renew an interest in Merton's approach to crime and deviance.

Three main criticisms have nonetheless been made of anomie theory. First, it has been observed to be a self-acknowledged 'theory of the middle range' that does little to trace the origins of criminogenic circumstances. Merton is accused of being a 'cautious rebel' who explains neither the initial existence of inequality, nor the exaggerated emphasis in society on making money (Taylor, Walton and Young, 1973). Indeed, it was criticisms of this kind that instigated the search for a more totalising, historically and politically aware criminology – or 'sociology of deviance' – in the late 1960s and 1970s: the rise, and indeed fall, of this mode of explaining criminal behaviour being the central focus of the third part of this book.

Anomie theory is not as comprehensive an account of crime and deviance as it may at first look. It quite simply fails to explain certain behaviours that are commonly labelled 'deviant', such as homosexuality or marijuana smoking, among people who are otherwise conforming members of society, sharing an acceptance of standard cultural goals and the institutionalised means of achieving them.

The second criticism is targeted at Merton's assumption that cultural goals and values are known and shared by all members of society. Lemert (1972), for example, argued that society is more accurately characterised by the notion of a plurality of values. If this is the case, then Merton's 'ends–means' approach becomes problematic and generally insufficient in explaining crime and deviance. He can be partially defended in that he did state that different goals are possible within his scheme, but he does not give sufficient emphasis to different groups and different values. Moreover, the assumption that it is the 'lower classes' who are most likely to suffer from frustrated aspirations and who are subject to strain and commit criminal or deviant acts may not be accurate. Later criminological studies reveal that there is a great deal more deviant behaviour in society than Merton's formula suggests. Anomie theory, we are told, is hard-pressed to account for business fraud and other 'white-collar' crimes, and also for 'lower-class' conformity. Thus, anomie theory predicts both too little deviance among the more privileged members of society, and too much among those potentially most subject to strain.

In defence of Merton, it would seem that he was motivated to explain those forms of highly visible and immediately apparent crime that have traditionally been committed by the poorer sections of society and which have been of immediate concern to the public and hence politicians and inevitably criminologists. Indeed, later researchers – predominantly working in the victimised actor model of crime and criminal behaviour tradition, which is the focus of the third part of this book – have sought to use the concept of anomie in an attempt to explain corporate crime.

From this perspective, it has been argued that explanations based on individual motivations are inadequate and that it is necessary to consider these in the context of corporate goals, the essential goal of which is to maximise profit over a long period (Etzioni, 1961; Box, 1983). Box, however, identifies five potential sources of 'environmental un-certainty' for the corporation that represent obstacles to the lawful attainment of its main goal. These are: competitors; the government; employees; consumers; and the public, especially as represented by protectionists. Box observes that confronted with such obstacles, the corporation adopts tactics that frequently involve breaking the law, in order to achieve its goal.

Staw and Szwajkowski (1975) compared the financial performance of 105 large firms subject to litigation involving illegal competition with those of 395 similar firms not so involved and concluded that environmental scarcity did appear linked to a whole range of trade violations. Box (1983) goes further and argues that adherence to the profit motive renders the corporation inherently criminogenic with the bulk of corporate crime initiated by high-ranking officials. He suggests that the very factors connected with career success in corporations – and the consequences of such success – are themselves criminogenic.

Gross (1978) conducted a survey of several studies of corporate career mobility and noted the relevance of personality differences. He found senior managers to be ambitious, to accept a non-demanding moral code, and to regard their own success at goal attainment as being linked to the success of the organisation. Box (1983) took this notion a step further, however, and argued that the very nature of the corporate promotion system means that those who reach the top are likely to have the very personal characteristics required to commit business crime. The greater success they achieve, the more free they feel from the bind of conventional values. In this way, we might observe that Box's interpretation of anomie seems to be closer to that of Durkheim than Merton.

Financial profit is not, however, the only goal relevant to anomie. Braithwaite (1984: 94) has described fraud as 'an illegitimate means to achieving any one of a wide range of organisational and personal goals when legitimate means … are blocked'. For example, he found a wide-spread willingness among pharmacologists to fabricate the results of safety tests. This could sometimes be attributed to financial greed, but there were other explanations. Some scientists have an intense commit-ment to their work. When the value of this is threatened by test results there could be considerable temptation to cover up in order to defend professional prestige.

This author is of the view that the notion of anomie – and the more contemporary manifestation of 'relative deprivation' developed by the highly influential populist socialists or 'left realists' and the focus of Chapter 15 – can be equally applied to white-collar offenders. We might like to contemplate the probability that it is not just the abject poor and objectively deprived who feel aggrieved by an unequal and non-caring society. Politicians have long recognised and pandered to the material insecurities of the relatively affluent middle-classes.

The third criticism of Merton is that he made no attempt to apply his typology to women and, at first sight it seems totally inapplicable to them. Leonard (1983) notes that the cultural goals of women in US society are relational goals – typified by successful relationships with others – rather than the financial goals sought by men. It is an argument revisited in Chapter 10.

Anomie theory has been subjected to many criticisms but is generally sympathetically regarded in the fields of sociology and criminology. Merton did a great deal to broaden the study of crime and criminal behaviour and to introduce the importance of social structure in shaping the life choices of individuals. Some have argued that he did not go far enough with this endeavour. However, it would seem that Merton – along with many liberal or social democratic critics of unrestrained egoism and conservative values both in his native USA and Britain – had no inclination to see a socialist transformation of society. The latter tends to be the ultimate goal of his critics working at the more radical end of the spectrum in the victimised actor model tradition. To criticise the substantial elements of his theoretical concerns on that basis is therefore rather unfair, particularly as many of those critics have since radically modified their views and come themselves to accept the explanatory potential of Merton's notion of anomie (see Chapter 15). In short, his work has provided a useful starting-point for subsequent researchers and this is clearly apparent in the discussion of deviant subcultures to which we now turn.

Deviant subculture theories

There have been different deviant subculture explanations of crime and criminal behaviour but all share a common sentiment that certain social groups have values and attitudes that enable or encourage delinquency. The highly influential US subcultural tradition was at its peak during the 1940s and 1950s, and it incorporated five main explanatory inputs.

First, there was Merton's concept of anomie with its proposition that people may either turn to various kinds of deviant conduct in order to gain otherwise unobtainable material rewards or, failing that, seek alternative goals.

Second, there were the case studies carried out by the Chicago school which had suggested that young males living in socially 'disorganised' areas had different moral standards from other people and that helped facilitate their willingness to become involved in offending behaviour. Moreover, some of these patterns of conduct were passed on – or 'culturally transmitted' – from one generation to the next.

Third, there was the 'masculine identity crisis theory' outlined by the then highly influential functionalist sociologist Talcott Parsons (1937) during a period when his work was highly influenced by Freud. Parsons argued that the primary social role of the adult male is job-centred while that of the adult female is home-centred. The father is consequently absent from the family home for much of the time and cannot therefore function as a masculine role model for his children. The outcome is that children of both sexes identify with their mother to the exclusion of their father. This is particularly problematic for the male child who encounters strong cultural expectations that he adopt a masculine role but has no real concept of what this involves. But he has, during his childhood, discovered that stealing, violence and destruction provoke the disapproval of his mother; hence he identifies these as non-feminine and therefore masculine characteristics. Offending behaviour satisfies these criteria of masculinity.

Fourth, there was the 'differential association theory' that Edwin Sutherland had developed from the social disorganisation thesis of the Chicago school and which was discussed at some length in the previous chapter. He proposed that a person was more likely to offend if they had frequent and consistent contact with others involved in such activities. Offending behaviour was likely to occur when individuals acquired sufficient inclinations towards law-breaking that these outweighed their associations with non-criminal tendencies.

Fifth, there were the early sociological studies of adolescent gangs carried out in the social disorganisation–cultural transmission tradition developed by the Chicago school. Thrasher (1947) argued that the adolescent gang emerged out of spontaneous street playgroups of young children in relatively permissive and socially disorganised slum areas. The young males involved were neither 'disturbed', 'psychopathic' or 'driven' by socio-economic forces beyond their control. They were simply looking for excitement, adventure and fun. This could be found on the streets but not at school or home.

Later studies of adolescent gangs followed in the tradition established by Thrasher. All argued that the young male gang was a natural response to a socially disorganised environment and that deviant behaviour when it occurred was learned from previous generations of adolescents (see for example, Yablonsky, 1962). These studies continued throughout the 1930s, 1940s and 1950s in the USA with a few minor examples in the UK. At the same time the concept of the 'delinquent subculture' was emerging in the USA.

Albert Cohen (1955) pointed out that previous research had focused on the process through which individual young males had come to adopt deviant values and had either ignored, or taken for granted, the existence of deviant subcultures or gangs. By analysing the structure of such subcultures he argued that juvenile offending was rarely motivated by the striving for financial success proposed by Merton. Cohen proposed that adolescent gang members in fact stole for the fun of it and took pride in their acquired reputations for being tough and 'hard'. The gang, or subculture, offers possibilities for *status* that are denied elsewhere.

Cohen noted that although society is stratified into socio-economic classes it is the norms and values of the middle class that are dominant and employed to judge the success and status of everybody in society. The young working-class male experiences a different form of upbringing and is unlikely to internalise these norms and values. He is nevertheless thrust into a competitive social system founded on alien and incomprehensible middle-class norms and values. As a result he experiences *status frustration.*

Since the young male is involved in a process of interaction with others who are faced with the same difficulties, a mutually agreed solution may be reached. A separate subculture with alternative norms and values with which young males can relate is formed. In this way the boy can achieve a status that legitimates all the things the official culture rejects: hedonism, aggression, dishonesty and vandalism. In short, there is a conscious and *active* rejection of middle-class norms and values.

Cohen's delinquent subculture theory has attracted its share of criticism. Fundamentally, it is observed that he failed to base his theoretical formulation on empirical data. Indeed, all attempts to test it have failed and it can be argued that it is inherently untestable. Kitsuse and Dietrick (1959) showed there was no real basis for the assertion that the young working-class male experiences 'problems of adjustment' to middle-class values. They point out that middle-class norms and values are simply *irrelevant* to young working-class men. There is simply no interest in acquiring status within the middle-class system and their aspirations are therefore *not frustrated.* They simply resent the intrusion of middle-class outsiders who try to impose their irrelevant way of life upon them. Offending behaviour should therefore be considered rational and utilitarian in the context of working-class culture.

Walter Miller (1958) argues that offending is the product of long-established traditions of working-class life. Thus, it is the very structure of working-class culture that generates offending behaviour, rather than responses to conflicts with middle-class values. The *focal concerns* of working-class society – toughness, smartness, excitement, fate and autonomy – combine in several ways to produce criminality. Those who respond to such concerns automatically violate the law through their behaviour. Thus, the very fact of being working class places the individual in a situation that contains a variety of direct influences towards deviant conduct. Implicit in this formulation is a significant attack on the notion that subcultures originate as a response to lack of status or thwarted aspirations. Delinquency is simply a way of life. It is a response to the realities of their lives.

Miller himself problematically offers no explanation for the origins of these highly deterministic working-class values from which there appears to be no escape. All he does is note their existence and explain that conforming to them will lead to criminal behaviour. His work was strongly influenced by Parson's masculinity identity crisis (Parsons, 1937). It had been noted, for example, that it is common in lower-class households for the father to be absent, often because he has transgressed against the criminal law. The home life is thus a female-dominated environment that leads working-class males to look for 'suitable' role models outside the home. These could be found in street gangs what Miller termed 'one-sex peer units'. These gangs took part in activities that uphold the working-class 'focal concerns' and give the adolescent male a sense of belonging and status.

Richard Cloward and Lloyd Ohlin's *Delinquency and Opportunity* (1960) was a major development in deviant subculture theory and provided one of the central foundations of labelling theory which itself is a central element of the victimised actor tradition (the focus of the third part of this book). They argue that it is necessary to have two theories in order fully to explain adolescent criminal behaviour. First, there is a need for a 'push' theory to explain why it is that large numbers of young people offend. Second, a 'pull' theory is required to explain the continuance of this behaviour and how it becomes passed on to others. The originality of their work lies in their use of a combination of Merton's anomie theory to explain the 'push' and Sutherland's differential association theory to explain the 'pull'.

Cloward and Ohlin observe that there is a discrepancy between the aspirations of working-class adolescent males and the opportunities available to them. When an individual recognises that membership of a particular ethnic group or social class and/or lack of a suitable education has seriously restricted his access to legitimate opportunities he will blame an unfair society for his failure and withdraw his belief in the legitimacy of the social order. It is this awareness that leads to a rejection of conventional codes of behaviour.

Cloward and Ohlin followed Cohen in stressing that individuals have to actively seek out and join with others who face the same problems.

Together these young makes will devise a collective solution to their predicament. For surrounded by hostile adults, they need all the support that they can obtain from each other. Moreover, they need to develop techniques to neutralise the guilt they feel and this is easier to achieve as the member of a like-minded group.

Underlying this reformulation of anomie theory is the assumption that illegitimate routes to success are freely available to those individuals who 'need' them. Cloward and Ohlin combine the cultural transmission theory of Shaw with the differential association theory of Sutherland to create an 'illegitimate opportunity structure' concept that parallels the 'legitimate opportunity structure' of Merton. From this theory the existence of three separate delinquent subcultures were predicted. First, *criminal* delinquent subcultures are said to exist where there are available illegitimate opportunities for learning the motivations, attitudes and techniques necessary in order to commit crimes. Second, a *conflict* subculture exists where adolescent males – denied access to the legitimate opportunity structure because of their social class, ethnic origin, etc. – have no available criminal opportunity structure. In this case young males work off their frustrations by attacking people (assault), property (vandalism) and each other (gang fights). Third, *retreatist* subcultures tend to exist where drugs are freely available and membership is composed of those who have failed to gain access to either the legitimate or criminal subcultures. These young males who retreat into drug misuse and alcoholism are considered to be 'double failures'.

Cloward and Ohlin predicted – and this was 1960 – that because the organisation within poor inner cities was collapsing and adult crime was becoming too sophisticated for adolescent males to learn easily, the criminal delinquent subculture would decline. The conflict or retreatist subcultures would on the other hand expand, with increased adolescent violence, 'muggings', vandalism and drug addiction.

Three main criticisms have been made of Cloward and Ohlin's work. First, it is observed that their notion of the criminal subculture is modelled on the fairly stable and structured adolescent gangs of the Chicago slum areas of the 1920s and 1930s and which had long since ceased to exist (Jacobs, 1965). Second, there is an inherent assumption that the working class is a relatively homogeneous group and this is simply not the case. Third, they, like their predecessors, provide a grossly simplistic explanation of drug misuse, which is, in reality, fairly common among successful middle-class professional people, particularly, if alcohol consumption is included under the generic term 'drugs'.

Coward and Ohlin's theory was nonetheless the focus of considerable academic debate, a major issue being the extent to which the actions of young males in delinquent gangs can be considered determined by their socialisation. Moreover, it was necessary to consider the extent to which they are committed to the delinquent norms of the group.

It was Ivan Spergel (1964) who provided at least a partial answer to these questions. Identifying an 'anomie gap' between aspirations measured in terms of aspired to and expected occupation and weekly wage, he found that the size of this gap differed significantly between offenders and non-offenders and between one subculture and another. He consequently rejected Cloward and Ohlin's subculture categories and replaced them with his own three-part typology. First, *a racket subculture* is said to develop in areas where organised adult criminality is already in existence and highly visible. Second, *a theft subculture* – involving offences such as burglary, shoplifting, taking and driving away cars – would develop where a criminal subculture was already in existence but not very well established. Third, *conflict subcultures* – involving gang fighting and 'rep'utation – would develop where there is limited or no access to either criminal or conventional activities.

Spergel significantly found that drug misuse was common to all subcultures as part of the transition from adolescent delinquent activity to either conventional or fully developed criminal activity among older adolescents and young adults. He found that people involved in drug misuse do not in themselves constitute a subculture. Moreover, the common form of deviant behaviour specific to a particular area depends on the idiosyncratic features of that particular district and not, as Merton and Cloward and Ohlin seem to imply, on *national* characteristics.

The general conclusion reached by critics of early US deviant subculture theories is that they fail to provide an adequate explanation of adolescent offending behaviour. A number of specific criticisms can also be identified. First, descriptions of the 'typical' offender make little sense. They are portrayed as being in some way different from non-offenders and are driven into offending behaviour by grim social and economic forces beyond their control. There is simply no attempt to explain why it is that many if not most young males faced with the same 'problems of adjustment' *do not* join delinquent gangs. Second, virtually all-deviant subculture explanations consider adolescent offending to be a gang phenomenon. In reality this is a very doubtful proposition. A lot of adolescent offending behaviour is a solitary activity or involves, at the most, two or three young males together. The fairly stable gangs identified by the deviant subculture theorists are in fact very difficult to find. Third, none of these explanations takes into account the roles of authority figures – the police, parents, social workers and teachers – in labelling these young people as offenders. Fourth, adequate explanations are provided of how it is that many young males appear to simply outgrow offending behaviour. Fifth, no explanation is provided for the offending behaviour of adolescent females. Sixth, there is an inherent assumption that adolescent offending is the preserve of the lower working classes. This is simply not the case. Indeed, some researchers have usefully used the early deviant subculture tradition in an attempt to explain corporate – or business – crime.

Aubert (1952) examined the attitudes of certain Swedish citizens towards violation of wartime rationing regulations. He found that two sorts of obligation influenced the behaviour of each research subject. First, 'universalistic' obligations affected their behaviour as a law-abiding citizen. These should have provided sufficient motivation to obey the law, but sanctions against those who transgressed were found to be invariably weak. Second, 'particularistic' obligations were considered due to business colleagues, and were supported by a philosophy that demanded only avoidance of certain blatant offences. Aubert (1952: 177) describes the groups to which white-collar criminals belong as having 'an elaborate and widely accepted ideological rationalisation for the offences and ... great social significance outside the sphere of criminal activity'. He found that corporate crimes are sometimes accepted and endorsed by group norms and certain types of illegal activity come to represent a normal response. Braithwaite (1984) found, for example, that bribing health inspectors was normal and acceptable business practice in the pharmaceutical industry.

However, these subcultural influences should not be seen as being fully deterministic. Irresistible forces beyond their control do not pressure executives who violate laws. Deviance may be encouraged and condoned but it is not automatic. Both Geis (1967) and Faberman (1975) found that even within industries where criminal practices are common, some employees were not prepared to get involved in spite of often quite extensive pressure from senior managers. It seems that individual characteristics, variations between groups within a subculture and the degree of exposure to subcultural values may be relevant.

The best and most comprehensive critique of the highly determinist early deviant subculture tradition is provided by David Matza. In doing so he provides an influential and crucial link with the later non-determinist explanations discussed in the third part of this book.

David Matza (1964) observes that all criminologists working in the predestined actor tradition – from Lombroso onwards – have made three basic assumptions about crime. These have some validity but have simply been taken too far. First, the focus has been on the criminal and their behaviour while the role of the criminal justice system has been ignored. The criminal justice system is part of the environment of the criminal and needs to be considered. Second, the predestined actor model is overly determinist in its rejection of the notion of rational free will. Human beings *are* capable of making rational choices but these are limited by structural constraints. Third, the predestined actor model considers criminals to be fundamentally different types of people from non-criminals. There are, of course, substantial variations on this theme. Lombroso considered the criminal to have been born bad. For the deviant subculture theorist, the actions of the offender are determined by a commitment to an alternative 'ethical' code that makes involvement in delinquent activity appear mandatory.

Matza notes that those working in the predestined actor tradition have simply failed to explain why it is that most delinquents 'grow out' of delinquency. From that determinist perspective, offenders would presumably continue to offend all the time, except of course when they have been incarcerated. This is clearly not the case but it is the logical deduction that can be made from the position taken by such writers as Cohen, and Cloward and Ohlin. In response, Matza proposes that delinquency is a *status* and delinquents are *role players* who intermittently act out a delinquent role. These young men are perfectly capable of engaging in conventional activity, and therefore the alleged forces that compel them to be delinquent are somehow rendered inactive for most of their lives. The young person simply 'drifts' between delinquent and conventional behaviour. He is neither compelled nor committed to delinquent activity but freely chooses it some times and not at others.

Matza accepted that there are subcultures whose members engage in delinquency. On the other hand, he denied the existence of a specific deviant subculture. Theories that propose the existence of such a subculture assume that this involves a contra culture, one that deliberately runs counter to the values of the dominant culture. Matza argued that this position is problematic for the following reasons. First, there is the implication that the young person does not experience feelings of guilt. This actually is not the case. Second, there is an assumption that young offenders have no respect for conventional morality. In fact most young people involved in offending behaviour recognise the legitimacy of the dominant social order and the validity of its moral standards. Third, it is argued that young offenders define all people outside the 'delinquent subculture' as their potential victims. In reality they distinguish special groups, mostly other delinquents, as legitimate targets to victimise. Fourth, it is proposed that delinquents are immune from the demands of the larger culture. In reality the members of these supposed 'delinquent subcultures' are *children* and cannot escape from disapproving adults. Their condemnation of delinquent behaviour must be taken into consideration and there is a strong probability that their demands for conformity will be internalised.

Matza found that young males could remain within the 'subculture of delinquency' *without* actually taking part in offending behaviour. When he showed a sample of photographs of various criminal acts to a group of delinquents – some of which the adolescents had themselves committed – their reactions ranged from mild disapproval to righteous indignation.

Matza argued that adolescents go through three stages in a process of becoming deviant. The first stage is the nearest the young male comes to being part of an oppositional subculture. Such a situation arises when he is in the company of other young males and where there appears to be an 'ideology of delinquency' implicit in their actions and remarks. In these circumstances he is motivated by his anxiety to be accepted as a member of the group and his concerns about his own masculinity and 'grown-up' status. In this condition of anxiety he reaches conclusions about what will be the 'correct' form of behaviour, the 'correct' attitude to present and the 'correct' motives for engaging in a particular form of behaviour from the remarks, gestures and behaviour of the other adolescents. He hears and perhaps sees others in the group approving of or doing daring, but illegal, acts and assumes that, to be accepted, he must join in and show that he is just as good (or bad), if not better than, all the others. So he steals things, vandalises things, hits people not because he 'really' wants to but because he feels he 'ought' to want to, because that is what being 'grown up' is all about. What this young man fails to realise is that the other members of the group feel exactly the same as he does. The others are also plagued by doubts about acceptance, masculinity and adulthood and, indeed, may be taking *their* cues from him. In other words, all the members of the group are trapped in a vicious circle of mutual misunderstandings. This circle can be broken when two young men confess to each other that they do not like offending or when the particular individual is sufficiently old to stop feeling anxieties about masculinity and adult status. At this stage of maturity a young man can decide to leave the group and cease involvement in deviant activity.

The second stage occurs when the young man, having overcome his original anxieties about masculinity, is faced with another problem. He must overcome his initial socialisation that has taught him not to be deviant and hence protect himself from feelings of guilt. He must find extenuating circumstances that will release him from conventional control and leave him free to choose to drift into deviancy. Thus, young males use 'techniques of neutralisation' to justify their own deviancy. Matza identifies five major types of neutralisation:

- denial of responsibility (I didn't mean it);
- denial of injury (I didn't really harm him);
- denial of the victim (he deserved it);
- condemnation of the condemners (they always pick on us); and
- appeals to higher loyalties (you've got to help your mates).

These techniques are by themselves merely excuses and not explanations of deviant behaviour. Matza argued that at a deeper level there is a commitment to 'subterranean values', which – like Miller's 'focal concerns' they resemble – exist in the wider culture of normal society. The most important of these values is what psychologists refer to as the 'need for stimulation', which means, in this context, the search for excitement. Young males commit deliberate criminal acts because they *are* criminal. Quite simply, being deviant is better than being bored. Deviancy is fun; it is exciting.

Matza argued that the operation of the criminal justice system and the actions of social workers might actually convince young people that deviant behaviour does not really matter. Deviant young males are not stupid. They are aware that many social workers, police officers, teachers and magistrates think that the young person is not fully responsible for their actions but will go ahead and punish – or rather 'treat' – them just the same. Deviant children are as quick as, or even quicker than, non-deviants to recognise this contradiction and to exploit it in their own defence.

The third stage in a deviant career has now been reached. The young male is now in a situation of 'drift'. He knows what is required of him and has learned the techniques of neutralisation, which justify his deviant behaviour. On the other hand, he is not automatically *committed* to deviant behaviour. He *could* just boast about previous and un-verifiable exploits, much as other young people boast about imaginary sexual encounters.

The missing impetus that makes actual deviant behaviour possible is 'free will'. It is this recognition that distinguishes Matza completely from those working in the predestined actor tradition. The deviant is *responsible* for their behaviour. They *know* that their activities are against the law. They *know* that they may be caught. They *know* that they may be punished. They probably accept that they *should* be punished. It is one of the rules of the game. If this is the case the question remains to be asked as to why the young person should continue to be involved in criminal behaviour.

In the first place, the young person has acquired certain skills partly from their older friends and partly from the mass media, for example, television, which has made involvement in criminal behaviour possible. They will have learned from their friends how to manage guilt and discount the possibility of capture. They assume that they will not be caught, and criminal statistics suggest that they are likely to be correct in this supposition. This state of *preparation* allows the young person to repeat an offence that they have committed before. Less frequently, the young person falls into a condition of *desperation* derived from a mood of *fatalism*, a feeling of being 'pushed around'. This feeling of being pushed around is sufficient for them to lose their precarious concept of their self as a 'real man'. They need to 'make something happen' in order to prove that they are a *cause* not merely an effect. It is this feeling that leads them directly to become involved in more serious, previously untried, delinquent behaviour. Even if caught they have still made something happen. The whole apparatus of police, juvenile court and social work department is concerned with them and has been activated by what *they themself* did. In a state of desperation the young person needs to do more than simply repeat an old offence; after all, as their peers would say, 'anyone can do that'. In the state of desperation, they need to do something that they have not tried before.

Matza's theoretical schema has also been usefully applied to the study of business crime. Corporate executives have been found to use 'techniques of neutralisation' to rationalise deviant acts and violate the law without feeling guilty (Box, 1983). Officials can deny responsibility by pleading ignorance, accident or that they were acting under orders. Vague laws that rest on ambiguous definitions and permit meanings and interpretation to shift help facilitate this. As a result it is difficult to distinguish praiseworthy corporate behaviour from illegal actions. Box (1983: 55) observes that in these circumstances, 'it is convenient for corporate officials to pull the cloak of honest ignorance over their heads and proceed under its darkness to stumble blindly and unwittingly over the thin line between what is condoned and what is condemned'.

Bandura (1973: 13) found that shared decision-making in an organisation allows people to contribute 'to cruel practices ... without feeling personally responsible'. 'Denial of the victim' may also be used. The nature of much corporate crime permits an illusion that there is no real person suffering, particularly when the victims are other corporations or people in far-off countries, especially if they are less developed countries (Braithwaite, 1984). Swartz (1975) has noted that company spokespersons have been prepared to blame industrial accidents on 'careless and lazy' workers or the development of brown lung in black workers on their 'racial inferiority'. The corporate criminal often denies that any harm has been caused. Geis (1968: 108) quotes an executive who described his activities as 'illegal … but not criminal … I assumed that criminal action meant damaging someone, and we did not do that'. Moreover, the corporate employee can 'condemn the condemners', by pointing to political corruption, or describing laws as unwarranted constraints on free enterprise. Acting for the good of the company, or following widespread but illegal business practices, seen as more important than obeying the law.

Early British deviant subcultural studies tended to follow the lead of the US theories discussed above. The main influences were the work of Miller and Cohen; the work of Cloward and Ohlin appears to have had little or no application in Britain.

John Mays (1954) argued that in certain, particularly older urban areas, the residents share a number of attitudes and ways of behaving that predispose them to criminality. These attitudes have existed for years and are passed on to newcomers. Working-class culture is intentionally criminal; it is just a different socialisation, which, at times, happens to be contrary to the legal rules. Criminal behaviour, particularly adolescent criminal behaviour, is not therefore a conscious rebellion against middle-class values. It arises from an alternative working-class subculture that has been adopted over the years in a haphazard sort of way.

Terence Morris (1957) argued that social deviants are common among the working classes and that it is the actual characteristics of that class that create the criminality. Forms of antisocial behaviour exist throughout society and in all classes, but the way in which the behaviour is expressed differs. He considered criminal behaviour to be largely a working-class expression. The family controls middle-class socialisation, it is very ordered and almost all activities are centred on the home and the family. In the working classes, the child's socialisation tends to be divided between family, peer group and street acquaintances. The latter child is thus likely to have a less ordered and regulated upbringing. The peer group is a much stronger influence from a much earlier age. They encounter controls only after they commit a crime, when they are processed by the criminal justice system. The whole ethos of the working class, according to Morris, is oriented towards antisocial and criminal, rather than 'conventional', behaviour.

David Downes (1966) conducted a study among young offenders in the East End of London. He found that a considerable amount of offending behaviour took place, but this mostly happened in street corner groups, rather than organised gangs. Status frustration did not occur to a significant degree among these young males. Instead, their typical response to lack of success at school or work was one of 'dissociation'. The process was one of opting out rather than reaction formation. Among these youths there was an emphasis on leisure activities, not on school or work. They tended to be interested in commercial forms of entertainment, not in youth clubs with their middle-class orientation. Access to leisure pursuits was nonetheless restricted by a lack of money. As an alternative, youths would take part in offending behaviour to find excitement. Peter Wilmott (1966) also conducted a study of teenagers in the East End of London and reached much the same conclusions as Miller. He found that adolescent offending behaviour was simply part of a general lower working-class subculture. Teenagers became involved in petty crime simply for the fun and 'togetherness' of the shared activity experience.

Howard Parker (1974) conducted a survey of unskilled adolescents in an area of Liverpool that official statistics suggested had a high rate of adolescent offending. He found there was a pattern of loosely-knit peer groups, not one of tightly structured gangs. Offending behaviour was not a central activity. Young males shared common problems, such as unemployment; leisure opportunities were limited. Some youths had developed a temporary solution in the form of stealing car radios. Furthermore, the community in which the young males lived was one that largely condoned theft, as long as the victims were from outside the area.

Ken Pryce (1979) studied African-Caribbean youngsters in the St Paul's area of Bristol. He suggested that the first African-Caribbeans to arrive in the 1950s came to Britain with high aspirations but found they were relegated to a force of cheap labour. They and their children were subject to racism and discrimination, which contributed to a pattern of 'endless pressure'. Pryce suggested there were two types of adaptation to this pressure. One was to be stable and law-abiding, the other was to adopt an expressive, disreputable attitude. Second and third generation African-Caribbeans were more likely, but not bound, to adopt the second response.

These earlier British deviant subculture studies were important because they drew our attention to specific historical factors, in particular the level of economic activity, and to the importance of a structural class analysis in the explanation of subcultural delinquency (Burke and Sunley, 1996; 1998). They also demonstrated that different groups within the working class had identified distinct problems in terms of negative status and had developed their own solutions to their perceived problems. However, these early studies also tended to neglect the involvement of young women in offending behaviour. Where young women are discussed, they tend to be dismissed as 'sex objects' or adjuncts to male offending behaviour, merely 'hangers-on'.

Studies of deviant youth sub-cultures carried out in the USA since the 1970s have predominantly focused on issues of violence, ethnicity and poverty. Wolfgang and Ferracuti (1967) identified a 'sub-culture of violence' where there was an expectation that the receipt of a trivial insult should be met with violence. Failure to respond in this way was greeted with social censure from the peer group. Curtis (1975) adapted this theory to explain violence among American blacks. Maintenance of a manly image was found to be most important in the sub-culture, and individuals unable to resolve conflicts verbally were more likely to resort to violence in order to assert their masculinity. Behaviour is seen to be partly a response to social conditions, and partly the result of an individual's acceptance of the ideas and values that he has absorbed from the sub-culture of violence. Maxon and Klein (1990) have more recently recognised that certain youth groups, for example, racist 'skinheads' and neo-Nazi organisations, engage in group-related violent behaviour for ideological – including political and religious – ends.

Recent American research has proposed that poverty is simply the root cause of gangs and the violence they produce. Miller (1958) had argued that lower-class delinquency was a normal response to socio-cultural demands; in his later writings he essentially adopts a 'culture of poverty' view to explain the self-perpetuation of gang life, a view that emphasises the adaptational aspects of the gang to changing socio-economic circumstances (Miller, 1990). However, the most popular current theory to explain criminal behaviour among poor young people in the American inner city is William Julius Wilson's 'underclass theory' where it is suggested that groups in socially isolated neighbourhoods have

> … few legitimate employment opportunities, inadequate job information networks and [where] poor schools not only give rise to weak labour force attachment but also raise the likelihood that people will turn to illegal or deviant activities for income.
>
> (Wilson, 1991: 462)

Wilson has been accused of failing to address the issues of gang formation or to explain the development of specific types of gang problems (Hagedorn 1992). Nevertheless, a number of observers assume a close correlation between gangs, gang violence and the development of a socially excluded underclass (Krisberg 1974; Anderson 1990; Taylor

1990). Poverty is central to the underclass thesis and various writers recognise that the absence of economic resources leads to compensatory efforts to achieve some form of economic and successful social adjustment (Williams 1989; Moore 1991; Hopkins Burke, 1999a). It is in this context that Spergel (1995: 149) argues that 'a sub-culture arises out of efforts of people to solve social, economic, psychological, developmental, and even political problems'. This thesis is revisited in Chapter 15.

The concept of deviant subculture was subsequently revised by radical neo-Marxist sociologists and criminologists – working in the 'victimised actor' tradition – and based at the Centre for Contemporary Cultural Studies in Birmingham during the 1970s. The approach was devised to explain what came to be termed 'spectacular' youth cultures, including Teddy Boys, Mods, Skinheads and Punks.

This new wave of subcultural studies argued that previous interpretations of youth had all neglected the relationship that groups of young people had to the economy at particular historical moments (see Hall *et al*, 1978; Hall and Jefferson, 1976). It is an approach developed by this author who has argued that young people, living in a fragmented society, have different life-experiences, different *problems* and in many cases are able to choose a *solution* offered by different coexisting deviant subcultures. Particular groups of young people, not all members of the traditional working class but in existence concurrently at the same historical moment, have had very different experiences of the radical economic change that has engulfed British society since the late 1970s (see Burke and Sunley, 1996, 1998).

Conclusions

The early sociological variants of the predestined actor model of crime and criminal behaviour have, like the early biological and psychological versions, been accused of being overly determinist. It is nonetheless a form of criminological explanation that has been extremely influential in informing the direction of later, less determinist, approaches. Moreover, the recognition that social factors external to the human being place constraints on that person's choice of action, has been particularly influential and, indeed, would be considered by many today to be an almost common-sense, if partial, explanation of criminal behaviour.

We have seen that the later subculture theorists came increasingly to recognise that human beings are able to make choices about the course of action that they will take. It is a recognition that does not, however, herald a return to unbridled purist variants of the rational actor model.

From the perspective of these later and more sophisticated versions of the predestined actor model there is recognition of limited constrained human choice. The choices available to the human being are restricted by their life-chances, such as their education, training and skills, place of upbringing, membership of ethnic group, gender and differential access to material resources. Thus, people do not enjoy free will – as in the rational choice actor conceptualisation – for no human being is ever totally free. They simply make choices that are constrained by their social circumstances. These issues are developed more fully in the following part of this book.

Suggested further reading

Sociological positivism is an extremely wide subject area and there are thus many relevant texts. Students are therefore again advised to use the references in the text as a guide to specific interests. However, for a comprehensive introduction to the increasingly rediscovered and currently highly influential social theory of Emile Durkheim it is well worth consulting the original text, Durkheim, *The Division of Labour in Society* (1933). Shaw and McKay, *Juvenile Delinquency and Urban Areas* (1972) provide a thorough introduction to the work of the Chicago school. Merton, 'Social Structure and Anomie' (1938) – subsequently reprinted in many different collections - provides a still essential introduction to anomie theory. The early US deviant subculture tradition is well represented by Cloward and Ohlin, *Delinquency and Opportunity* (1960), Cohen, *Delinquent Boys* (1955), Miller, 'Lower-class Culture as a Generalizing Milieu of Gang Delinquency' (1958) and Spergel, *Racketsville, Slumtown, Haulburg* (1964). Matza, *Delinquency and Drift* (1964), however, in a text widely regarded as one of the best criminology books ever written, provides both an excellent critique of that tradition and an excellent link with both the rational actor and victimised actor models. Spergel, *The Youth Gang Problem* (1995) provides a comprehensive overview of more recent US work in that tradition. Early UK research is well represented by Downes, *The Delinquent Solution* (1966), Mays, *Growing up in the City* (1954), Morris, 'The Criminal Area: a Study in Social Ecology' (1957), Parker, *View from the Boys* (1974) and Pryce, *Endless Pressure: a Study of West Indian Life-styles in Bristol* (1979). A key text representing the later Marxist-influenced Birmingham CCCS approach is Hall and Jefferson (eds), *Resistance through Rituals* (1976), while Burke and Sunley, 'Hanging Out' in the 1990s (1998) provide a comprehensive but concise overview of the various formulations of deviant subculture theory while introducing the notion of postmodernism into the debate.

Part Three

The victimised actor model of crime and criminal behaviour

Definitions of serious crime are essentially ideological constructs. They do not refer to those behaviours which objectively and *avoidably* cause us the most harm, injury and suffering. Instead they refer only to a sub-section of these behaviours, a sub-section which is more likely to be committed by young, poor educated males who are often unemployed, live in working-class impoverished neighbourhoods, and frequently belong to an ethnic minority.

(Box, 1983: 10)

We saw in the first part of this book that the rational actor model of crime and criminal behaviour understands human beings to possess free will and thus have the capacity to make rational decisions to engage in activities of their choice. Criminal behaviour is simply a rationally chosen activity. The predestined actor model on the other hand proposes that crime emanates from factors – be they biological, psychological or social – that are outside the control of the offender and which determine their behaviour. Thus, the major concern of this tradition is to identify and analyse what they consider to be the *causes* that drive individuals to commit criminal acts. A major criticism of this tradition has centred on its acceptance of the conventional morality and criminal laws as self-evident truths. In other words, if a particular action is defined as a crime, it is necessarily wrong because the state decreed it to be so.

The third model of crime and criminal behaviour provides a challenge to the predestined actor notion of determined human behaviour and its uncritical acceptance of the socio-political status quo. This victimised actor model proposes that the criminal is in some way the victim of an unjust and unequal society. It is the behaviour and activities of the poor and disadvantaged that are targeted and criminalised while the actions of the rich and powerful are simply ignored or not even defined as criminal.

The victimised actor model has two theoretical foundations. First, there is the critique of the predestined actor model of human behaviour offered by symbolic interactionists and which was to become increasingly influential during the latter-half of the twentieth century. The labelling theories that provide the first and earliest component of the victimised model tradition – and which are the focus of the following chapter – have their roots in symbolic interactionism in general and the work of George Herbert Mead (1934) in particular.

Symbolic interactionism primarily analyses the way individuals conceptualize themselves and others around them with whom they interact. Of central importance in that analysis is the concept of the 'procedural self'. This broadly speaking is the view that a person's self-identity is continuously constructed and reconstructed in interaction with 'significant others' – those who have an influence on the individual – and that human behaviour can only be understood by reference to this process. Moreover, it is proposed that meanings do not reside within objects or within the psychological elements of the individual person, but rather emerge out of the social processes of interpretation by which definitions of objects are created and used (Plummer, 1975).

Symbolic interactionists conclude that deviance is not a property *inherent* in certain forms of behaviour but one that is *conferred* on certain forms of behaviour by an audience. Thus, in this way, the focus of criminological inquiry was to shift away from the qualities and characteristics of the deviant actor and towards that of the audience, that is, the *response* of society to the deviant act. Of particular relevance here were the responses of the various agencies of social control such as the police, courts, psychiatrists, social workers and teachers.

The work of those writers most closely identified with the labelling/interactionist perspective, such as Lemert (1967), Becker (1963) and, in particular, Erikson (1962, 1966), Kitsuse (1962) and Cicourel (1968) were also influenced by *phenomenological* and *ethnomethodological* approaches.

Phenomenology is a philosophical approach that arose out of a general debate about the character, scope and certainty of knowledge. The most influential proponent of the sociological variant was Alfred Schutz, who argued that sociology should not attempt to establish the 'reality' of social phenomena. Such, phenomena are only 'real' if they are defined as such by individuals who then act on the basis of those definitions. Since the reality that lies behind the way individuals interpret the world can never be penetrated, the positivist goal of objectivity should be abandoned in favour of a quest to ascertain subjective *meaning*.

The focus on deviant meanings involved the recognition that negative or stigmatic responses to a deviant act may well affect the way that deviants see themselves. This in turn led to a widening of the focus to include the creation of deviant meanings by agencies of social control (Rock, 1973).

Ethnomethodology draws on and further develops these phenomenological concepts and methods in order to describe social reality. It is a method of sociological study concerned with how individuals experience and make sense of social interaction. Central to this approach is the notion that *all* expressions of reality are 'indexical'; that is, they are based upon a set of assumptions specific only to the social context in which they are used. Perhaps the major significance of this approach to criminology lies in its profound questioning of the utility of criminal statistics. Unlike other perspectives, which viewed these as reasonably objective and independent of theory, ethnomethodologists treated them as social constructions produced, as are all phenomena, by interpretative work and social organisation.

The second theoretical foundation of the victimised actor model is a critique of the orthodox predestined actor model notion that society is fundamentally characterised by consensus (see Talcott Parsons, 1951). That view had been based on the simple assumption that there is fundamental agreement concerning the goals of social life and the norms, rules and laws that should govern the pursuit of these objectives. There is, however, another long-established tradition in the social sciences that considers society to be fundamentally conflict-ridden.

Max Weber (1864–1920) had influentially argued that conflict arises in society from the inevitable battle within the economic market place over the distribution of scarce resources. Karl Marx (1818–83) had taken a much more radical stance and argued that conflict involves an inherent struggle by people to abolish the social divisions imposed by the material arrangements within society.

The conflict theorists (who are the focus of the earlier sections of Chapter 9) had, however, little recourse to these traditions in sociology and preferred to concentrate on examining and commenting on the world around them, even though their explanations are often strongly resonant of this heritage. The one acknowledged influence was the work of the German sociologist Ralph Dahrendorf whose work follows very much in the tradition established by Weber.

Dahrendorf (1959) proposes that there is conflict in society over the control of authority. Writing at a time when there were spectacular signs of disorder emerging in many economically developed countries in both eastern and western Europe, and in the USA, he accepted the inevitability of conflict. However, he was confident that new accommodations could emerge to moderate and ameliorate the resulting disorder. Conflict in this formulation was therefore seen positively as a motor for change, towards the development of more effective mechanisms and structures to integrate people and groups into society. While keen to distance himself from consensus thinkers who refused to accept the validity, and indeed utility, of conflict in society, Dahrendorf was at the same time critical of those 'utopian' Marxist modes of thought that promised an end to crime with the arrival of socialism (Dahrendorf, 1958).

Dahrendorf held a pluralist view of society, a perspective that recognises the many and varied interest groups in society and that these may conflict over who should hold authority. The challenge for the pluralist is to develop institutions that can best accommodate these varied interests. On a number of occasions Dahrendorf celebrated the flexibility of British institutions to respond to shifts in the balance of interests and authority and commented on this unusual capacity to minimise conflict and generate a relatively high level of sustained social stability.

Dahrendorf disagreed fundamentally with Marxism on the question of inequality. He located the source of inequality in power and authority relationships within a society and did not see these factors as necessarily linked to injustices in economic systems. Unlike Marx, who had argued for the abolition of inequality, Dahrendorf was of the view that because cultural norms always exist and have to depend on sanctions if they are to be enforced, some people must have more power than others so as to make these sanctions work. Thus, it is not the economic inequality resulting from capitalism that produces social inequality. Inequality is an inescapable fact of any society where the basic units, the family, or institutions such as the criminal justice system, necessarily involve dominance–subjection relationships.

Many of the founding principles of the USA have led to a deep-rooted aversion to socialist or Marxist forms of analysis. Evidence of this can be found in the manner in which many European immigrants to the United States were screened for 'radical sympathies', most notably following the Bolshevik revolution in Russia in 1917. Subsequently the post-Second World War 'witch hunt' for radical socialist and communist sympathisers in public life spearheaded by Senator Joseph McCarthy, produced a climate hostile to theories based on class conflict.

By the late 1950s, however, there was clear evidence of conflict in the USA, despite a high level of general affluence. The black civil rights movement and a steadily rising crime rate were but two examples. In this context a theoretical approach that offered a non-socialist or non-Marxist explanation for conflict appeared welcome to many American social theorists and criminologists. It was at the time that Dahrendorf was writing that George Vold presented his version of conflict theory. Subsequently, Austin Turk developed the approach with direct reliance on the work of Dahrendorf. Richard Quinney was to follow. Their work is the focus of the earlier part of Chapter 9.

The later radical criminology tradition has its roots in an attempt to develop an understanding of crime in response to the rapidly changing and chaotic circumstances of the late 1960s and 1970s. Criticisms of Western societies as being overly concerned with wealth creation and material consumption were hardly new in the 1960s, but the decade saw evidence in the West that the apparent political consensus that had typified post-war politics was disintegrating. Concern began to emerge about the quality of life in societies that encourage the pursuit of material acquisition above the fulfilment of human need and satis-faction. The burgeoning student movement was at the forefront of this criticism, although many of its claims could be traced back to the con-cerns of social reformers and philosophers over the whole of recorded history. Alternative lifestyles were embraced and celebrated and these concerns were reflected in the arts and entertainment industries, making anti-materialism appear interesting and even fashionable.

It was a period characterised by anti-authoritarianism with its roots in an increasing recognition of the failings of the modern state in western countries to cure human ills and address human needs. In countries such as the United Kingdom – and to a lesser extent the USA – there had been a dramatic post-war shift towards an acceptance of the role of the state in the provision of welfare services to ameliorate poverty, ill-health, poor educational provision and other human wants. Undoubtedly major improvements had been made, but none of these had fully met public expectations. In most cases welfare benefits were distributed according to strict entitlement rules that attached conditions to the delivery of services. Many argued that benefits should be received as rights due to any citizen, rather than being conditional on obeying life-style rules. Hence, radical critics came to see the welfare states of many western countries as being oppressive.

Many critics of the socio-political consensus came to search for broad political, economic and social theories to explain how western societies had come to be as they were. Hence, there emerged a complex range of minority interest groups concerned with attempting to explain the circumstances in which social inequality came about. These groups began by mounting protests to push for the fulfilment of equal rights in society and gradually developed historical, political, social and economic theories to support their efforts to argue for change. The black civil rights movement in the United States developed and then frag-mented into different wings, each holding differing views on the origins and solutions to the problems that faced black people. The Northern

Ireland civil rights movement similarly began with an assertion of equal rights for Catholic citizens in Northern Ireland, before different interpretations of the nature of the problems facing this group led to divisions based on differing views concerning the range of possible solutions. The movement to secure equal rights for women also began to take on a new momentum in the late 1960s. More recently, we have seen further issues being raised and fragmentation caused by varying interpretations of the problems within the peace movement, animal rights, the environmental movement and an increasing array of other interest groups.

Chapter 8

Labelling theories

Labelling explanations of crime and criminal behaviour are theoretically informed by the various concepts and insights of interactionism, phenomenology and ethnomethodology. It is an approach that focuses on three central concerns. First, there is a consideration of why and how it is that some acts come to be defined as deviant or criminal while others do not. To this end there is an examination of legal codes and practices, and the social and professional interest groups that shape the criminal law. The second concern recognises that certain people and groups are more likely to attract deviant, criminal and stigmatizing labels than others are. Thus, there is an examination of the differential applications of laws and labels by the various social control agencies and the relationship of this to organisational context. Unfortunately, labelling theorists – with the limited exception of Becker (1963), Kituse (1962), Piliavin and Briar (1964) and Cicourel (1968) – have not addressed these concerns as thoroughly as they might have done, although they have contributed substantially to the development of the radical criminology discussed in Chapter 9. Most of the energy of the most active phase of labelling theory was directed towards the third concern that assesses the experience of being labelled for the recipients of the label. We will consider each of these concerns in turn.

The social construction of crime

Before labelling theories achieved prominence, most criminologists had a non-problematic conception of crime. Criminal behaviour was simply a form of activity that violates the criminal law. Once crime was thus defined, theorists – working in the predestined actor model tradition – could concentrate on their main concern of identifying and analysing its causes. This whole approach was nonetheless far too simplistic for proponents of the labelling perspective. They argued that what is defined as 'criminal' is not fixed but varies across time, culture and even from one situation to the next. From this perspective, the conventional morality of rules and criminal laws in any given society should be studied and questioned and not merely accepted as self-evident.

Labelling theorists argued fundamentally that no behaviour is *inherently* deviant or criminal, but only comes to be considered so when others confer this label upon the act. Thus it is not the intrinsic nature of an act, but the nature of the societal reaction that determines whether a 'crime' has taken place. Even the most commonly recognised and serious crime of murder is not universally defined in the sense that anyone who kills another is everywhere and always guilty of murder. The essence of this position is neatly summarised in a well-known passage by Becker (1963: 4) who, unlike most other labelling theorists, was concerned with the creators and enforcers of criminal labels and categories:

> Social groups create deviance by making the rules whose infraction constitutes deviance, and by applying those rules to particular people and labelling them as outsiders. From this point of view ... the deviant is one to whom the label has been successfully applied; deviant behaviour is behaviour that people so label.

Becker argued that rules, including criminal laws, are made by people with power and enforced upon people without power. Thus, even on an everyday level, rules are made by the old for the young, by men for women, by whites for blacks, by the middle class for the working class. These rules are often imposed upon the recipients against their will and their own best interests. Moreover, the rules are legitimised by an ideology that is transmitted to the less powerful in the course of primary and secondary socialisation. As a result of this process, most people internalise and obey the rules without realising – or questioning – the extent to which their behaviour is being decided for them.

Becker also argues that some rules may be cynically designed to keep the less powerful in their place. Others may have simply been intro-duced as the outcome of a sincere, albeit irrational and mistaken, belief on the part of high-status individuals that the creation of a new rule will be beneficial for its intended subjects. Becker termed the people who create new rules for the 'benefit' of the less fortunate, 'moral entrepreneurs'.

Becker noted two closely interrelated outcomes of a successful 'moral crusade'. First, there is the creation of a new group of 'outsiders', those who infringe the new rule. Secondly, a social control agency emerges charged with enforcing the rule, and with the power to impose labels on transgressors, although more often this simply means an extension of police work and power. Eventually the new rule, control agency and 'deviant' social role comes to permeate the collective consciousness and be taken for granted. This leads to the creation of negative stereotypes of those labelled 'deviant'.

Becker (1963) cites the campaign by the US Federal Bureau of Narcotics (FBN) to outlaw marijuana use through the Marijuana Tax Act of 1937. The campaign was justified on the grounds of protecting society – particularly young people – from the ill effects of this drug and relied heavily on propaganda of one sort or another to get its message across. In Becker's view, however, the campaign was undertaken primarily as a means of advancing the Bureau's organisational interests. Moreover, the successful conclusion of the campaign led to 'the creation of a new fragment of the moral constitution of society, its code of right and wrong' (Becker, 1963: 145).

Other studies have looked at the process whereby previously 'acceptable' forms of behaviour have been brought within the remit of the criminal law. Platt (1969) shows how contemporary approaches to 'juvenile delinquency' – indeed even the very concept itself – is the outcome of a nineteenth-century moral crusade undertaken by largely upper-class women. This successful campaign established juveniles as a separate category of offender with their own courts, which in turn enabled the scope of the state's powers of intervention to be extended beyond mere breaches of the criminal law to cover 'status offences' such as truancy and promiscuity.

Tierney's (1982) analysis of domestic violence also provides evidence of the process of criminalisation. She argues that 'wife battering' only emerged as an important social issue worthy of criminal justice intervention after the mid-1970s, mainly because of the increasing strength of the women's movement and the determination to secure the provision of refuges, legislation and other measures aimed at protecting women.

In short, what these and similar studies show, is not the inherent harm of behaviour or its pervasiveness that prompts changes in the law, but rather the concerted efforts of sufficiently motivated and powerful social groups to redefine the boundaries of what is considered acceptable and legal.

Others have adopted a macro perspective in order to explain these processes. Erikson (1962) draws upon Durkheim in arguing that all social systems place certain boundaries on culturally permissible behaviour. Deviant behaviour is simply that which is defined as crossing these boundaries. Indeed, deviant behaviour may be the only way of *marking* these boundaries. Thus, transactions between deviants and social control agents are 'boundary maintenance mechanisms' which attract a good deal of publicity. By acting outside of these system boundaries deviants demonstrate to society where the perimeters lie, at the same time giving those inside a sense of identity or 'belongingness'. These processes in turn help preserve social stability. Thus, in viewing deviance as essentially 'boundary maintenance activity', the work of Erikson marks a point of convergence between the labelling perspective and the functionalism of Durkheim.

Quinney (1970) also employed a macro sociological perspective but one that combined labelling theory with conflict theory, differential association and deviant subculture theories. He was also influenced by Durkheim's notion of mechanical and organic solidarity in proposing two ideal types of society (or social organisation): *singular* and *segmental*. According to Quinney, in a singular or homogeneous society all crime must necessarily occur outside any value system since by definition all members of the society adhere to this value system. In a segmental or heterogeneous society some segments will share common values with others, but because there is unlikely to be a complete consensus, value systems will be in conflict to a certain extent. Thus, the criminal laws and their enforcement are a product of this conflict and the associated unequal distribution of political power.

From Quinney's perspective, society is segmentally organised or pluralistic, therefore the criminal law tends to represent the values of politically powerful sections of society. Quinney went on to suggest a direct relation between the possibility of someone being labelled as criminal and their relative position in the social structure.

The recipients of deviant labels

It is the conventional wisdom that those who break the law will be labelled as criminal. Becker (1963) exposed the inadequacy of this line of thinking, noting that the innocent are sometimes falsely accused and, more importantly, that only some of those who violate the criminal law are eventually arrested and processed through the system. Kitsuse (1962), in a study of homosexuality that has much wider criminological ramifications, found that it is not behaviour *per se* that is the central issue. Rather it is the interactional process through which behaviour is both defined as deviant and through which sanctions are initiated. Thus distinguishing deviants from non-deviants is not primarily a matter of behaviour but is contingent upon 'circumstance or situation, social and personal biography, and the bureaucratically organised activities of social control' (Kitsuse, 1962: 256).

A number of important studies conducted in the USA have confirmed that actual behaviour is not the only factor in determining whether a deviant or criminal label is conferred, and that official responses are shaped by a range of extra-legal variables, such as appearance, demeanour, ethnic group and age. For example, Piliavin and Briar (1964) looked at police encounters with juveniles and found that arrest decisions were based largely on cues – demeanour, dress and general appearance – from which the officer inferred the character of the youth. *Structural* factors, such as gender, social class, ethnic group, and time of day were also significant. Thus a young, working-class, black male in a 'high delinquency area' at night was seen to have a very high chance of being at least stopped and questioned, if not arrested. He is quite simply *assumed* to be delinquent unless he can prove otherwise (Piliavin and Briar, 1964: 206). More recent studies undertaken in the UK have also shown that some police officers show class and/or race bias in the performance of their duties (see for example Smith and Gray, 1986; Institute of Race Relations, 1987).

Cicourel (1968) found that in the course of their interactions with juveniles, the 'background expectations' of the police – that is, their lay theories as to the typical delinquent – led them to concentrate the activities on certain 'types' of individuals. A further factor in deter-mining how that encounter developed was found to be dependent on how the individual officer defined his or her own role. Those who defined their role in terms of a 'due process' model that emphasizes the rights of the defendant attempted to follow the *letter* of the law and, therefore, tended to react only to specific, concrete evidence of the commission of a crime. In contrast, when officers perceived their role primarily in terms of a 'crime control' model that considers the control of crime to be of primary importance they were more concerned with the *spirit* of the law. Thus, they were more likely to respond on the basis of their subjective definition of a situation and the personalities involved.

Cicourel found this process to be essentially class-biased, as it was generally working-class areas and their inhabitants that most closely mirrored the typifications and expectations of the police. Moreover, other criminal justice practitioners, such as probation and social workers, court officials and the organisational context within which they work reinforced such practices. Cicourel found probation and social workers subscribed to a theory of delinquency causation that focused on factors such as 'broken homes', 'permissive parenting' or 'poverty'. Thus, juveniles with this sort of background were seen as the likeliest candidates for a delinquent career and were often, albeit unwittingly, launched upon one. These findings had serious implications for the validity of crime statistics.

Many criminologists from quite different perspectives had previously acknowledged that official statistics were not a wholly accurate reflection of the reality of crime. For example, there was much concern over the hidden figure of unrecorded crime. Nevertheless, official statistics had been widely considered as reasonably objective and as providing a reliable basis for discerning patterns in crime and sug- gesting associations. From a labelling perspective, however, official statistics were seen to be just another interpretation of the world and their only utility lay in the light they inadvertently shed on the agencies of social control that 'constructed' them. Quinney (1970) suggested four societal structures – age, gender, class and ethnic group – that would enhance the likelihood of someone receiving a criminal label. Thus, there is a high probability that a young black working-class male will be defined as deviant. Moreover, that this group is over-represented in the official crime statistics is not surprising since these figures are produced by agencies whose personnel, operating criteria and rationale are drawn from the more politically powerful segments of society. What Quinney was essentially arguing is that some people have the facilities for applying stigmatizing labels to other people, ostensibly because these other people violate norms the labellers wish to uphold. This is only possible, however, because these others are identified as members of society with little or no political power.

The consequences of labelling for the recipients

It was noted earlier that labelling theories have for the most part concentrated on their third area of concern: assessing the consequences of the labelling process for the future conduct of the recipient. This aspect is certainly the most widely discussed and best documented.

Frank Tannenbaum (1938) – who is usually regarded as founder of the labelling approach – noted that of the many young males who break the law only some are apprehended. His 'dramatisation of evil' hypothesis described the process whereby a community first defines the *actions* of an individual as evil, but eventually goes on to define the *individual himself* as evil, thus casting suspicion on all his future actions. The evil is further 'dramatised' by separating the individual from his usual group and administering specialised treatment to 'punish' or 'cure' the evil. This leads to further isolation and the confirmation and internalisation of his new 'tag'. Eventually he will redefine his self-image in line with the opinions and expectations of others in the community and thereby come to perceive himself as criminal. This idea that in reacting to people as 'criminal' society actually encourages them to become so, and that criminal justice intervention can therefore deepen criminality is the central contention of the labelling approach.

Edwin Lemert (1951) made a crucial distinction between *primary* and *secondary* deviance. The former – with affiliations to the predestined actor model of criminal behaviour – could arise out of a variety of socio-cultural, psychological or even physiological factors. However, because these initial acts are often extremely tentative and certainly not part of an organised way of life, offenders can easily rationalise them as a temporary aberration or see it as part of a socially acceptable role. For example, a worker may observe that everyone pilfers a little from work. Thus such behaviour will be of only marginal significance in terms of the status and self-concept of the individual concerned. In short, primary deviants do not view their deviance as central to themselves and do not conceive of themselves as deviant.

However, if these initial activities are subject to societal reaction, and with each act of primary deviance the offender becomes progressively more stigmatized through 'name calling, labelling or stereotyping', then a crisis may occur. One way of resolving this crisis is for the individual to accept their deviant status and organise their life and identity around the facts of deviance. It is at this stage that the individual becomes a 'secondary deviant'. In short, a youth who steals something and is not caught may be less likely to persist in this behaviour than one who is apprehended and officially sanctioned. Deviance is simply the end result of a process of human interaction. Primary deviance may or may not develop into secondary deviance: it is the number of criminal transgressions and the intensity and hostility of societal reaction that determines the outcome.

It was with the influential work of Becker (1963), Erikson (1966) and Kitsuse (1962), and their use of Merton's concept of the 'self-fulfilling prophecy' – a false definition of a situation, evoking a new behaviour that makes the original false assumption come true – that the labelling perspective was to gain widespread popularity. These writers argued that most offenders are falsely defined as criminal. That is not to say that they are innocent in the sense of having not committed offences, but rather that the system, and thus society, not only judges their actions as criminal and 'bad', but extends this judgement to them as people. The consequences are that once someone has been deemed by society to be 'bad', there is an expectation that this 'badness' must again find expression in some way or another, leading to the commission of further offences. Armed with these stereotypes of offenders as wholly criminal and incapable of law-abiding behaviour, the general population reacts to them on this basis and treats them accordingly. Consequently, offenders may face discrimination in employment, often even where their offence bears no relation to the type of work being sought. Moreover, a person's previous social status, such as parent, spouse or worker, is hidden under the criminal label until that becomes their 'master status' or controlling public identification.

In summary, labelling theorists claim that the false definition of offenders as uncompromisingly criminal fulfils this very prophecy by evoking hostile and negative societal reactions that render conformity difficult, and criminality attractive. Thus, the processes and means of social control that are intended to induce law-abiding behaviour can have the ironic and unintended consequence of achieving the very opposite. It would be misleading to suggest, however, that in general, the labelling perspective views the processes outlined above as in any way deterministic or unavoidable. It is quite possible that some of-fenders may react to being labelled and stigmatized by refraining from the type of conduct that elicited such a reaction. As Downes and Rock (1997: 183) have noted in a sympathetic commentary:

> Interactionism casts deviance as a process which may continue over a lifetime, which has no necessary end, which is anything but inexorable, and which may be built around false starts, diversions and returns. The trajectory of a deviant career cannot always be predicted. However constrained they may seem to be, people can choose not to err further.

The key point from a labelling perspective is that *many* offenders *do* internalise their criminal labels, and thus stable or career criminality arises out of the reaction of society to them.

Moral panics and deviance amplification

The labelling perspective has also been applied at the group level. A useful analytical tool in this context is that of the *deviancy amplification* feedback or spirals (Wilkins, 1964) where it is argued that the less tolerance there is to an initial act of deviance, the more similar acts will be defined as deviant. This process will give rise to more reactions against criminals resulting in more social *alienation,* or *marginalization* of deviants. This state of affairs will generate more crime by deviant groups, leading to decreasing tolerance of deviants by conforming groups.

Deviancy amplification feedback is central to the phenomenon known as the 'moral panic'. Jock Young (1971) first coined the term in his study of recreational drug users in north London and it was later developed by Stanley Cohen (1973) in his study of the societal reaction to the 'mods and rockers' disturbances of 1964. These studies marked a significant break with those approaches to delinquency – favoured by proponents of the predestined actor model of criminal behaviour – that were primarily concerned with finding the causes of delinquent behaviour. By contrast, definitional and structural questions relating to why certain groups define certain acts as deviant, and the consequences of this process were asked.

Cohen (1973) found the press to be guilty of exaggeration and distortion in their reporting of the events in Clacton over the Easter bank holiday weekend in 1964. The sense of outrage communicated by such misrepresentation had set in motion a series of interrelated responses. First, there was increased public concern about the issue, to which the police responded by increasing their surveillance of the groups in question – mods and rockers. This resulted in more frequent arrests, which in turn appeared to confirm the validity of the original media reaction. Second, by emphasising the stylistic differences and antagonisms between the groups, the press reaction encouraged polarisation and further clashes between the groups. Finally, these further disturbances attracted further sensationalised media coverage, increased police activity and greater public concern. Thus, the way the media distorted the initial events resulted in an amplification of deviance – both perceived *and* real.

The concept of moral panic is also central to Hall, Critcher, Jefferson, Clarke and Roberts' (1978) study of 'mugging'; however, the concept is used within a very different theoretical framework. While conceding that there can be no deviance without an agency of condemnation and control, it is argued that the notion of moral panic is limited if employed without reference to the social and political structures that empower a dominant minority to construct and implement the process of labelling. Within labelling theories, therefore, moral panic is expressed in terms of a 'society' that creates rules. Within the Marxism that informs Hall *et al*'s approach, it is expressed in terms of a 'state' that has the power to criminalise (Cohen, 1985: 272). Given its theoretical basis, this analysis falls more within the scope of the radical theories discussed in the following chapter. That the labelling perspective neglects the structures of power that ultimately allow the construction of deviance is one of a number of limitations identified by its critics.

The limitations of labelling theories

As the labelling approach became more influential during the 1960s and early 1970s it attracted criticism from a variety of sources. Plummer (1979) noted that because the perspective is so loosely defined, it could harbour several diverse theoretical positions and thus open itself to internal contradiction and criticism from all theoretical sides. Such ambiguity and eclecticism has led some critics to claim that labelling is at best a vague perspective that does not contain consistent and inter-related concepts, and which fails to make precise distinctions between mere description and causal statements (Taylor, Walton and Young, 1973). On the other hand, proponents of labelling theory such as Schur (1971) contend that the strength of the approach lies in its ability to analyse aspects of social reality that have been neglected, offer directions for research and thus complement other theoretical approaches.

Others argue that labelling theories do not clearly define deviance. According to Gibbs (1966), labelling theorists claim that an act is deviant only if a certain reaction follows, yet at the same time refer to 'secret deviants' and 'primary deviants', and suggest that certain groups of people are licensed to engage in deviant behaviour without negative reactions. This implies, it is argued, that deviance can be identified not merely in terms of societal reactions to it but in terms of *existing social norms*. There may be ambiguity about certain kinds of 'soft' deviance, where criminal definitions are relative to time and place, but there is no such ambiguity regarding 'hard' deviance, such as violent assault, robbery and burglary, which have always been universally condemned. 'Hard' deviants at least are fully aware that what they are doing is deviant or criminal but freely choose this course of action because it is profitable or exciting. Labelling is therefore an irrelevance.

Taylor *et al* (1973) accept the notion that deviance is not simply an inherent property of an act but they do not agree that it is as arbitrary as labelling theories imply. They take the view that the deviant is not a passive actor but a decision-maker whose rule-breaking reflects initial motives and choices, and thus has meaning. This approach overlaps with a further criticism that the emphasis on the negative repercussions of labelling implies an individual totally at the mercy of official labellers. A consequence of this overemphasis on societal reaction at the expense of individual choice has been the tendency to elevate the offender to the status of victim. Labelling theories have 'the paradoxical consequence of inviting us to view the deviant as a passive nonentity who is responsible neither for his suffering nor its alleviation – who is more "sinned" against than sinning' (Gouldner, 1968: 38). Yet, as previously noted, labelling theories do not on the whole argue that the effects of labelling are determinant, but rather that negative societal reaction can, and in many cases will, deepen criminality. Thus as Downes and Rock (1998: 190) quite correctly observe, 'criticisms of the species offered by Gouldner really reflect a response to only the most narrow versions of interactionism'. As for the charge that labelling theorists take the side of the deviant and overlook the 'real' victims of crime some, most notably Becker (1967), make no apologies for this and argue that they are merely balancing out traditional approaches within criminology that are severely biased *against* the deviant.

Many of the criticisms of labelling theories would seem more justified had the approach been promoted as a developed theory rather than as a perspective comprising loosely connected themes. In the light of this, perhaps the most telling criticism of the perspective is that, though it focused on societal reaction, it stopped short of offering a systematic analysis of social structure and power relations. While acknowledging that political interest and social disadvantage influenced societal reaction, labelling theorists failed to make explicit the connection of the criminal justice system to the underlying capitalist economic order and the inequalities of wealth and power rooted therein. These issues are addressed in the following chapter.

Suggested further reading

Becker, *Outsiders* (1963) still provides an essential introduction to the labelling tradition in criminology, with Erikson, *Wayward Puritans* (1966), Kitsuse, 'Societal Reaction to Deviant Behaviour' (1962) and Lemert, *The Social Reality of Crime* (1972) being other key texts. Quinney, *The Social Reality of Crime* (1970) provides an early link with conflict theory. Cohen, *Folk Devils and Moral Panics* (1973) is a milestone text on 'moral panics'; the concept importantly developed from a radical/critical perspective by Hall *et al*, *Policing the Crisis* (1978).

Chapter 9

Conflict and radical theories

Conflict and radical versions of the victimised actor model have sought to explain crime and criminal behaviour in terms of the unequal nature of the socio-political structure of society. Again this is not a homogenous theory but a diverse collection of perspectives united by a common tendency to see societies as being characterised by conflict rather than consensus. Nonetheless, two broad categories or groupings can be identified. First, conflict theorists take a *pluralist* stance and propose that society consists of numerous groups all involved in struggle to promote their interests. Second, *radical* accounts are invariably informed by various interpretations of Marxist social and economic theory. However, notwithstanding these differences, writers in both camps see social consensus as a temporary situation engineered by those with substantial power in a society. The main concern for both groups of writers is with the social struggle for power and authority.

Among the critics of the labelling perspective were those who had argued that it had just not gone far enough. In essence, it had failed to account for the origins of the differential power to label or stigmatize people. It was in response to that critique that conflict and radical writers came to explore and apply wider economic and political science ideas to the consideration of crime and criminal behaviour.

Conflict theories

George Vold (1958) produced an explanation of crime and criminal behaviour that emphasised the group nature of society and stressed the fact that groups compete with each other in order to secure what they identify as their interests. He argued that they become ever more wary and watchful of their interests vis-à-vis other groups, and become engaged in a continuous struggle to improve their standing in relation to others. The whole process of law-making, law-breaking and law enforcement directly reflects deep-seated and fundamental conflicts between these group interests and the more general struggle between groups for control of the police power of the state. Since minority groups lack the power to have a strong influence on the legislative process, their behaviour is that most often defined as criminal, or deviant. This process of criminalisation then legitimises the use of the police and other control agencies to enforce these laws on behalf of the most powerful groups in society.

For Austin Turk, the theoretical problem of explaining crime lies in not in understanding varieties of criminal behaviour – for he observes that definitions will vary over time and place – but in explaining the actual process of criminalisation. Specifically this involves examining the process of the assignment of criminal status to individuals, which results in the production of criminality. There is an obvious resonance with labelling theory in Turk's work. He nevertheless went much further in seeking to explain why it is that labels come to be widely accepted as legitimate, often by those who are so labelled.

Turk saw the social order as the outcome of powerful social groups who successfully control society in their own interests. He argued that social control is exercised by providing a normative – moral or value-laden – justification for law, which is then enforced by controlling agencies such as the police. In his earlier work, Turk (1964) suggested that those people who have an unclear view of how their behaviour will impact on others, especially on the powerful, and who go on to break rules, norms or laws, will be the most likely to be caught and processed by control agencies. It is an argument that explains why it is that young people are more likely to fall foul of the law than most adults.

In his later work, Turk (1969) described two ways in which control is exercised in society: first by *coercion* and, second, by the *control of legal images* and *living time*. The control of society by *coercion* – or the threat and exercise of physical force – is perhaps the most obvious form of control. But the more that force is applied, the less likely it is to be accepted as legitimate and therefore the more difficult it will be to control society. The control of legal images, on the other hand, is an altogether more subtle exercise. Legal systems have formal laws, breaches of which are legally punishable, and there are established procedures for exercising those laws. There are also degrees of discretion as to how the law is exercised. Turk argues that the subtle interplay of the formal and informal allows the powerful to manipulate the legal system in their own interests while still preserving an image of due process and impartiality.

The concept of the control of living time suggests that people will become accustomed to forms of domination and control, especially if it is maintained and legitimised over generations. New generations will gradually forget that social control conditions were ever any different from those with which they are familiar.

Richard Quinney was originally a traditional conflict theorist – heavily influenced by social reaction/labelling theory and later identified with a more radical Marxist-inspired perspective – who considered crime to be the product of legal definitions constructed through the exercise of political power. In this way actions that may cause harm to others and be similar to forms of behaviour which are subject to the criminal law, may be dealt with less seriously, or not at all, if they are conventionally activities carried out by, or in the interests of, the powerful. Thus, while the causing of death by a less powerful individual may well be defined as murder or manslaughter if committed by a corporate body or high-status individual, it may be interpreted as a civil law violation, or simply an accident. Quinney pointed to numerous examples of harm-generating activities committed by the powerful that are not investigated, are excused or effectively treated as misdemeanours and fail to come under the auspices of the criminal law.

Quinney, like many of the later radical criminologists, paid a good deal of attention to the role of the mass media in shaping the way in which people perceive crime. He observed that both crime and non-crime definitions are spread throughout the media. With their pervasive effect, the media select and construct a commonly held view of reality that certain actions are naturally crimes and others non-crimes.

Quinney outlined six propositions that summarise his particular version of conflict theory. First, crime is a definition of human conduct created by authorised agents in a politically organised society. Second, these criminal definitions are applied by the segments of society that have the power to shape the enforcement of the criminal law. Third, these criminal definitions are applied by these segments of society that have the power to shape the administration of the criminal law. Fourth, behaviour patterns are structured in segmentally organised society in relation to criminal definitions, and within this context people engage in actions that have relative probabilities of being defined as deviant. Fifth, conceptions of crime are constructed and diffused in the segments of society by various means of communication. Sixth, the social reality of crime is constructed by the formulation and application of criminal definitions, the development of behaviour patterns related to criminal definitions and the construction of criminal conceptions (Quinney, 1970: 15–23).

Criticisms of conflict theories

For later radical criminologists much of early conflict theory, while accepting the inevitability of social conflict, was still seen as essentially conservative and complacent about the possibility of conflict leading to more successful social integration. It was also to an extent founded on predestined actor model notions that denied the possibility that victims of an unfair social and economic system might simply rationally choose offending behaviour as a way of coming to terms with a system which had failed to accommodate their interests. Conflict theorists had simply failed to explain why the law is as it is in the first place. Moreover, they proffered no acceptable explanation as to why it is that those sections socially of society who do not have their interests represented by established social institutions should choose to accept 'stable authority relationships' out of which they benefit little.

In seeking an answer to that last criticism, Turk had argued that it is a 'lack of sophistication' among the subordinate groups that is to blame for the problems they pose for established society. They may simply choose to break laws or norms that do not fit in with their perceptions of their situation.

By promoting the idea that offenders have a limited capacity to express themselves to authority, we are encouraged to see their accounts of their actions as less valid than those of authority-holders. This is a perspective strongly countered by labelling theorists such as Howard Becker, who had argued that it is the task of the social researcher to give voice to the 'underdog' in the face of more than adequate representation of the account of 'superordinate groups'. The essentially predestined actor model 'correctionalist' stance implicit in the work of Turk is illustrated by his view that deviant subcultures should be forcibly broken up by the authorities in order to coerce deviants back into an integrated consensus (Turk, 1969). This should happen apparently, regardless of whether or not they see such integration as being in their interests or not.

This same criticism cannot be directed against Quinney. He proposes that the actions of those who are criminally labelled are not so much the outcome of inadequate socialisation and personality problems but rather as conscientious actions taken against something – generally the established, unequal social order. Taking this rather more rational actor model-oriented approach, Quinney saw what these acts defined as criminal as perhaps the only appropriate means for expressing thoughts and feelings concerning powerlessness and inequality. Also, somewhat romantically, Quinney considered that deviant, or criminal, behaviour provides the only possibilities for bringing about social change.

Radical criminology

Radical criminology – like conflict theories – encompasses a broad range of ideas. The seminal book in the field, Taylor, Walton and Young's *The New Criminology* (1973) was an attempt to link the concerns of labelling theory with Marxism, while in the United States the work of William Chambliss and Richard Quinney was based on somewhat different foundations.

William Chambliss had become interested in the socio-political context in which the criminal law had developed while undertaking a study of the development of the vagrancy laws in Britain. He observed that the origin of this body of legislation could be traced to vested interests:

> There is little question that these statutes were designed for one express purpose: to force labourers to accept employment at a low wage in order to ensure the landowner an adequate supply of labour at a price he could afford to pay.
>
> (Chambliss, 1964: 69)

It was an approach influenced by the American school of *legal realism*, which concerned itself with the distinction between the 'law in books' and the 'law in action'. In his 1971 work *Law, Order, and Power* – written in collaboration with Robert Seidman – an almost Durkheimian argument is presented. They proposed that the complexity that comes with technological development and which necessitates more complicated, differentiated and sophisticated social roles actually operates to put people at odds with one another. This increasing social complexity requires that sanctioning institutions be designed to keep order among the conflicting interests. In their view, the basis of the sanctioning would be organised in the interests of the 'dominant groups' in society but the actual application of the sanctions are enforced by bureaucratic institutions who have their own interests. The 'law of action' thus comes to reflect a combination of the organisations created to enforce the rules.

Chambliss (1969) had previously argued that criminal justice bureaucracies tend to deal with members of the lower social classes more harshly than other people because the latter have little to offer in return for leniency and they are also in no position to fight the system. Chambliss and Seidman (1971) later concluded, however, that the police act illegally and breach the norms of due process at every stage of their activities. This occurs because they are neither committed to the notion of due process in the first place and at the same time they have an enormous potential for making discretionary decisions. Moreover, there are no real safeguards. Bargains struck with the prosecutor before the trial begins tend to reflect the relative political and economic power of the defendant. Furthermore, considerable pressure is applied to the accused to plead guilty, leading the powerless to surrender the 'right' to trial by jury in nine cases out of ten.

Chambliss (1969) had observed that much of the criminal legal effort is devoted to processing the very people least likely to be deterred by legal sanctions. He observed that the use of lengthy prison sentences against drug addicts and capital punishment against murderers are instances where sanctions have little deterrent effect. On the other hand, he noted the reluctance to impose severe sentences against white-collar and professional criminals, the very offenders who are deterred by sanctions. Chambliss argued that such a policy went directly against the formal logic of deterrence, but fits perfectly the bureaucratic logic of demonstrating 'effectiveness' by harsh treatment of the powerless while avoiding the organisational tensions that would follow from confronting the powerful.

By the mid-1970s there was a significant shift in Chambliss's perspective at a time when a number of important social theorists were returning to the Marxist tradition that had virtually disappeared during the 1940s and 1950s in the USA. This shift in perspective was reflected in nine specific propositions.

1 Acts are defined as criminal because it is in the interests of the ruling class to define them as such.

2 Members of the ruling class will be able to violate the laws with impunity while members of the subject class will be punished.

3 As capitalist societies industrialise and the gap between the ruling-class and the working-class widens, penal law will expand in an effort to coerce the latter class into submission.

4 Crime reduces the pool of surplus labour by creating employment not only for the criminals but also for law enforcers, welfare workers, professors of criminology, and a horde of people who live off the fact that crime exists; an analysis later developed by Christie (1993), who coined the term 'the crime industry' to describe this multitude of interested professional groups.

5 Crime diverts the attention of the lower classes from the exploitation they experience and directs it toward other members of their own class rather than toward the capitalist class or the economic system.

6 Crime is a reality that exists only inasmuch as those who create it in society have an interest in its presence.

7 People involved in criminal behaviour are acting rationally in ways that are compatible with the life conditions of their social class position.

8 Crime varies from society to society depending on the political and economic structures of society.

9 Socialist countries should have much lower rates of crime because the less intense class struggle should reduce the forces leading to, and the functions of, crime (Chambliss, 1975: 152–5).

At this time during the late 1960s, similar concerns and conclusions were emerging among a group of radical young criminologists in the UK who were beginning to question the role of orthodox criminology in helping to legitimate unequal social relations in capitalist societies. The law, police and social workers in particular were highlighted as having an important role in preserving the *status quo*, and the proponents of the predestined actor model of criminal behaviour that dominated social work and probation training; the British Home Office and the Cambridge Institute of Criminology were observed to give these crucial criminal justice agencies academic support.

There developed among these young radicals an increased concern to restore some dignity to the deviant person. They were no longer to be seen as the 'poor wee things' of the predestined actor model, nor the inevitable and terrible pathological creatures deserving of harsh containment – or even death – proposed by a great deal of right-wing criminology. There was a concern to restore meaning to the deviant actors, to regard them as knowing people responding rationally, albeit sometimes rebelliously, to their circumstances.

This concern for the 'authenticity' of the deviant's position was combined with a concern for the nature of the state and its agencies in labelling deviance, in the passing of legislation, apportioning blame and prosecuting individuals, in the interests of those who already hold political power. The ideas were by no means new and many of them can be traced back to the Chicago school. The work of Howard Becker – discussed in the previous chapter – in such work as *Outsiders* (1963), and other symbolic interactionists and labelling theorists, was very influential, as was the entire phenomenological and ethnomethodological tradition. Further influences were the anti-psychiatry movement and radical psychology epitomised by the work of R.D. Laing (1960).

Notable practitioners in this field emerged from a series of meetings held by the New Deviancy Conference at York University in the late 1960s and early 1970s. Those involved included Paul Rock, David Downes, Laurie Taylor, Stan Cohen, Ian Taylor and Jock Young. These new criminologists – or 'sociologists of deviance' – moved from a purely symbolic interactionist, labelling theory position to one more heavily influenced by Marxism. At the same time, however, Marxism itself was going through something of a revision.

There had been earlier writers – in particular Wilhelm Bonger (1916) – who attempted to explain crime and criminal behaviour from a Marxist perspective. These had, however, tended to over-predict the amount of crime that would occur under capitalism by noting that an alienating social structure would inevitably lead to criminal and anti-social behaviour. Bonger's work was crudely deterministic and ignored the possible diversity of responses to adverse social conditions – such as drug-taking, retreatism, and ritualistic accommodations by those with little stake in society – as described by Merton and others working in the anomie theory tradition. The new criminologists sought a 'totalising' explanation of crime and criminal behaviour, one that accounted for social structural power and history. They considered that they had found the solution – 'a fully social view of deviance' – in the combination of a labelling theory based sociology of deviance and what was seen at the time as a modern Marxism.

The classic text in this tradition is Taylor, Walton and Young's *The New Criminology* (1973), which provides an impressive summary of previous criminological ideas and a provision of indicators that the authors considered would give rise to a crime-free society. The book is founded on a set of assumptions that can be summarised as follows. First, crime is a two-sided affair – the cause of criminal behaviour *and* the identification of the power to criminalize. Second, capitalism itself is crime-producing – or criminogenic – as crime is a product of the material and social inequalities that are inherent to the logic of capitalism. Third, the only way to eliminate crime is to destroy inequality and thus the power and need to criminalize.

Drawing heavily on labelling theory, it was argued that the power to criminalize, make laws and prosecute offenders, or particular groups that are perceived as offenders, was a function of the state. The state was seen to vary in form during different historical periods, and the techniques that it employs to maintain social discipline, ultimately in the interests of the powerful, also varies.

In summary, the New Criminology represented a 'global', 'macro' approach that locates the causes of crime and criminal behaviour within the social structure. The labelling perspective nonetheless retains a great deal of importance in this explanatory model. Indeed, it appears to be at least as important as the underlying structural considerations that determine the nature of the labelling process. But this approach does have the advantage of ensuring that there is an appreciation that individuals do possess a great deal of freedom of action within broad social circumstances. However, decisions to act are left to the rationality of the individual themselves.

Criticisms of radical theories

The New Criminology provided a very generalised prescription for a crime-free, socialist 'good society'. From the standpoint of the twenty-first century, it can be seen to be utopian, reflecting the optimistic nature of the times in which it was written; while, the generality of the work itself meant that it could offer very little to substantive theory at all. Indeed, it can be argued that since its publication very little has been achieved to produce a 'truly social view of deviance'. The subsequent text, edited by *Taylor, Walton and Young* (1975), appears to have marked something of a retreat into smaller concerns and away from the 'grand theory' and meta-vision of the original programme. Five possible explanations as to why this should have been the case can be identified, while the reader will note that these are not necessarily mutually exclusive.

First, some have doubted the legitimacy of merging and synthesizing labelling theory and Marxist analysis, as the philosophical under-pinnings of the two traditions are fundamentally different. Hirst (1980) argues that Taylor *et al* are simply labelling theorists who have raided the works of Marx in order to provide a synthesis of the two perspectives.

Second, others have argued that the new criminologists failed to provide an adequate definition of crime and deviance. For proponents of the predestined actor tradition this was not a problem; crime is either the outcome of 'pathological behaviour' or simply behaviour that transgresses against the law. The notion of crime as consisting of any behaviour that causes social harm is, however, highly problematic. The fundamental question is whether it is possible to have a theory of crime causation that legitimately encompasses such diverse activities as working-class theft, rape and 'white-collar' fraud. If we accept such an expansive definition of crime, the problem arises as to how we are to accurately measure social harm. Some have argued that once the label 'crime' has become problematic, it becomes clear that separate areas of criminal behaviour require different explanatory frameworks. In that case, the ability to develop any central all-encompassing criminology begins to dissolve and this inevitably leads to a retreat from grand theory.

Third, the retreat from grand theory was encouraged by the diverse accounts of criminal activity emerging from sociologists and social historians. Studies carried out by researchers such as Thompson (1975) and Hay (1981) reveal that criminal behaviour is not a homogenous concept and thus the 'rule of law' cannot be simply conceptualised as an external coercive force repressing the working class. Indeed, it could possibly offer protection from certain abuses of power while constraining action in the interests of maintaining order. Examples offered by these authors from the eighteenth and nineteenth centuries demonstrate that state power was a far more complex concept than the authors of the *New Criminology* had at first envisaged. In short, there are many parasitic and diverse forms of crime from which the working class seek protection in law and order.

Fourth, changes in Marxist theory during the 1970s left the first wave of New Criminologists intellectually stranded. The state had traditionally been seen as the political form of class domination. In the 1970s, however, the focus of Marxist theorising changed to encompass such areas as culture, ideology and hegemony, a much more complex analysis. Law was no longer conceptualised as an entirely bourgeois concept, but as a more differentiated idea.

New Criminology revisionists addressed many of these complex new issues, some working at Birmingham University's Centre for Contemporary Cultural Studies under its charismatic director, Professor Stuart Hall. This group was responsible for producing the controversial *Policing the Crisis* (1978) an attempt to rework many of the utopian aspects of the New Criminology into a more modern and sophisticated theoretical package. They incorporated ideas from the recently available work of the Italian Marxist Antonio Gramsci – originally published during the 1920s – in a discussion of the substantive issue of street robbery or 'mugging'. In doing so, they investigated the relationship between ethnicity, class and the state. This body of work forms such a crucial element in the intellectual origins of critical criminology – one of two contemporary variants of the radical tradition – that it is the focus of Chapter 11. It is a perspective that has nonetheless had little impact outside academic criminology.

Fifth, in response to an apparent substantial increase in crime rates and a general perception among vast sections of the population that crime levels were at an unacceptable level, a great deal of popularism came to infiltrate criminological debate. We saw in Chapter 3 that the conservative populists – or 'right' realists – came to take seriously the problems that ordinary people, notably working-class people, had experienced, and in doing so managed to capture much of the ground that the political left had always regarded as their natural constituency. We shall see in Chapter 15 that in an effort to recapture the issue of crime from the political 'right', the populist socialists – or left realists – influentially came to reconsider radical criminology. This second contemporary variant of the radical tradition recognises that capitalism may well be responsible for the relative inequality and absolute poverty that shape so much of British culture and provides the root cause of crime. On the other hand, it is noted that the bulk of that crime is predatory on the very people that they would wish to defend, the working class and the poor.

Suggested further reading

The US conflict and radical theory approach is well represented by Chambliss, *Crime and the Legal Process* (1969) and 'Toward a Political Economy of Crime' (1975), Chambliss and Seidman, *Law, Order and Power* (1971), Quinney, *The Social Reality of Crime* (1970) and Turk, *Criminality and the Social Order* (1969). The radical UK tradition is best represented by Taylor *et al*, *The New Criminology* (1973) and Taylor *et al* (eds), *Critical Criminology* (1975). Christie, *Crime Control as Industry* (1993) provides an excellent more recent radical discussion of the notion of crime control as industry in a tradition established by Cohen, *Visions of Social Control* (1985).

Chapter 10

Feminist perspectives

We have seen in the previous two chapters that the victimised actor model of crime and criminal behaviour proposes that the criminal is in some way the victim of an unjust and unequal society. It is the activities of the poorer sections of society that are criminalised while the actions of the rich and powerful are simply ignored or not even defined as criminal. From a feminist perspective, it is argued that it is men who are the dominant group in society and it is they who make and enforce the rules to the detriment of women.

Feminism has had a considerable impact on criminology in recent years, providing both critiques of traditional explanations of crime and criminal behaviour while at the same time offering its own perspectives. It is, however, important to recognise that feminism is not a unitary system of thought but a collection of different theoretical perspectives with each explaining the oppression of women in a different way. Consequently, there is no one feminist explanation of female crime and criminal behaviour and therefore before examining these debates it will be useful to consider briefly the different variations of feminist thought – or feminisms. A further word of caution should be noted at this stage.

The various versions of feminism tend to be united in their rejection of the term 'victim' to describe the oppression of women in a male-dominated society. There is a preference for the far more positive term 'survivor'. It is a linguistic device that suggests that by working together in pursuit of the common cause women can successfully contest male supremacy.

Perspectives in feminist theory

Feminism is generally perceived to have emerged in western societies in two waves. The first emphasised equality within rational individual rights and was most notably characterised in the British context by the suffrage movement that lasted from the 1860s to the First World War. Subsequently, there was the opening up of educational opportunities, the provision of social legislation providing rights over property and the marital home. In 1928 there was the provision of the vote for those women over the age of 21. Nonetheless, while the social position of women was enhanced they were not to enjoy equality with men.

The second wave of feminism emerged in the USA and was brought to the UK in the late 1960s. The emergence of the Women's Liberation Movement in the wake of the civil rights and student movements demanded nothing less than the wholesale transformation of society. Consciousness-raising groups and the development of women's collectives provided the arena for debate and discussion that formed the basis of contemporary feminist thought and action.

Feminist thought has subsequently had a considerable impact on the social sciences and other academic fields. It has essentially involved a challenge to traditional male-dominated perspectives and arguments have been proposed both for the integration of women into theoretical perspectives and the development of new approaches that analyse and develop an understanding of issues specifically related to the lives of women. Essentially new areas of research have been opened up designed to make previously invisible women visible.

There are a number of contemporary variants of feminism. *Liberal feminism* has its roots in the notions of individual rights and freedoms that were central to the rise and consolidation of modern societies in the eighteenth and nineteenth century. The subordination of women is examined as part of an analysis of wider social structures and in-equalities. The central concern is to locate discrimination in social practice, specifically within the public sphere, and extend rights to women to equal those enjoyed by men through the process of legal reform. It is a perspective nonetheless criticised for its inability to confront the deep-rooted levels of gender inequality. In short, there is an identified failure to challenge male values, while solutions offered are limited and to some extent superficial. However, the legacy of sex discrimination and equal pay legislation, for example, can be attributed to the influence of liberal feminism.

Radical feminism emerged in the 1970s and focuses on the importance of *patriarchy*, or the 'set of hierarchical relations between men, and

solidarity between them, which enables them to control women'
(Hartmann, 1981: 447). The slogan 'the personal is political' has been
used to identify the basis of women's oppression within the private
realm of personal relationships and private lives. Thus, the need to
expose the hidden secrets of personal relationships and social practice
within the private sphere is recognised by radical feminists and has led
to the examination of issues such as reproductive freedom, pornography,
domestic violence and child abuse. Radical feminists advocate sep-
aratism from men to different degrees. This can be seen either partially,
in the provision of women-only institutions or events, or wholly,
including the withdrawal of women from personal and sexual relationships with men.

Radical feminism has been criticised for its biological determinism,
that is, the belief that by nature all men are the same and all women are
the same. Further criticism is directed at the notion that patriarchy is an
all-pervasive universal principle operating in the same way in all places
at all times. It thus fails to recognise differences in the experiences of
women across time and space accounting for class and ethnic differences
(Jaggar, 1983).

Marxist feminists argue that the subordination of women is located in
the capitalist exploitation of their domestic role. They observe the existence of a dominant ideology that presents women as primarily carers
within the domestic sphere and which is used to justify low wages, low
status and part-time jobs, and, in turn, is used to deny women the right
to economic independence (Beechey, 1977). Women are also considered
to be part of a reserve army of labour, available to be drawn into the
workforce when the needs of capitalism demand it and to be easily
rejected when there is surplus labour (Bruegel, 1978).

Marxist feminists have been criticised for their over-use of economic
explanations of women's oppression while failing to examine the
complexity of family relationships. Tong (1988) notes, however, the
increasing relevance of the Marxist feminist critique, as more and more
women have become employed in the market economy.

Socialist feminism provides a synthesis of the radical and Marxist
feminist perspectives with recognition that both capitalist and patriar-
chal systems play a part in the subordination of women. 'Dual systems
theory' recognises the systems of capitalism and patriarchy to be separate but at the same time mutually accommodating systems of oppression. More recent 'unified system theorists', on the other hand, have
developed unifying concepts as central categories of analysis. Jaggar
(1983), for example, identified the concept of 'alienation' that provides a
theoretical synthesis of Marxist, radical and liberal feminist thought.

The potential of socialist feminism to bring together the diverse accounts of different feminist approaches is significant. It has nonetheless been criticised by black feminists for the tendency to deny the diversity of experiences that different women have.

Black feminism examines the structures of domination prevalent in the personal, cultural and institutional levels and experiences of the lives of black women. The axes of race, gender and class are identified as forming the basis of black women's oppression, within which, it is argued, there exists a 'more generalised matrix of domination'. This matrix was described by bell hooks (the writer spells her name in the lower case) (1988: 174–6)) as a 'politic of domination' which is grounded in a hierarchical, ideological belief system.

In their critique of the feminist accounts of the family, education, reproduction and patriarchy, black feminist writers have identified the relationship of black women to the structures, ideologies and institutions of oppression. Accusations of racism made by black feminists towards the broader, often white middle-class feminist movement has been productive for it opened up a discourse of difference, recognising the diversity of female experience.

The notion of difference is also central to any understanding of the relationship of feminism to postmodernism (see the final chapter in this book). We shall see later that Carol Smart has welcomed postmodernism but that other feminists have found it problematic. Radical feminists have criticised the emphasis on, and celebration of, individual difference by arguing that it is the collective voice that makes women strong. Other feminists argue that the challenge is to find a way to think both women and 'women' recognising diversity *and* collective experience.

It has been the purpose of this section to sensitise the reader with little or no knowledge of contemporary feminism to the diversity of thought that co-exists within that paradigm. The main differences between these accounts centre on factors identified as providing the basis of women's oppression and the proposed solutions. Black feminism and post-modernist feminism provide both critiques of other feminist accounts and also their own perspectives that recognise the different experiences of women and of their subordination. We now return to our discussion of women and criminality.

Early explanations of female criminality

Late twentieth-century criminology has been described as the 'most masculine of all the social sciences, a speciality that wore six-shooters on its hips and strutted its machismo' (Rafter and Heidensohn, 1985: 5). Thus, the most significant characteristic of feminist work has been its critique of mainstream male 'malestream' criminology. The main concern has been the 'intellectual sexism in theories of female crime and the institutional sexism in the juvenile and criminal justice systems' (Daly and Chesny-Lind, 1988: 508).

Bertrand (1967), Heidensohn (1968) and Klein (1976) were among the first feminists to draw attention to the relative neglect of women in the study of crime and the stereotyped distortions imposed on females in those studies that did address the issue; although it should be noted that a more traditional but eminent woman criminologist – Barbara Wootton (1959) – had first made similar observations during the 1950s. It was nonetheless the publication of Carol Smart's *Women, Crime and Criminology* (1977) that is widely acknowledged to be the turning point. Highlighting the failure of much of traditional criminology to recognise women while identifying the sexual stereotypes imposed on women and girls in those studies that did consider female criminality, the agenda was set for future feminist work.

Lombroso and Ferrero (1885) had produced the earliest criminological study of female criminals, measuring their skulls and studying their appearance from photographs, looking for signs of degeneration or atavism. Finding few 'born' female criminals they concluded that true female criminals were rare. They argued that women offenders showed fewer signs of degeneration because they had evolved less than men due to the inactive nature of their lives. It was suggested that the 'natural' passivity of women deprived them of the initiative to break the law.

The female criminal was seen to be more cruel and sinister than the male. She is described as unnatural, masculine and 'an inversion of all the qualities which specially distinguish the normal woman; namely reserve, docility and sexual apathy' (Lombroso and Ferrero, 1885: 153). The ultimate degenerative sign of a female criminal was a lack of maternal instinct, a deficiency viewed as evidence that the criminal woman belonged more to the male than the female sex. Moreover, those women who did degenerate into atavism were most likely to become prostitutes 'whose type approximates so much to that of her primitive ancestress' (Lombroso and Ferrero: 107). In this way, the 'distinctive sub-species of women was defined as "good" and "bad", "natural" and "abnormal" and these were equated with conformity and crime' (Heidensohn, 1985: 115).

The early work of Thomas (1907) was much influenced by Lombroso and Ferrero, making similar assumptions concerning the passive nature of women. His later work is less based on such a simple biologically determinist perspective. There remains, however, a particular emphasis on the sexual nature of female criminal behaviour. Thomas (1923) identified four basic 'wishes', which he argued to be fundamental to human nature – the desire for new experience, for security, for response and for recognition – and these are derived from the biological instincts of anger, fear, love and the will to gain power and status. These instincts are channelled towards appropriate goals through socialisation, with women, it was argued, having a stronger desire for the biological instinct of love than men. For Thomas it was this intense need to give and feel love that led women into crime, particularly sexual offences like prostitution. Smart (1977: 41) observes that the source of female criminality – believed to be mainly sexual – was the 'breakdown of the traditional constraints on women who formerly would not have thought of working outside the home or marrying outside the ethnic or community group'. With women being more repressed they were likely to become 'unadjusted' with the removal of social sanctions. Thomas thus advocated early intervention in the lives of 'pre-delinquent' girls by welfare agencies so as to allow for their readjustment to society.

Otto Pollak (1950) was mainly concerned with the hidden or 'masked' nature of female criminality. He proposed that female crime had been greatly under-estimated and argued that women are equally as criminal as men but the type of offences they commit and their social roles protect them from detection. It is again an analysis dependent on the biological variant of the predestined actor model of criminal behaviour. Women are viewed as being more deceitful and cunning than men, the basis of this deceitfulness being their capacity to simulate sexual arousal. It is thus this devious nature that enables women to successfully conceal their crimes and avoid detection. Moreover, the traditional caring role of a woman also allows her to 'cover' for a variety of crimes. For example, as the preparers of meals they are able to administer poisons to their unsuspecting victims.

Finally, Pollak proposed that there should be a greater leniency in the prosecution and sentencing of female offenders in comparison to men. He refers to the 'general protective attitude of man towards women … [where] … men hate to accuse women and thus indirectly send them to their punishment' (Pollak, 1950: 151). This 'chivalry' hypothesis claims that the police and courts are 'both self-deceiving and deceived about the essentially passive nature of women' (Downes and Rock, 1998: 278).

Early feminists criticised traditional criminology for assuming women to be controlled by their biology and incapable of rational action.

While the rest of the criminological world had moved on from a slavish adherence to the prescriptions of the biological variant of predestined actor model, female crime had been cut off from most of this development (Heidensohn [1994]. At the same time, as Downes and Rock (1998: 274–75) note, 'policies and attitudes towards female criminality mirrored such determinisms and lent undue prominence to "sexual deviance" as the focus of enquiry'. Early feminists emphasised these undesirable consequences as a direct outcome of the approach to the study of female criminality adopted by traditional criminological theorists.

The feminist critique of traditional criminology

Until the late twentieth century criminologists had failed to consider two salient issues relating to female criminality. First, there is the 'problem of generalisability', that is the extent to which theories created to describe male criminality can be applied to female offending behaviour. Second, there is the 'gender ratio' question of why it is that women commit less crime than men. Leonard (1983) observes that 'theoretical criminology is sexist ... it unwittingly focused on the activities, interests and values of men, while ignoring a comparative analysis of women'.

We have seen that one of the most enduring distinguishing features of explanations of female criminal behaviour has been the continuing emphasis on biological variants of the predestined actor model. From this perspective their emotions, reliability, maturity and deviancy have all been seen to be dependent on their hormonal and reproductive systems. Indeed, this analysis is still apparent in some more recent explanations of female criminal behaviour. For example, some have followed up the work of Pollak and suggested a link between hormonal changes in pregnancy, menstruation and female criminal behaviour (see Dalton, 1961). Furthermore, the use of hormonal imbalances as a defence in criminal cases is in fact specific to women. The case of infanticide is a particular example of where a woman in her defence can use post-natal depression as a partial excuse. Feminists argue nonetheless that while this may benefit in some instances the individual woman, it at the same time reinforces the belief that women are driven by their biology and denies for them a full analysis of the social, economic and political factors that determine their lives.

The psychological variant of the predestined actor model – with its origins in the work of Freud and later Thomas – gained later credence with the widespread acceptance of Bowlby's maternal deprivation thesis. This theory emphasised the importance of an early loving and enduring mother-child relationship – and hence the crucial notion that the mother should be at home to look after her children during their early years – if they are to develop into mature and well-adjusted adults. It is a theory that has continued to receive approval from some quarters and remains a popular 'common-sense' explanation of adolescent offending. Indeed, fairly unsophisticated versions of the psychological variant of the predestined actor tradition continue to inform common-sense explanations of female criminal behaviour. Campbell (1981), for example, identified research that has used psychological and sexual factors in the explanation of female shoplifting. She observes that while the great majority of the women in the studies reviewed were single, divorced or widowed none of the accounts recognised the social and economic deprivation predominantly suffered by this group.

Merton's version of anomie theory had proposed that those individuals who do not possess the legitimate means of achieving what they have been taught to desire, turn to crime in frustration. However, as Leonard (1983) observes it is a theory that applies in the main to men and their central goal of financial success. She consequently attempts to insert women into anomie theory by incorporating an alternative female aspiration of marriage and children. Leonard suggests that the lower aspirations and more accessible goals of women could therefore help to explain the lower female crime rate.

The problem is of course that not all women desire marriage and motherhood. There are also substantial problems with any attempt to use anomie as an explanation of the actual offending behaviour of women. For example, can involvement in prostitution or shoplifting be legitimately viewed as an alternative means of attaining the female goal? Leonard suggests that they cannot. Illegal means of reaching the goals of marriage and motherhood are rarely attempted. Anomie perspectives therefore appear to apply mainly to men and the goal of financial success.

Labelling theories have considered why it is that society labels some people as criminal and not others. It is claimed that it is the powerless who suffer the detrimental effects of labelling but at the same time there is a failure to explain why it is that powerless women are less involved in crime than powerless men (Gregory, 1986). Heidensohn (1985) concludes that labelling theorists only found male deviants to be interesting; which is probably the case.

Sutherland (1947), in his theory of differential association, had stressed the importance of understanding the social processes by which individuals become criminals. Crime is simply learned in exactly the same way as any other behaviour. Leonard (1983) observes that this theory usefully draws attention to the different associations of women compared to men and observes that this could help explain the differing crime rate between the two. However, there is a crucial failure to explain exactly why it is that women and men have different associations in the first place. Subcultural explanations are fundamentally criticised for being based primarily on studies of male delinquency that make it difficult to apply them to women. For example, Albert Cohen (1955) claimed that a woman's only role was to seek both a partner and a family.

Leonard (1983) observes that 'radical criminology', while challenging traditional explanations of crime and criminal behaviour on many issues, gave little attention to women. Pointing to the classic critique of criminology proposed by Taylor, Walton and Young (1973), she notes that it contains not one word about women. She concludes that applying radical criminology to an understanding of women and crime is impossible due to it being extremely generalised.

In summary, from a feminist perspective it is argued that traditional explanations of crime and criminal behaviour are 'deformed by the almost unrelieved focus on the criminality of males and the invisibility or, at best, marginalisation of women and girls' (Gelsthorpe and Morris, 1988: 281).

The impact of feminist critiques

An area where feminism has been particularly influential has been in focusing our attention on the nature of crimes committed against women by men. The two areas most frequently studied are rape and domestic violence. In the former case feminists have campaigned for anonymity and protection for women against having their character tested in court – although in practice it is still possible to agree with Adler (1982) that few women are actually protected – and the setting up of specialist rape suites in police stations where victims can be dealt with in a sympathetic manner. These changes have encouraged some improvement in the reporting of offences to the police, although the incidence of rape is still greater than officially recorded (Jones, Newburn, and Smith, 1994). In the case of domestic violence the whole issue is now considered far more serious than previously by the criminal justice system. First, there are now special legal provisions established in order to protect women and children from this behaviour, although some critics have argued that this body of legislation has actually worsened matters, for it allows these offences to be less seriously dealt with than would be the case in incidents of street violence. Second, although the greater emphasis than before in dealing with these cases has led to some increased reporting of such offences, it still remains one of the least reported (see Hamner and Saunders, 1984; Dobash and Dobash, 1992).

Separate studies of women and their experiences of crime have none-theless had a threefold influence. First, there has been the development of different explanations of female criminality and conformity. Second, there has been a general gendering of crime and therefore gendered explanations of certain male criminality. Indeed, we might note that in some respects men have also been gender-stereotyped in explanations of crime and criminal behaviour. Third, there has been recognition of a different female 'experience' of crime, victimisation and the criminal justice system. In particular, feminist criminologists have been very influential in the development of the left realism that is the focus of Chapter 15 of this book, in particular the emphasis of that perspective on the use of victim studies, even though the application of the information is not always acceptable to feminists (see Schwatz and DeKeseredy 1991; Carlen, 1992).

Downes and Rock (1998) identify several specific areas where the feminist perspective has contributed to theoretical criminology. First, there is the 'female emancipation leads to crime' debate. Adler (1975) and Simon (1975) both focused on increases in female crime since the late 1960s and early 1970s, and the increasing aggression involved in much female offending. They claimed that such variations could be explained by the influence of the emerging women's movement. Thus, it was argued that liberation, or emancipation, causes crime. Box and Hale (1983) neatly summarise the many and varied criticisms by noting merely an historical overlap between women's liberation and an increase in female crime. It has also been noted that the rate of male violent crime has continued to rise faster than the female rate (Mukjurkee and Fitzgerald, 1981). Thus, the 'new violent' female is considered to be a myth (Box, 1983).

Second, there is the invalidation of the 'leniency hypothesis' proposed by Pollak (1950). Much feminist work has examined how women are dealt with by the criminal justice system, the issue being whether they are treated more leniently for reasons of 'chivalry'. Farrington and Morris (1983), for example, found that court leniency towards women was an outcome of their lesser criminal records; while Carlen (1983) found that Scottish Sheriffs justified imprisonment more readily for female offenders whom they viewed as having 'failed' as mothers.

Downes and Rock (1998: 285–6) conclude that rather than being treated leniently by the courts, 'women – by comparison with men – are under-protected and over-controlled'.

Third, there has been the emergence of gender-based theories. Some writers, in seeking to understand female criminality, have modified the 'control theory' originally proposed by Hirschi (1969) – and discussed more fully in Chapter 14 – and applied this to the situation of women. Heidensohn (1985) significantly argues that the reason why there are so few women criminals is because of the formal and informal controls that constrain them within male-dominated society. She argues that in order to understand more about the transmission of gender inequality and the control of women by familial roles, it is necessary to consider the practical and ideological constraints imposed by family life. It is the very practices and policies that limit the involvement of women in activities outside the home that propel them back into the family where they are subject to greater control. Heidensohn observes that while women can be seen as responsible for the behaviour of others within the home and within the community, they are acting as the agents of male authority when carrying out that control function. Thus exists the stereotype of mother reprimanding a child by saying 'wait until your father gets home'.

Heidensohn notes that while women may act as agents of control on behalf of men, they are themselves controlled both at home and outside. The sexual division of labour is related to the notion of separate spheres – public and private – for men and women. The latter are expected to function chiefly within the 'private' sphere of the home. Moreover, the privacy afforded this sphere is a contributing factor in the oppression which women experience. Within the home they are vulnerable to isolation and its consequences. Lacking alternative definitions of themselves and their roles, they are affected by those around them, particularly their husbands. Male dominance may result in the subtle undermining of the woman's confidence and self-esteem and this may lead to overt violence and bodily harm (Dobash and Dobash, 1980). Wives, who are housebound, isolated and dependent are also the major victims of neurosis and depression (Brown and Harris, 1978). Furthermore, paid employment for women often means subjection to male power and supervision. In short, Heidensohn argues that their socialisation and the conditions of their existence effectively control women. It is little wonder that so few women engage in criminal activity.

Is there a feminist criminology?

Some writers have noted the existence of an identifiable feminist criminology (Brown, 1986). Others suggest that to have a few writers calling themselves or their work feminist does not constitute a 'feminist criminology' (Smart, 1977). Furthermore, where attempts to create such a 'feminist criminology' have been made, there has not been any consensus about its success. Pat Carlen (1988) identified two problems with the endeavour. Most feminists, she suggests, identify crime as a male problem – ironically agreeing with the great body of traditional criminology – and where there has been an attempt to identify a universal explanation of crime that applies to both men and women, she argues that it has been theoretically unsound.

Other feminist writers have identified the wider feminist debate as the ideal location for examining the position of women in society and their social control. They argue that a feminist analysis should be central to any examination of women and crime, rather than the development of a 'feminist criminology' as a separate discipline (Heidensohn. 1985). Alison Morris (1987) takes this further, suggesting that since the nature of feminism, like criminology itself, is diverse the idea of a unified feminist criminology is erroneous. Gelsthorpe and Morris (1988) suggest that a more appropriate position is to talk about feminist perspectives within criminology, thereby recognising the diversity within both feminism itself and among the writers examining women as subjects within criminology.

The notions of diversity and difference are crucial to any understanding of the relationship of feminism to postmodernism (itself discussed in the final chapter of this book). Postmodernism has been welcomed by some feminists but viewed as problematic by others. Radical feminists have criticised the arguments of postmodernists, by suggesting that the voices of women would be lost and that it is collectively that women are strong. Other feminists suggest, however, that the challenge for feminism is to find a way to think women and 'women', recognising diversity and collective experience. Criticising the mystification and glorification of distinct female traits is identified as the limitation of this approach.

For postmodern feminists, all-encompassing feminist theory is itself of concern as it draws together and attempts to provide, in some instances, a universalistic account of the experience of all women. However, the rejection of 'malestream' assumptions of truth and reality – an essential feature of feminist postmodernism – has been identified as a potential weakness.

We have seen that Carol Smart (1977) had considered the possibility of creating a 'feminist criminology' and a few years later decided that this was an unnecessary task as there were 'more important goals to achieve than the one of constructing a sub-discipline to rank alongside other criminologies' (Smart, 1981: 86). She was however to take this argument a step further in a later article entitled 'Feminist approaches to criminology or postmodern woman meets atavistic man' (1990) where she argues that feminism has actually transgressed, or gone beyond, criminology. Smart outlines the advances of feminist thought and contrasts it with the limited horizons of criminology. She argues that 'the core enterprise of criminology is problematic, that feminists' attempts to alter criminology have only succeeded in revitalising a problematic enterprise' (Smart, 1990: 70). She focuses on 'the continuing "marriage" of criminology to ... positivistic paradigms' and 'highlights criminology's isolation from some of the major theoretical and political questions which are engaging feminist scholarship elsewhere'. Smart points out that 'for a long time we have been asking "what does feminism have to contribute to criminology?" '; she suggests that this question should be 'rephrased to read "what has criminology got to offer feminism?" ' (Smart, 1990: 83). In this case her reply is that criminology actually has very little to offer.

Gender issues have nonetheless broadened the field of criminological enquiry, opening up opportunities for the examination of female criminality but at the same time the possibility of an examination of masculinity, male power and violence drawing on broader feminist debates. Pat Carlen (1992) – although critical of what she describes as the anti-criminology and libertarian, gender-centric and separatist tendencies of contemporary feminist 'criminologists', also recognises the benefits of a feminist perspective to an understanding of women, law and order. She advocates the recognition of women's crimes as those of the powerless, of the stereotypical notions of femininity integral to women's oppression. She also points to the active contributions of some feminist writers to campaigns around women and crime. The influence of these can be observed in the 'left realism' that is the focus of Chapter 15.

Masculinity and crime

Maureen Cain (1989, 1990) agrees with Smart (1990) that feminism has 'transgressed criminology' and has proposed a need to answer the fundamental question of what it is about maleness that leads a disproportionate number of men to become criminals.

In response to this feminist discourse a small but growing literature has begun to emerge that seeks to 'take masculinity seriously'. Central to this development is the work of the Australian academic Bob Connell (1987, 1995) who – in response to the one-dimensional notion of male dominance presented by radical feminism – has recognised the existence of 'multiple masculinities'. In short, he argued that masculinities could be black as well as white, homosexual or heterosexual, working-class or middle-class. Moreover, all are subject to challenge and change over time. Connell accepts that there is a dominant masculinity in society that is based on the notions of heterosexual power and authority but proposes that other forms can challenge this and that male power is not absolute but is historically variable.

Messerschmidt (1993) applied this analysis of diverse and contested masculinities to youth crime, arguing that the types of offences committed by young males are patterned through various interpretations of masculinity generated by 'structures of labour and power in class and race relations'. In an apparent development of Robert Merton's anomie theory, he argues that crime provides a means of 'doing masculinity' when there is no access to other resources. However, the nature of the actual offence committed takes on different forms according to how different class and ethnic groups define their masculinities. Thus, for white working-class youth, masculinity is constructed around physical aggression and, for some, hostility to all groups considered to be inferior in a racist and heterosexual society. Lower working-class ethnic minorities, on the other hand, find their masculinity in the street gang. Whereas the white middle-class may envisage a future in mental labour and the white working-class in manual labour, both of these routes are seen as inaccessible to many youths from ethnic minority backgrounds. Therefore, offences, such as robbery provide the opportunity to accomplish a particular form of masculinity based on toughness and physical power.

Messerschmidt argues that each form of masculinity represents an attempt to meet the cultural ideal of the dominant form of masculinity that is denied to young people elsewhere whether it is in the home, school, or even work.

Jefferson (1997) is, however, critical of such structurally determinist arguments which he observes tell us little of why it is that only a particular minority of young men from a given ethnic group or social class choose to accomplish their masculinity by 'doing crime' while the majority do not. He follows Katz (1988) and Presdee (1994) in noting that criminological knowledge has repeatedly failed to recognise the pleasure that is involved in 'doing masculinity' and 'doing crime'. These writers all argue that unless we come to understand these pleasures we will never have a complete picture of why it is that particularly young people become involved in criminal behaviour.

Suggested further reading

Key feminist texts in the field of explaining crime and criminal behaviour are Carlen, *Women, Crime and Poverty* (1988) and 'Criminal Women and Criminal Justice' (1992), Gelsthorpe and Morris, *Feminist Perspectives in Criminology* (1988), Heidensohn, *Women and Crime* (1985) and 'Gender and Crime' (1994), Leonard, *Women, Crime and Society* (1983) and Smart, *Women, Crime and Criminology* (1977), 'Response to Greenwood' (1981) and 'Feminist Approaches to Criminology' (1990). Dobash and Dobash, *Women, Violence and Social Change* (1992) and Hanmer and Saunders, *Well-founded Fear* (1984) are essential reading on violent crime against women. For key texts on masculinity and crime consult Connell, *Gender and Power* (1987) and *Masculinities* (1995), Messerschmidt, *Masculinities and Crime* (1993) and Jefferson, 'Masculinities and Crime' (1997).

Chapter 11

Critical criminology

There are at the time of writing two contemporary manifestations of the radical tradition in criminology. One version, 'left realism', is the focus of Chapter 15. The other, critical criminology – or 'left idealism' as it is now termed by their former colleagues and now 'realist' opponents – is, however, the only version that it can be argued has unequivocal foundations in the victimised actor model of crime and criminal behaviour.

There are also a number of different variations of critical criminology but in general it can be said to be a perspective where crime is defined in terms of the concept of oppression. Some groups in society – the working-class (in particular, the poorer sections), women (especially, those who are poor, sole parents and socially isolated) and ethnic minority groups (especially, those from non-English-speaking backgrounds and refugees) – are seen to be the most likely to suffer oppressive social relations based upon class division, sexism and racism.

Critical criminologists focus their attention on both the crimes of the powerful and those of the less powerful. Crime is viewed as being associated with broad processes of the political economy that affect the former and the latter in quite different ways. For the powerful, there are pressures associated with the securing and maintaining of state and corporate interests in the context of global capitalism. In the case of the less powerful, criminal behaviour is seen to be the outcome of the interaction between the marginalisation or exclusion from access to mainstream institutions and that of criminalisation by the state authorities. Particular attention is paid to the increasing racialisation of crime, in which the media and police in the 'war against crime' and public disorder target certain communities.

Critical criminologists thus link offending behaviour to a social context that is structurally determined by the general allocation of societal resources and by the specific nature of police intervention in the lives of its citizens.

The origins of critical criminology

From the late 1960s onwards, many radical criminologists in the UK had developed an idealist view of the working class that allowed them to appreciate and even condone deviant acts committed by members of this group. It was argued that offenders do not respond mindlessly to stimuli, but are engaged in meaningful activity that so happens to have been labelled as criminal by the dominant groups in society. Thus, Stan Cohen (1980: 1) argued that 'our society as presently structured, will continue to generate problems for some of its members – like working-class adolescents – and then condemn whatever solution these groups find'.

Thus the labelling and deviant subculture perspectives with their tradition of ethnographic observation were a considerable influence on this 'new idealism'. Actual day-to-day contact with so-called deviant adolescents convinced researchers that these young people were simply involved in activities regarded as legitimate by their perpetrators, but which had been prohibited by the state. In stigmatizing sections of young people, the legislature was responding to a moral panic fanned by sensational and exaggerated media reporting. Cohen (1973) had written about the stigmatization of mods and rockers and exaggerated news-paper and television reports of their behaviour, the damage they caused and the holiday-makers they terrorised back in 1964. Today, critical criminologists might claim that 'ravers' and New Age travellers are the new 'folk devils' and the targets of an overly enthusiastic and crimi-nalising criminal justice intervention. Thus critical criminologists have argued that crime rates are far from being a perfect measure of the actual amount of criminality in society – being more a measure of the level of police activity – and can create a misleading image of horrific rises in certain types of crime. Figures purporting to show that black people are responsible for a disproportionate number of street robberies, for example, may be seen to reflect racist police stereotyping rather than reality (Hall, Critcher, Jefferson, Clarke and Roberts, 1978).

During the 1970s, orthodox criminology, with its roots firmly founded in the predestined actor model of crime and criminal behaviour, was undergoing a crisis of confidence of aetiology (Young, 1994). It had quite simply failed to explain why it was the case that the crime statistics appeared to increase ever upwards even during periods of societal affluence. Criminologists had, as we have seen in this book, proposed many – varied, apparently incompatible and sometimes even more impractical – solutions to an ever-increasing crime problem for many years without any visible success. A cynic might have observed that the numbers of books offering explanations of crime and criminal behaviour – and indeed ways of successfully responding to the crime problem – had grown accordingly on the shelves of academia in direct proportion to the ever-increasing crime figures. Indeed, one of their own number had influentially noted that 'nothing works' (Martinson, 1974); an observation that had been seized upon eagerly at the British Home Office (Mayhew, Clarke, Sturman and Hough, 1976) and which had subsequently become official orthodoxy. This new 'administrative criminology' (Young, 1994) had supposedly signalled an end to grandiose projects to change and rehabilitate criminals. The emphasis – highly influenced by contemporary manifestations of the rational actor model of criminal behaviour discussed in the first part of this book – was now on reducing the opportunity to offend while catching and in-carcerating those who still managed to transgress. A new and 'useful' role was now found for academic criminologists. They could be employed in assessing and evaluating the success of these usually small-scale situational crime prevention schemes. Explaining crime and criminal behaviour – and thus developing grandiose and expensive proposals for its elimination – had been dismissed as an academic exercise without practical application and not worthy of support.

If the 'nothing works' argument was becoming increasingly popular with politicians, critical criminologists had their own answers to the aetiological crisis. They argued that an analysis of the processes and situations within which the labelling of certain individuals and groups takes place does not go far enough. It is necessary to examine the structural relations of power in society, and to view crime in the context of social relations and political economy (Scraton and Chadwick, 1996, originally 1992). It was at this point that much work was done from a Marxist perspective to identify the causal basis of crime, and to make the link between dominant institutions and ruling-class interests. There was, however, a tendency at times either to romanticise crime – as acts of rebellion or resistance – or to see the crime solely in economic terms. Later work was to explore in more detail the specific contexts and lived experiences of people involved with the criminal justice system (Hall and Scraton, 1981).

The issues of racism, sexism and masculinity had been virtually ignored by much of academic Marxism. At the other end of the spectrum there was a need to keep the focus on the actions of those in power, not only in relation to those marginalised in society but more generally in the area of what has come to be known as white-collar crime or crimes of the powerful.

Crimes of the powerful

Edwin Sutherland – as we saw in Chapter 6 – was the first to use the phrase 'white-collar crime' in 1939, when he launched an attack on the actions of the respectable in society which, had they been performed by the less powerful in a different context, would have been labelled as criminal. Sutherland basically observed a need to address the inequalities in the treatment of people who engaged in harmful behaviour between those in power and those without power.

The pioneering work of Sutherland was to lead to a steady increase in research and writing – in particular, as we have seen, among those working in the differential association, anomie and deviant subculture traditions – initially in the USA and then worldwide (Geis and Goff, 1983). Critical criminology has built upon that tradition but located it firmly in the context of a contemporary critique of the nature of global capitalist society.

Swartz (1975: 115) has unambiguously observed that because capitalism involves the maximisation of corporate profits, 'its normal functioning produces … deaths and illnesses'. He is unequivocal; the commission of business crime is linked to the values of capitalism and legitimate business goals. In the same vein, Mars (1982) observes that there is only a fine line between 'entrepreneurialism and flair' and 'sharp practice and fraud'. Indeed, many such activities are not greeted with widespread disapproval; for example, an electrician who overcharges for services is often not perceived as a thief but an entrepreneur, and in this way such behaviour is excused and distinguished from the activities of 'real' criminals.

Corporations can practice a policy of law evasion. This may include the setting up of factories in countries that do not have pollution controls or stringent safety legislation – for example, the Union Carbide plant in Bhopal (Pearce and Tombs, 1993) – or the selling of goods that have been banned by the developed nations to markets in the developing world (Braithwaite, 1984). An example of this involved the Dalkon Shield intra-uterine device that was sold overseas for a considerable period when it had been declared unsafe in the USA (Hagan, 1994). In other words, multinationals dump some of their products, plants and practices, illegal in industrialised countries, on to undeveloped or underdeveloped countries (Box, 1987).

Such practices occur because the recipient nations are dependent on the capital investment of multinationals, they have fewer resources to check the claims of manufacturers and their government officials are more susceptible to bribery and corruption (Braithwaite, 1984). Corporations therefore export their illegal behaviour to where it is legal or at least where laws are not so rigorously enforced. In addition, multinational corporations often have sufficient economic resources and political influence to instigate or curtail legislation or at least its enforcement. In fact, many of the world's multinationals are wealthier than some of the less developed countries where they have subsidiaries, which means they hold tremendous economic and political influence in those countries (Carson, 1980; Box, 1983). Box (1983) observes a need to penetrate the process of mystification that perpetuates the myth that corporate crime is both not serious and harmless and which protects the powerful segments of society who benefit from such crime. He himself provides a readable account of the ability of corporate crime to kill, injure and rob; arguing forcefully that the competitive environment in which businesses operate actively encourages employees to break the law:

> Not only does the promotion system mean that people who rise to the top are likely to have just those personal characteristics it takes to commit corporate crime, but these are reinforced by the psychological consequences of success itself, for these too free a person from the moral bind of conventional values.
>
> (Box, 1983: 39)

In short, critical criminologists argue that working-class crime is insignificant when compared to the 'crimes of the powerful' that largely go unpunished. Price-fixing, tax evasion, white-collar crime, environmental pollution, deaths at work and other offences, they contend, cost society far more than, for example, youth offending, a regular source of societal condemnation. Moreover, the powerful perpetrators of these offences stand to gain far more material advantage from their misdemeanours. Nevertheless, fewer resources are used to combat white-collar crime and some questionable activities are not even criminalised, but are instead portrayed as examples of wealth-creation and enterprise. In addition, offenders in this category can hire accountants and lawyers to protect them and have powerful friends to lobby on their behalf.

Crimes of the less powerful

Critical criminologists recognised that although the general level of affluence as measured by gross domestic product per head, public spending and welfare benefits had increased, relative deprivation still existed among a substantial minority of society, who were well below 'the average' and accepted standard of living of the majority. Now the definition of relative deprivation changes over time and between societies. Absolute poverty was admittedly being eliminated, but relative poverty continued to exist as the rich claimed a seemingly unfair slice of the larger cake. Thus, according to critical criminologists, attempts by the less powerful to claim their just rewards, or to protest about their lot, were simply criminalised; thus Reiman (1979) claimed that 'the rich get richer and the poor get prison'.

Critical criminologists explain crime among the less powerful in society by reference to an interaction between *marginalisation*, or the exclusion from access to mainstream institutions, and *criminalisation*, which occurs with the intervention of the state authorities. The latter involves a process in which the law, agencies of social control and the media associate crime with particular groups who are subsequently identified and targeted as a threat. Scraton and Chadwick (1996 originally 1992) argue that this process is used to divert attention from economic and social conditions, particularly at times of acute economic change that could provide the impetus for serious political unrest. Moreover, it is argued that overtly political protests are criminalised and political terrorists termed 'common criminals' in order to neutralise the political nature of their actions. Hillyard (1987) observes that this criminalisation process helps to engender public support for anti-terrorist measures, as it is easier to mobilise state intervention against criminal acts than for the repression of what might be seen as a just political cause.

Criminalisation can therefore be used to justify harsher social control measures that are often taken against economically and politically marginalised groups who have few means of resisting these initiatives. Major economic changes occurred during the last quarter of the twentieth century in most advanced industrial societies and in particular in the UK that were to impoverish many in the lower, and less powerful, social classes. Critical criminologists observe that it is this group that has always been seen, since at least the beginning of the modern era, as the 'dangerous classes'. It is through criminalising their activities that their situation can be attributed to their own weaknesses, thus justifying harsher control measures.

Crime, according to some critical criminologists, is therefore a reassuring sign that the perpetual struggle against inequality continues. It is an idea with its origins in the writings of Durkheim (1964: 72) who claimed that crime could be 'functional' for the needs of society:

> Crime must no longer be conceived as an evil that cannot be too much suppressed. There is no occasion for self-congratulation when the crime rate drops noticeably below the average level, for we may be certain that this apparent progress is associated with some social disorder.

Durkheim's concept of the functionality of crime has survived in 'conflict theories' that depict crime as symptomatic of an ongoing struggle between powerful groups and the weak. This essentially needs to take place so that social control does not become an unchecked oppression of citizens by the state.

Critical criminology of 'left idealism'?

For critical criminologists – such as Scraton and Chadwick (1996 originally 1992) – the growing disparities between rich and poor, and the expansion in the sheer number of the poor constitute a legitimation crisis for the capitalist system as a whole. *Actual* deprivation is again seen as the cause of working-class crime with the perceived state response involving a substantial move toward 'law-and-order' politics, which has exacerbated the process of identifying and punishing members of particular groups within the working class and ethnic minorities.

Critical criminologists propose that a legitimate response to crime must be built upon a strategy of social empowerment. This means involving people directly in decisions about their future through direct participatory democracy. It also requires a redistribution of social resources to communities on the basis of social need and equity.

To counter crimes committed by the powerful, there must be open and public accountability of all state officials. Furthermore, as part of wealth redistribution, there has to be a transfer of wealth from private hands to public ownership under community control.

As a general crime prevention measure, and to reduce the prevalence of certain crimes, there need to be anti-racist and anti-sexist campaigns. These include the re-education and retraining of agents of the state such as the police. Strong emphasis is given to extending and protecting basic human rights and institutionalising these by means of watchdog agencies and developmental policies.

In summary, critical criminologists propose that the function of the criminal justice system is not to solve crime but to unite the people against a rump in their midst, defined as deviant, and hence in this way maintain the legitimacy of the existing social order. The true function of prisons, it is argued, is not to reform criminals but rather to stigmatize them and cause them to be seen as the enemy in our midst (Foucault, 1980). Likewise, it is not the real function of the police to prevent crime and apprehend criminals but rather to maintain the social order, being used to control industrial disputes, political demonstrations or any other activities that may threaten the community. They are also used to widen the net of social control so that the state – in the form of the criminal justice system – brings under surveillance and control more of those individuals and groups that can be considered potentially deviant (Cohen, 1985). In order to achieve this overall intention, the authorities, in particular the police, will require the necessary powers and be relatively free of control by local and central governments (Scraton, 1985).

Many would consider this view of social order, the law and the criminal justice system to be too simplistic and a denial of the reality that most people experience. The individual nature of criminality, it will be argued, cannot simply be regarded as a construction of the state. Critical criminologists have nevertheless posed a number of important questions. They have attempted to critically interrogate dominant and orthodox perceptions of crime and criminal behaviour, arguing that crime should not be perceived as a problem of individual offenders in society but as a process related to wider economic and social structures of power. This is nonetheless a problematic analysis; most criminal behaviour is not targeted against the dominant social order, while the criminal law is not just directed at keeping the less powerful in their place. Indeed, many of the weaker and poorer sections of our society need both the law and its agents in the criminal justice system to protect them from criminal elements living in their midst (Hopkins Burke, 1998b). Other former radical proponents of the victimised actor model were to come to recognise that reality and eventually came to reconsider their stance and the very meaning of radicalism. These subsequently highly influential 'left realists' came to constitute the second variant of the former radical tradition – terming their former radical colleagues as 'left idealists – and are themselves the focus of attention in Chapter 15.

Suggested further reading

Box, *Recession, Crime and Punishment* (1987), Cohen, *Folk Devils and Moral Panics* (1980) and *Visions of Social Control* (1985), Hall *et al, Policing the Crisis* (1978), Reiman, *The Rich get Richer and the Poor get Prison* (1979) and Scraton and Chadwick, 'The Theoretical Priorities of Critical Criminology' (1996) all make essential contributions to critical criminological explanation of crime and criminal behaviour. Those interested in the crimes of the powerful should consult the following body of work not necessarily written by those identifying themselves as critical criminologists: Braithwaite, *Corporate Crime in the Pharmaceutical Industry* (1984), Geis, *White-collar Crime* (1968) Mars, *Cheats at Work* (1982) and Pearce and Tombs, 'US Capital versus the World' (1993).

Part Four

Integrated explanations of crime and criminal behaviour

As positivism evolved, it eventually encompassed, under the term 'deviance', the many forms of behaviour left behind by the Classical tradition. Lacking the Classical theory of behaviour, however, positivists have not been able to deal with the connections among the many acts that make up deviance and crime. Consequently, they have tended to develop behaviour-specific theories and to treat the relations between deviance and crime as cause and effect rather than as manifestations of a single cause. One purpose of this [*theory*] is to reunite deviance and crime under a general theory of behaviour.

(Gottfredson and Hirschi, 1990: 3–4)

The first three parts of this book each considered a different model of explaining crime and criminal behaviour. The first, the rational actor model, proposed that people choose to engage in criminal behaviour in the same way that they choose to become involved in any other form of activity. The second, the predestined actor model, proposed that the behaviour of the person is in some way determined by factors either internal or external to them in a way over which they have very little or no control. Criminal behaviour is the destiny of that person. The third, the victimised actor model proposes that the offender is the victim of an unequal society that has in some way chosen to target and criminalise his or her activities while ignoring those of other invariably more powerful individuals and groups.

Within the parameters of these three models a range of different theories have been identified that have sought to explain criminality. There are essentially three principal ways in which these theories can be developed and their predictability value validated. The first is to consider each theory on its own. If the data obtained by empirical research confirms the predictions of the theory then it is generally accepted. If the data fails to support those predictions then the theory can be either modified or rejected.

Theory competition involves the logical, conceptual, or empirical comparisons of two or more theories to determine which offers the best explanation of the phenomenon to be studied (Liska, Krohn and Messner, 1989). In the first three parts of this book, the focus has been on single-theory explanation, albeit it the context of the particular model, or tradition, of criminal behaviour in which it can be best located.

Moreover, it should be noted that theory building, like the development and acquisition of knowledge in general, is usually incremental, each theory building on its predecessors.

Evaluation of the evidence on a single theory has rarely led to its total rejection. On the other hand, no one theory cited has been able to explain all incidences or forms of crime. In reality, the evidence in support of, or contra to, most theories lies somewhere in between these two extremes.

The central issue is how well a theory performs when compared with others either internal or external to its model of behaviour. Criticism of one approach from the perspective of another is common, and direct competitive testing of rival perspectives often occurs. For example, the older biological variants of the predestined actor model of criminality have been largely discredited. Even the more recent and sophisticated biological explanations of criminal behaviour have tended to perform badly in comparison with sociological theories. Psychological approaches that rely on emotional disturbance or personality traits have also been found to be less successful than sociological or social-psychological explanations (Akers, 1997).

The third way to assess and construct en explanation of crime and criminal behaviour is through theoretical integration. The objective is to identify commonalities in two or more theories to produce a synthesis that is superior to any one theory individually (Farnsworth, 1989). However, while theory integration often involves such deliberate attempts to fuse together two closely related theories, it may well also stem from theory competition. Upon closer examination, two theories may not be as compatible as at first thought.

Certainly, all of the theories discussed in the first three parts of this book have been subjected, to some degree, both to competition and integration. For example, there has long been competition between the proponents of biological, sociological and social learning theories as to which approach best provides an explanation of criminal families. On the other hand, most theories have come to at least tacitly – but usually more explicitly – incorporate concepts and notions from their supposed competitors. For example, Cesare Lombroso, that much-maligned early biological positivist, came to accept social factors to such an extent that by the fifth edition of *L'Uomo Delinquente (On Criminal Man)* they account for eighty per cent of his explanation of criminal behaviour.

Moreover, when a theory is first formulated, it tends to build upon other explanations within the context of the particular model of criminal behaviour in which it is situated. For example, critical criminologists provided a radical re-working of labelling perspectives incorporating structural concepts. At the same time, each theory tends to draw upon a range of different sources. For example, labelling theorists incorporate ideas and concepts from symbolic interactionism, phenomenology and ethnomethodology.

All theories have been revised to some degree after their original formulations. These revisions almost always borrow from the insights and explanations found in other theories and the sources can be both internal and external to their host model of criminal behaviour. For example, later criminologists working within the predestined actor tradition came increasingly to recognise that people are capable of making – albeit limited – choices. On the other hand, the converse is also true. Later rational actor model theorists came to recognise the limitations of individual rationality. At the same time, the proponents of each theory implicitly or explicitly compare its explanatory power with that of alternative explanations.

Liska *et al* (1989) identify different types of theoretical integration. First, there is conceptual integration where concepts from one theory are shown to have meanings similar to those within another theory. For example, there has been a long debate about the similarities between Durkheim's concept of anomie and Marx's notion of alienation. Second, *propositional* integration relates propositions from different theories. This can be accomplished by showing how two or more theories make the same predictions about crime, even though each begins with different concepts and assumptions. For example, both anomie theory and con-flict theories predict higher crime rates among the lower social classes. This form of integration can also be achieved by placing the explanatory variables from different theories into some kind of causal or explanatory sequence. The sequence starts with the variables from one theory (for example, social disorganisation) to explain the variations in variables from another theory (for example, attachment to family) that can be used to explain offending behaviour.

Theoretical integration can be *within level* (only micro-level or only macro-level), *across level* (micro-macro) as well as *within model* or *across model*. The following chapters in this fourth part of the book consider some of those explanations of crime and criminal behaviour where theorists have deliberately set out to integrate different approaches. This has been done in an attempt to provide a stronger explanatory tool than that offered by one individual theory.

Chapter 12

Socio-biological theories

It was shown in Chapter 7 that proponents of the biological variant of the predestined actor model sought explanations for crime and criminal behaviour in the measurable, organic part of individuals, their bodies and brains. It was acknowledged that some of the studies reviewed in that chapter really do point to biological explanations of criminality but only in a tiny minority of offenders. Moreover, a closer investigation of individual cases suggests that social and environmental background is at least equally as important. Consequently, in recent years there has been a concerted attempt to rehabilitate biological explanations by incorporating social and environmental factors into a 'multi-factor' approach to explaining crime and criminal behaviour (Vold, Bernard and Snipes, 1998). Thus, from this contemporary perspective, it is argued that the presence of certain biological factors may increase the likelihood but not determine absolutely that an individual will engage in criminal behaviour. These factors generate criminal behaviours when they interact with psychological or social factors.

Biosocial theory

The work of Sarnoff Mednick and associates (1977, 1987) provides a good example of the orientation of more recent biologists. Mednick argues that the biological characteristics of an individual are only part of the explanation of criminal behaviour. The other factors involved are the physical and social environment:

> Where the social experiences of the antisocial individual are
> not especially anti-social, biological factors should be examined.
> The value of the biological factors is more limited in predicting
> antisocial behaviour in individuals who have experienced
> criminogenic social conditions in their rearing.
>
> (Mednick, 1987: 68)

Mednick proposes in his *biosocial theory* that all individuals must learn to
control natural urges that drive us toward antisocial and criminal
behaviour. There is an acknowledgement that the learning process takes
place in the context of the family and during the course of interaction
with peer groups, and is based on the punishment of undesirable
behaviours. However, the punishment response is mediated by the
automatic nervous system. If the reaction is short-lived, the individual is
said to have rewarded him or herself, and criminal behaviour is in-
hibited. A slow physiological recovery from punishment does little
nonetheless to teach the individual to refrain from undesirable
behaviour. Mednick ultimately proposes that criminals are those who
have slow automatic nervous system responses to stimuli.

Jeffery (1977) has argued strongly that this new biological criminology is not 'neo-Lombrosian' and is highly critical of those
criminological theories that ignore or reject biological components. He
proposes that biological, psychological and sociological characteristics
should be seen as interacting together in a systems model to produce
criminal behaviour. Central to his argument is the notion that individuals are born with particular biological and psychological
characteristics that not only may predispose them to, but also may
actually cause, certain forms of behaviour. This 'nature' is independent
of the socialisation process present in the social environment. There is,
however, a good deal of interaction between nature and nurture through
the physical environment and the feedback mechanisms that exist in
human biochemical systems.

Jeffery notes that poor people tend to experience a poor quality diet
and are more likely to be exposed to pollutants. The resulting nutrients
and chemicals are transformed by the biochemical system into neuro-
chemical compounds within the brain. Poverty, therefore, leads to
behavioural differences through the interaction of individual and
environment. It is an argument that has been taken up and developed by
key 'right realist' criminological theorists.

Biosocial theory and the 'new right'

James Q. Wilson was – as we noted in Chapter 3 – a major influence on the development of the 'right realist' perspective on crime and criminal behaviour that was so influential in the rehabilitation of the rational actor model after many years in the explanatory wilderness. However, it was his work with Richard Herrnstein (Wilson and Herrnstein, 1985) that offers a more definitive account of what they consider to be the underlying causes of crime.

Three elements are defined. First, there are constitutional factors; these are not necessarily genetic but they have some biological origin. Observing that crime is an activity disproportionately carried out by young men, Wilson and Herrnstein (1985: 69) observe that:

> It is likely that the effect of maleness and youthfulness on the tendency to commit crime has both constitutional and social origins: that is, it has something to do with the biological status of being a young male and with how that young man has been treated by family, friends and society.

It is therefore an explanation of criminal behaviour that is not solely rooted in biology. There is a concern to construct an explanation in which factors such as gender, age, intelligence, body type and personality are inserted as potential biological givens of human beings projected into a social world. These factors are, however, not necessarily determiners of human action. It is a social world in which the individual learns what kind of behaviour is rewarded in what circumstances. This is the second element of the theory.

Wilson and Herrnstein are heavily influenced by the psychological behavioursim of B.F. Skinner (see Chapter 6). It is thus proposed that individuals learn to respond to situations in accordance with how their behaviour has been rewarded and punished on previous occasions. From this 'operant conditioning' perspective, the environment can operate to produce the kind of behavioural response most wanted from an individual. In order to understand the propensity to commit crime it is important therefore to understand the ways in which the environment might operate on individuals – whose constitutional make-up might be different – to produce this response. Within this general learning framework the influence of the family, the school and the wider community is located.

The third element in the theory is that of the conscience. Wilson and Herrnstein (1985: 125) support the conjecture made by Eysenck that 'conscience is a conditioned reflex' by proposing that some people during childhood have so effectively internalised law-abiding be- haviour that they could never be tempted to behave otherwise. For others, breaking the law might be dependent upon the particular circumstances of a specific situation suggesting less effective inter- nalisation of such rules. For yet others, the failure to appreciate the likely consequences of their actions might lead them into criminal behaviour under any circumstances. In other words, the effectiveness of something termed 'the conscience' may vary in terms of the particular constitution of the individual and the learning environment in. which people find themselves.

These three elements – constitutional factors, the presence and/or absence of positive and negative behavioural reinforcers alongside the strength of the conscience – provide the framework in which Wilson and Herrnstein seek to explain crime. For them the interplay between these factors can explain why crime rates may increase both in times of prosperity and recession since the equation between the social and the individual is a complex one. They suggest that:

> Long-term trends in crime rates can be accounted for primarily by three factors. First, shifts in the age structure of the population will increase or decrease the proportion of persons – young males in the population who are likely to be temperamentally aggressive and to have short horizons. Second, changes in the benefits of crime … and in the cost of crime will change the rate at which crimes occur, especially property crimes. … Third, broad social and cultural changes in the level and intensity of society's investment (via families, schools, churches, and the mass media) inculcating an internalized commitment to self control will affect the extent to which individuals at risk are willing to postpone gratification, accept as equitable the outcomes of others, and conform to rules.
>
> Wilson and Herrnstein (1985: 437)

Conclusions

Biologically oriented and sociologically oriented criminologists have in the past been in fundamental disagreement. Both have tended to defend their own positions and disciplines while completely refusing to acknowledge those of their adversaries. Increasingly, however, there has been recognition of the need for biological theories which examine the interaction of sociological, psychological and biological phenomena in the production of criminal behaviour. Vold *et al* (1998: 87) pertinently observe that:

> This emerging synthesis of perspectives will probably benefit biological criminology, since extreme biological views often raise images of determinism among some audiences, who subsequently react negatively to the furthering of such research and to any policies based on it.

In short, the future of biological explanations of crime and criminal behaviour probably only lies in its rejection of its old predestined actor model pretensions and a willingness – however grudgingly – to incorporate notions from the other two models.

Suggested further reading

Jeffery (ed.), *Biology and Crime* (1979), Mednick, 'A Biosocial Theory of the Learning of Law-Abiding Behaviour' (1977) and Mednick (eds), *The Causes of Crime* (1987) are essential introductory readings for those interested in socio-biology. Wilson and Herrnstein, *Crime and Human Nature* (1985) provide the links between this approach and right realism.

Chapter 13

Environmental criminology

The environmental criminologists Brantingham and Brantingham (1981) have argued that criminal incidents essentially occur when four different dimensions of crime – a law, an offender, a target and a place – are all in concurrence. They describe environmental criminology as the study of the fourth dimension, the study of where and when crimes occur. However, while academic interest in environmental explanations of crime and criminal behaviour has grown considerably since the 1970s, the recognition of the relevance of geographical setting to levels of crime is far from new.

Early environmental explanations

The earliest environmental explanations of crime and criminal behaviour occurred during the nineteenth century. In France, Guerry (1833) and Quételet (1842) had analysed conviction rates for crimes committed in different geographical areas and had made a number of important findings. First, crime rates varied greatly in different geographical areas. Second, when violent crimes and property crimes were separated, a further variation in patterning was found. Third, these patterns remained stable over time. Similar studies were carried out in England and these also showed variations in crime rates between different counties, towns and villages (Plint, 1851; Mayhew, 1968 originally 1862).

Mayhew (1968) conducted a study of parts of London and identified the existence of areas – known as 'rookeries' – with a high proportion of criminal residents. Moreover, the tendency of crime levels to persist over time in these areas was confirmed by later studies. In short, the significance of geographical settings to the incidence of crime was confirmed. Moreover, the tendency for spatial patterns to persist suggested an element of predictability and therefore the possibility of adopting preventive policies.

The later Chicago school variant of environmental criminology – which we encountered in Chapter 7 – had also proposed that social disorganisation and social pathology tend to be more prevalent in certain geographical areas. Researchers in that tradition argued that crime and delinquency are transmitted by frequent contact with criminal traditions that have developed over time in disorganised areas of the city (see Shaw and McKay, 1972 originally 1931).

Developments in environmental explanation

A number of British studies conducted during the 1950s – Mays (1954), Morris (1957), Wootton (1959) – made repeated attempts to explain the relatively high incidence of crime in urban working-class areas. However, what was distinctive about this approach was the attempt to combine three different sociological explanatory perspectives. First, there was the ecological approach that considers why it is that people live where they do. Second, there was the deviant subculture approach that considers the development of distinctive life-patterns and their relationship to local and environmental factors. Third, there was the social reaction – or labelling approach – which considers the effects of classifying certain individuals and residential groups as different or simply bad (Gill, 1977).

In reality, this integrated theoretical perspective had rather unequivocal theoretical foundations in the predestined actor model. The notion that aspects of social disorganisation and anomie characterised the 'criminal areas' led to the familiar determinist tautology that proposed crime to be caused by levels of social pathology already in existence in these areas. Yet this was by no means a simple or crude environmental determinism. It was rendered more 'open' and complex by adding the rational actor model notion of 'free will' to the environmental predestined actor model 'influences' affecting the city, and ordering and disordering its behaviour patterns. In short, from this perspective influences such as the varying indices of social disorganisation affect group and individual action in these criminal areas. But in the last resort the individuals themselves decide whether to become criminal or not. They can choose to disregard the surrounding influences, even if – as Rex and Moore (1967) have shown – there is little real choice over their area of residence in the ecological struggle between the city 'housing classes'.

A summary of the significant features of this post-Second World War reconstitution of the ecological approach to crime in a British context includes the following points. First, there was a modified use of the core Chicago school concept of the 'struggle for space' in studies of city life. Second, the focus of this concept was on studies of housing allocation and 'housing classes': in ecological terms the competition and differential access to residential space (Morris, 1957). Third, there was an emphasis on the importance of market situation, race relations and the 'class struggle for housing' in the work of Rex and Moore (1967) in Sparkbrook, Birmingham, a study which broke with the determinism of the Chicago school while still retaining its distinction of differential urban areas. Fourth, there was the further theoretical refinement of Lambert (1970), who revealed how high crime rates in inner Birmingham were not primarily instigated by the arrival of new and unemployed black immigrants, but through the activities of the permanent black and white residents. Newcomers merely adjusted the nature of their activities to fit in with those already taking place in the locality. Again, explanations for crime are located in the market for jobs, housing and leisure. The problems culminating in the Bristol, Brixton and Toxteth (Liverpool) disturbances in 1981 provide good examples of this type of explanation.

Fifth, there was the existence by the early 1970s of two further significant theoretical developments. Taylor, Walton and Young (1973) proposed that criminal area delinquency reflects the availability of opportunities/gratifications that exist in particular urban contexts; rather than being a natural outgrowth of the demoralisation of the less able, the biologically inferior or the individually pathological. At the same time, a more dynamic view of culture was being developed. The notions of change, conflict and struggle were coming to replace the static, predestined actor model notion of a social disorganisation-induced 'pathology' disturbing a harmonious and monolithic 'normal' culture.

Sixth, area studies conducted since the mid-1970s show a changed focus on 'the manufacture of neighbourhood reputation', notably in the work by Damer (1974) and Gill (1977). The focus of these studies remains on the housing area and the neighbourhood unit but includes new notions. These include 'hierarchies of desirability' of housing area 'types' and types of tenant, the ideology of manufactured reputation, as in Damer's (1974) 'dreadful enclosures', and the differential policing of such areas as prime agents in the production of offending behaviour.

These British ecological analyses did not in themselves purport to provide a causal explanation. Morris (1957) stresses their importance as a method of calculating the likelihood of offending behaviour taking place. Baldwin and Bottom (1976) note that they provide descriptive information without any explanation. Later North American studies sought a more sophisticated examination of the geographical distribution of crime and criminals.

Brantingham and Brantingham (1981) observe a distinct break between the earlier ecological research and the later environmental criminology and this is characterised by at least three shifts in perspective. First, there has been a significant shift away from the tendency for academics to keep their research into crime and criminal behaviour contained within the parameters of their own specific discipline. In contrast, environmental criminologists have introduced techniques and knowledge from many different disciplines. Second, there has been a move away from the traditional predestined actor model search for causes of criminal motivation. Environmental criminologists simply assume that some people are criminally motivated. The focus is now on the actual criminal event, to find patterns in where, when and how crimes occur. Third, there has been a shift in emphasis away from the sociological imagination to the geographical imagination. This does not mean, however, a simple replacement of the former by the latter. The two are now used together in an attempt to gain a more comprehensive understanding of crimes, and ultimately an increased capacity to control them.

In summary, the field of environmental criminology includes studies of:

- the spatial patterning of crime at different levels of aggregation; the 'journey to crime';
- the processes by which potential offenders recognise potential crime sites and specific opportunities;
- the creation and maintenance of areas of criminal residence.

Environmental criminology should not, however, be equated with a crude environmental determinism. Rather, the sequence by which potential criminals recognise and act on criminal opportunities is seen as a 'multi-staged decision process situated within a more general environmental learning and evaluation process' (Brantingham and Brantingham, 1981:25).

Closely linked with environmental criminology are the notions of environmental design and environmental management.

Environmental design

It is through the work of writers like Jacobs (1965), Jeffery (1977) and Newman (1976) that the concept of preventing crime through environmental design has become influential. These various writers propose that the nature of the built environment can affect the level of crime both by influencing potential offenders and by affecting the ability of a person to exercise control over their surroundings. There is essentially a powerful belief in the capacity of surveillance to help control crime.

Oscar Newman (1972, 1976) suggests that part of the explanation for urban crime lies in a breakdown of the social mechanisms that once kept crime in check, while the inability of communities to come together in collective action hampers crime prevention. The proposed solution is to restructure 'the residential environments of our cities so they can again become liveable and controlled ... not by the police but by a community of people sharing a common terrain' (Newman, 1976: 2).

Newman advocates action to foster (i) territoriality, (ii) natural surveillance, (iii) a safe image and (iv) a protected milieu. First, the notion of *territoriality* is defined as the 'capacity of the physical environment to create perceived zones of influence' (Newman, 1976: 51), that is, the ability and desire of legitimate users to claim control of an area. It is claimed that the design of buildings and their sites can encourage residents to adopt ownership attitudes, and also that certain layouts inform outsiders that particular areas are for the private use of residents. Newman argues that such design features as narrowed street entrances – real and psychological boundaries – and the use of cul-de-sacs to project a 'private' image, can enhance the environment. The use of raised, coloured paving on residential streets provides such an example. Territoriality is diminished by the existence of public thoroughfares and open spaces that provide access to and from residential areas while giving the impression that they are owned and cared for by nobody.

Second, design features such as overlooked entrance lobbies and well-placed windows, which allow residents to identify and observe strangers, provide *natural surveillance*. Newman urges the avoidance of high-rise blocks to which outsiders can gain easy access, and enclosed entrances where offenders can operate unseen.

Third, the *safe image*: good design should seek to convey one of a safe and invulnerable neighbourhood in which residents know and look after each other. Where the distinctive image is negative 'the project will be stigmatized and its residents castigated and victimized' (Newman, 1976: 102). It is suggested that public sector housing is particularly affected because such estates or projects are designed to stand out. This image combines with other design features that reduce territoriality and surveillance opportunities and with the socio-economic characteristics of the population to make this type of housing particularly vulnerable to crime.

Fourth, a *safe milieu* is a neighbourhood situated in the middle of a wider crime-free area, which is thus insulated from the outside world by a 'moat' of safety. Jacobs (1962) had suggested that residential areas should be sited alongside commercial areas in the expectation of enhancing safety because of increased activity. Newman (1976: 112) argued that the success of a particular mixture of land uses 'depends as much on the degree to which residents can identify with and survey activity in the related facility as it does on the nature of the users of that facility and the activities they indulge in'.

Attempts by researchers to evaluate the effectiveness of the 'defensible space' thesis have often proved problematic because environmental design usually involves the simultaneous implementation of a number of measures. One initiative that was tested – in Hartford, Connecticut – featured enhanced police patrols and citizen mobilisation as well as design improvements. Large reductions in the relative rates of burglary and robbery were achieved in the redesigned area (Fowler, McCall and Mangione, 1979), but a follow-up study found that the effects of the scheme on offence rates were short-lived (Fowler and Mangione, 1982).

Other studies have found even less support for the effectiveness of environmental design schemes (Evans, Fyfe and Herbert, 1992). Merry (1981) has noted that the advantages of 'defensible space' are largely dependent on the residents who must report or challenge strangers. Therefore, in order to reduce crime, 'defensible' space must actually be defended.

Other features of environmental design may have a secondary impact on crime. Traffic-calming measures, increasingly seen in residential areas, prevent a quick exit for offenders as well as giving the impression of ownership. Moreover, systems of barriers and one-way schemes to prevent traffic using residential areas as short cuts have the same effect. They also reduce easy and casual access to the area and reduce the chance that a burglar, for example, will select a house in the area while passing through.

The concept of offenders as products of their environment has, as we have seen, firm foundations in the predestined actor model. However, the concept has enjoyed a renaissance through collaboration between 'routine activity theorists' and rational choice/opportunity theorists located theoretically within the rational actor tradition (Felson, 1994). Brantingham and Brantingham have commented extensively on Canadian experiments that have sought to curb crime through environmental design and note that many of these initiatives have stemmed from the observation that people travelling from one place to another, normally between home, school/work and place of entertainment commit much crime.

Environmental management

The concept of 'environmental management' rests largely on the premise that – apart from encouraging offending by their 'indefensibility' – certain districts may suffer simply because they give the impression that their residents no longer care. The difference between environmental design and environmental management is subtle but nevertheless important. The former requires implementation at the planning stage, before a district is built or developed. The latter can be practised on an existing neighbourhood and also commercial environments where there is less prospect of using informal surveillance.

Essentially, the theory that informs the notion of environmental management proposes that evidence that crime has been committed, if allowed to remain in place, will itself lead to further offences being committed. The argument is applied especially to such offences as vandalism, public drunkenness, vagrancy and begging: offences collectively known as 'incivilities'. Wilson and Kelling (1982: 3) describe the problem as witnessed in urban America in their 'broken windows' thesis:

A piece of property is abandoned, weeds grow up, and a window is smashed. Adults stop scolding rowdy children; the children, emboldened, become more rowdy. Families move out, unmarried adults move in. Teenagers gather in front of the corner store. The merchant asks them to move, they refuse. Fights occur. Litter accumulates. People start drinking in front of the grocery store; in time an inebriate drunkard slumps to the sidewalk and is allowed to sleep it off. Pedestrians are approached by panhandlers.

(Wilson and Kelling, 1982: 32)

Incivilities, according to this hypothesis, lead to crime, the evidence of which causes further incivilities. Environmental management involves striving to remove the evidence of incivilities by, for example, cleaning up graffiti and other signs of vandalism, cleaning the streets and avoiding property falling into decay. The thesis has relevance beyond residential areas: refusing to allow its effects to accumulate, for example, could reduce vandalism in schools (Knights, 1998). The attraction of the theory is its plausibility; so plausible is it, in fact, that it has been accepted despite very little research support. One study, however, suggested that immediate removal of graffiti from subway cars in New York deprived the 'artists' of the expressive benefits of seeing their work travelling around the system, and substantially reduced the problem (Felson, 1994).

Matthews (1992) questions whether the Wilson and Kelling hypothesis should have been so readily accepted. He points out that, according to British Crime Survey data, incivilities such as drunks, beggars, litter and vandalism seem to be linked more to the fear of crime than its actuality. The point is also made that some inner-city areas have attracted young professional people searching for an exciting and vibrant place in which to live. Street musicians and performers, noisy bars and the other trappings of inner-city life are as attractive to some people as they are a cause of fear to others.

Hopkins Burke (1998a, 2000) nonetheless notes the ambiguity surrounding the issue of street incivilities. Beggars invariably choose specific urban areas where their close proximity to the public enables them to use tacit intimidation as an aid to their activities. Different groups undoubtedly differentially receive the resultant aura of menace. Old people may be fearful and genuinely scared while cosmopolitan young professionals might consider it to be just a colourful segment of the rich tapestry of life. Likewise drunken vagrants gathered menacingly in a bus shelter may force by their presence – albeit silently – young mothers with pushchairs outside into the rain. Those openly urinating in the street after a hard day's drinking in the full view of mothers collecting their young children from a nearby nursery should surely experience some regulation, management and restriction placed upon their activities. Radical proponents of the victimised actor model would recognise that these people are among the poorest and disadvantaged people in society and are invariably targeted by agents of the criminal justice system. On the other hand the wider public surely deserve some protection from their more antisocial activities. This latter 'left realist' perspective is revisited in Chapter 15.

Suggested further reading

Key texts in environmental criminology are Brantingham and Brantingham (eds), *Environmental Criminology* (1981), Jacobs, *The Death and Life of Great American Cities* (1965), Jeffery, *Crime Prevention through Environmental Design* (1977) and Newman, *Defensible Space: Crime Prevention through Urban Design* (1972) and *Defensible Space: People and Design in the Violent City* (1976). Felson, *Crime and Everyday Life* (1994) provides links between this approach and routine activities theory. Wilson and Kelling, 'Broken Windows' (1982) provide a classic text on environmental criminology with a left-realist critique from Matthews, 'Replacing "Broken Windows" ' (1992). Hopkins Burke, 'Begging, Vagrancy and Disorder' (1998a) and 'The Regulation of Begging and Vagrancy' (2000) discusses this approach in terms of the policing of begging and vagrancy.

Chapter 14

Social control theories

Social control theories of crime and criminal behaviour have a long and distinguished pedigree with strong foundations in both the rational actor and predestined actor models of crime and criminal behaviour. More recent variants have entailed explicit attempts to integrate notions from both of these models and even more recently elements from the victimised actor model.

The origins of social control theories

The origins, or at least the underlying assumptions, of social control theories can be traced back to the work of Hobbes (1968 originally 1651) in the rational actor tradition, Freud (1927) and Durkheim (1951 originally 1897) from respectively the psychological and sociological variants of the predestined actor model.

Hobbes had been concerned with the apparent incompatibility between human nature and the notion of legal restraint. The answer to his question, 'Why do men obey the rules of society?' was, however, simple enough. 'Fear … it is the only thing, when there is appearance of profit or pleasure by breaking the laws that makes men keep them' (Hobbes, 1968: 247).

One of the central ideas of Freud that deviant impulses arise naturally when the id is not sufficiently constrained by the other components of the personality, the ego and super-ego, is also apparent in much of the work on control theory. This is particularly true of those earlier models that draw more explicitly on psychological rather than sociological factors (Reiss, 1951; Nye, 1958; Reckless, 1961).

The roots of the more sociologically oriented control theories lie partly in the work of Durkheim (1951) who had argued that needs, desires or aspirations arise naturally within the individual, are unlimited and restrained only by the socialised moral norms of a given society. At the same time, it is society itself that creates needs and ambitions that are incapable of realisation in the particular social framework of the time. Merton (1938) later developed this idea in his analysis of anomie as a cause of crime.

Social control theory is fundamentally derived from a conception of human nature that proposes that there are no natural limits on elementary human needs and desires. People will always want and seek further economic reward. It is not necessary, therefore, to look for special motives for engaging in criminal activity. Human beings are born free to break the law and will only refrain from doing so under particular circumstances. It is these fundamental assumptions that provide the foundations of modern social control theories.

Most of the explanations of crime and criminal behaviour that we have encountered previously in this book view conformity as the normal or natural state of humanity. Criminal behaviour is simply abnormal. It is this orthodox way of thinking about crime that social control theory seeks to challenge. Therefore, in taking deviance for granted and treating conformity as problematic, social control theory offers not so much a theory of *deviance* but one of *conformity*. The central question asked is not the usual, 'Why do some people commit crimes?' but rather, 'Why do most of us conform?' The unifying factor in the different versions of control theory is the assumption that crime and deviance is to be expected when social and personal controls are in some way inadequate.

Some writers in the rational actor tradition, for example Hobbes (1588–1678) and Bentham (1748–1832), had viewed human nature in general as essentially amoral and self-serving. Modern social control theories, on the other hand, do not on the whole depict people in this way. They merely reject the underlying assumption contained in many of the theories discussed earlier in this book – for example, anomie and subcultural theories – that people are basically moral as a result of having internalised pro-social norms and values during socialisation.

Because they remove the assumption of morality and the positively socialised individual, control theories are not dependent on ex-planations such as 'relative deprivation', 'blocked opportunities', 'alienation' or 'status-frustration' to account for the motivated deviant. Crime is seen as a product of the weaknesses of the forces restraining the individual rather than of the strength of the impulse to deviate. It is the *absence* of control and the fact that delinquent or criminal behaviour 'usually results in quicker achievement of goals than normative behaviour' that leaves the individual free to calculate the costs of crime (Hirschi, 1969). Again, the influence of the rational actor model is apparent in this core idea of the 'rational' individual choosing crime only after a careful appraisal of the costs and benefits of such activity.

Early social control theories

It was observed earlier that social control theories draw on both social and psychological factors in order to explain conformity and deviance. Probably the earliest sociological control theory was Durkheim's theory of anomie.

Durkheim proposed that inadequate forms of social control are more likely during periods of rapid modernisation and social change because new forms of regulation cannot evolve quickly enough to replace the declining force of social integration. The outcome is anomie or the complete collapse of social solidarity when the insatiable desires and aspirations of individuals can no longer be adequately regulated or controlled by society.

Many of Durkheim's central concerns and ideas were also present in the work of the Chicago school, particularly in its use of the concept of social disorganisation, itself a theoretical perspective that influenced many of the later theories encountered in this book. There have nonetheless been fundamental differences in how these different theorists have used the concept. For example, anomie theorists argued that social disorganisation generates pressure, which in turn, *produces* crime and deviance (a predestined actor model argument). Social control theorists, on the other hand, consider that social disorganisation causes a weakening of social control, making crime and deviance more *possible* (a rational actor model argument).

The early control theories reviewed in the remainder of this section attach much more importance to psychological factors in their analysis of deviance and conformity. Albert Reiss (1951) distinguished between the effects of 'personal' control and 'social' control. He proposed that the former comes about when individuals internalise the norms and rules of non-deviant primary groups to such an extent that they become their own. The latter are founded in the ability of social groups or institutions to make rules or norms effective. Thus, conformity derived from social control tends to involve mere submission to the norms in question and does not necessarily require the internalisation of these within the value system of the individual. Reiss tested his theory on 1,110 children between the ages of 11 and 17 who were subject to probation orders and found that personal controls were much more important in preventing deviance than social controls.

Ivan Nye (1958) developed a much more systematic version of control theory. In attempting to locate and identify the factors that encourage conformity in adolescents, he focused on the family, which, because of the affectional bonds established between members, were considered to be the most important mechanism of social control. He identified four modes of social control generated by the family:

1 *direct control* is imposed through external forces such as parents, teachers and the police using direct restraint and punishment;

2 individuals themselves in the absence of external regulation exercise *internalised control*;

3 *indirect control* is dependent upon the degree of affection that an individual has for conventional significant others;

4 *control through alternative means of needs satisfaction* works by reducing the temptation for individuals to resort to illegitimate means of needs satisfaction.

Though independent of each other, these four modes of control were considered mutually reinforcing and to work more effectively in tandem.

Walter Reckless's (1967) containment theory sought to explain why – despite the various 'push' and 'pull' factors that may tempt individuals into criminal behaviour (for example, psychological factors such as restlessness or aggression, or adverse social conditions such as poverty and unemployment) – most people resist these pressures and remain law-abiding citizens. Reckless argued that a combination of control factors, both internal and external to the individual, serve as insulators or 'containments' against these 'push' and 'pull' factors. The factors involved in outer containment were identified as being (a) reasonable limits and expectations, (b) meaningful roles and activities, and (c) several complementary variables, such as a sense of belonging and identity, supportive relationships especially in the family, and adequate discipline.

Reckless nonetheless attached much more importance to factors in inner containment as he argued that these would tend to control the individual irrespective of the extent to which the external environment changed. Four key components of inner containment were identified:

1 individuals with a strong and favourable *self-concept* are better insulated against those 'push' and 'pull' factors that encourage involvement in criminal activity;

2 *goal orientation* is the extent to which the individual has a clear direction in life oriented towards the achievement of legitimate goals such as educational and occupational success;

3 *frustration tolerance* is where contemporary society – with its emphasis on individualism and immediate gratification – might generate considerable frustration. Individuals have different capacities for coping with this factor;

4 *norm retention* is the extent to which individuals accept, internalise and are committed to conventional laws, norms, values and rules and the institutions that represent and uphold these.

Reckless described the process, by which norm retention is undermined, thus making deviance more possible, as one of norm erosion. This involves 'alienation from, emancipation from, withdrawal of legitimacy from and neutralisation of formerly internalised ethics, morals, laws and values' (Reckless, 1967: 476). This idea of individuals being able to neutralise formerly internalised norms and values to facilitate deviant or offending behaviour had been a prominent element in Matza's drift theory (see Chapter 7).

Modern control theories

Travis Hirschi (1969) that has made the most influential contribution to the development of modern social control theory. He asserts that at their simplest level all control theories share the assumption that 'delinquent acts result when an individual's bond to society is weak or broken' (1969: 16).

Hirschi identified four elements of the social bond: *attachment, commitment, involvement* and *belief*. However, unlike other control theorists who had emphasized the internal psychological dimension of control, these terms were employed in a much more sociological sense. The idea that norms and attitudes can be so deeply internalised as to constitute part of the personality is simply rejected. For Hirschi, an individual's bonds to conventional society are much more superficial and precarious.

1 The term *attachment* refers to the capacity of individuals to form effective relationships with other people and institutions, in the case of adolescents, with their parents, peers and school. When these attachments are sufficiently strong, individuals are more likely to be concerned with the opinions and expectations of others and thus more likely to behave in accordance with them. Since this bond of attachment is considered by Hirschi to lie not in some psychological 'inner state', but in ongoing social relationships with significant others, the strength of these attachments can and may vary over time.

2 The notion of *commitment* refers to the social investments made by the individual to conventional lines of action that could be put at risk by engaging in deviant behaviour. This is essentially a rational actor model cost–benefit type of argument: those investing most in conventional social life have a greater stake in conformity, and thus most to lose by breaking the rules.

3 The element of *involvement* again refers not to some psychological or emotional state, but to the more mundane reality that a person may be too busy doing conventional things to find time to engage in deviant activities.

4 *Beliefs* are not – as we might expect – a set of deeply held convictions but rather a set of impressions and convictions in need of constant reinforcement. In this context, beliefs are closely bound up with and dependent upon the pattern and strength of attachments an individual has with other people and institutions.

These four variables, though independent, are also highly interrelated and are theoretically given equal weight: each helps to prevent law-breaking activities in most people.

For many the main strength of Hirschi's work is empirical rather than theoretical (see Box, 1981; Downes and Rock, 1998). This view tends to be based on the results of a large-scale study conducted by Hirschi of over 4,000 adolescents from mixed social and ethnic backgrounds where a variety of propositions derived from control, strain and cultural diversity theories were tested. For the most part it was the control variables that appeared to correlate most closely and consistently with offending behaviour. Hirschi's data indicates that the closer a relationship a child enjoyed with its parents, the more it is attached to and identifies with them, the lesser the likelihood of involvement in delinquent behaviour. Moreover, it is those who do not like school and do not care what teachers think of them who more likely to commit delinquent acts. Not that attachment to delinquent peers is, in itself, found to undermine conventional bonds and lead to offending behaviour. It is, rather, weak social bonds and a low stake in conformity that leads to the acquisition of delinquent friends. The data showed that high aspirations give a stake in conformity that ties an individual to the conventional social order, and not the reverse suggested by the anomie theory tradition. Moreover, social class and ethnic background were found to be 'very weakly' related to offending behaviour.

Numerous other attempts have been made to test the theoretical and empirical adequacy of Hirschi's original theory and the models derived from it. One notable example is Thomas and Hyman's (1978) study, which is particularly illuminating as it employed a much more sophisticated methodology than Hirschi's original. The authors concluded that, 'while control theory does not appear to provide anything like a full explanation, its ability to account for a significant proportion of delinquency cannot be ignored' (1978: 88–9).

Overall, subsequent research has tended to find that the aspects of the social bond most consistently related to offending behaviour are those of the family and the school. There is substantial evidence that juveniles with strong attachments to their family are less likely to engage in delinquency. The evidence on the association between attachment and commitment to the school, particularly poor school performance, not liking school and low educational and occupational aspirations and delinquency, is even stronger.

Despite its impressive empirical support, Hirschi's original formulation of control theory has not entirely escaped criticism. He himself conceded that it overestimated the significance of involvement in conventional activities and underestimated the importance of delinquent friends. Moreover, both of these problems appeared to have stemmed from the same conceptual source, the taken-for-granted assumption of a natural motivation towards offending behaviour (Box, 1981; Downes and Rock, 1998). There have been other criticisms. First, the theory cannot account for the specific form or content of deviant behaviour, or 'why some uncontrolled individuals become heroin users, some become hit men, and others price-fixing conspirators' (Braithwaite, 1989: 13). Second, there is a failure to consider the underlying structural and historical context in which criminal behaviour takes place (Elliot, Ageton and Canter, 1979; Box, 1981, 1987). Third, while it plainly considers primary deviance among adolescents, habitual 'secondary deviance' appears to be outside its conceptual boundaries (Box, 1981).

Subsequently other researchers have sought a remedy for these various identified defects by integrating control theory with other theoretical perspectives.

Integrated theoretical perspectives

Elliot *et al* (1979) developed a model that sought to expand and synthesize anomie theories, social learning and social control perspectives into a simple explanatory paradigm. Their model begins with the assumption that individuals have different early socialisation experiences, leading to variable degrees of commitment to, and integration into, the conventional social order: to strong and weak social bonds. These initial bonds can be further reinforced or attenuated by subsequent experiences. Bonds can be strengthened and reinforced by such factors as positive experiences at school and in the wider community, positive labelling in these new settings and continuing stability in the home.

The structural dimension of Elliot *et al*'s model is most explicit in their analysis of the factors that serve to attenuate social bonds. Limited or blocked opportunities, negative labelling experiences at school, for example streaming, social disorganisation at home and in the wider community, high rates of geographic mobility, economic recession and unemployment, are all identified as experiences that may weaken or break initially strong ties to the conventional order.

Such structural impediments to achieving conventional success goals will constitute a source of strain and can of themselves – where commitment to conventional goals is strong enough – provide *the* motivational stimulus to delinquency. In most cases, however, and specifically for those whose ties and commitments to conventional groups and goals are weak in the first place, some further motivation is necessary for sustained involvement in delinquent behaviour. For Elliot *et al* it is 'access to and involvement in delinquent learning structures that provides this positive motivation and largely shapes the form and content of delinquent behaviour' (1979: 15).

Elliot *et al* propose two primary explanatory routes to delinquency. The first and probably most frequent represents an integration of control theory and social learning theory. It involves weak bonds to conventional society; and exposure and commitment to groups involved in delinquent activity. The second path represents an integration of traditional strain and social learning perspectives. This involves strong bonds to conventional society; conditions and experiences that attenuate those bonds; and in most cases exposure and commitment to groups involved in delinquency.

Stephen Box (1981, 1987) sought to explain the discrepancy between the findings of self-report studies, such as Hirschi's, that suggest only a weak relationship between social class and delinquency, and official statistics that show strong links. By integrating control theory with a labelling/conflict perspective – incorporated from the victimised actor model of crime and criminal behaviour – Box showed how the 'primary' deviants of the self-report studies become the largely economically disadvantaged and minority group 'secondary' deviants of the official statistics. He argues that differential policing practices, and institutional biases at different stages of the criminal justice system, all operate in favour of the most advantaged sections of a society and to the detriment of less favoured citizens. However, this is not merely a product of discriminating decision-making criteria made on the basis of a suspect's individual characteristics. Employing a more macro and historical view of the criminalization process, Box suggested it may be plausible to view such outcomes as a response to social problems of which the individual is merely a symbol:

> Thus, the economically marginalised and the oppressed ethnic minorities – because they will also be economically marginalised – will be treated more harshly by the judicial system not simply because of who they are, but also because of what they symbolise, namely the perceived threat to social order posed by the growth of the permanently unemployed.
>
> (Box, 1981: 200)

This relationship is viewed as being fully interactive as the stigma, disadvantage and sense of injustice engendered by the criminalization process, particularly when it is perceived as discriminatory, provides a further impetus towards criminal behaviour.

In his later work, Box (1987) showed how the impact of economic recession – such as that experienced in Britain during the 1980s – could lead to an increase in criminal activity. First, by further reducing legitimate opportunities and increasing relative deprivation, recession produces more 'strain' and thus more individuals with a motive to deviate, particularly among the economically disadvantaged. Thus, the commitment of a person to society is undermined because his or her access to conventional modes of activity has been seriously reduced.

Second, by undermining the family and conventional employment prospects the ability and motivation of an individual to develop an attachment to other human beings, who might introduce a controlling influence in his or her life, is substantially reduced.

John Braithwaite's (1989) theory of 'predatory' crime – that is, crimes involving the victimization of one party by another – builds upon and integrates elements of control, labelling, strain and subcultural theory. It is argued that the key to crime control is a cultural commitment to shaming in ways that are described as 'reintegrative'. Thus, 'societies with low crime rates are those that shame potently and judiciously' (1989: 1).

Braithwaite makes a crucial distinction between shaming that leads to stigmatizing 'to outcasting, to confirmation of a deviant master status' and shaming that is 'reintegrative, that shames while maintaining bonds of respect or love, that sharply terminates disapproval with forgiveness. The latter controls crime while the former pushes offenders toward criminal subcultures' (1989: 12–13).

Braithwaite argues that criminal subcultures become attractive to those who have been stigmatized by their shaming because they can provide emotional and social support. Participation in these groups can also supply criminal role models, knowledge on how to offend and techniques of 'neutralisation' (see Matza, 1964, discussed in Chapter 7) which taken together can make the choice to engage in crime more attractive and likely. Therefore, a high level of stigmatization in a society is a key factor in stimulating the formation of criminal subcultures. The other major societal variable that encourages this configuration is the 'systematic blockage of legitimate opportunities for critical factions of the population' (1989: 103).

Braithwaite claims that individuals are more susceptible to shaming when they are enmeshed in multiple relationships of *interdependency* and, furthermore, societies shame more effectively when they are *communitarian*. It is such societies or cultures – constituted of dense networks of individual interdependencies characterised by mutual help and trust – rather than individualistic societies that are more capable of delivering the required more potent shaming, and more shaming that is reintegrative. This is a crucial observation.

Both Box and Braithwaite have sought to rescue the social control theory perspective from its emphasis on the individual – or more accurately family – culpability that had made it so popular with conservative governments both in the UK and the USA during the 1980s. Box (1981, 1987) located his radical reformulation of social control theory within the victimised actor model. But it is the notion of 'reintegrative shaming' developed by Braithwaite that has been central to the populist socialist perspective that is the focus of the following chapter. Significantly, neither Box nor Braithwaite – like Hirschi whom they sought to improve upon – manage to offer a satisfactory explanation of all crime and criminal behaviour. More recently Hirschi himself, in collaboration with Michael Gottfredson, has sought to do just that.

A general theory of crime

In their *General Theory of Crime*, Gottfredson and Hirschi (1990) manage to combine rational actor model notions of crime with a predestined actor model theory of criminality. In line with the hedonistic calculus of rational actor model thinking, crime is defined as acts of force or fraud undertaken in the pursuit of self-interest. The authors propose that the vast bulk of criminal acts are trivial and mundane affairs that result in little gain and require little in the way of effort, planning, preparation or skill. Moreover, their 'versatility construct' points to how crime is essentially interchangeable. The characteristics of ordinary criminal events are simply inconsistent with notions of specialisation or the 'criminal career'. Since the likelihood of criminal behaviour is also closely linked to the availability of opportunity, the characteristics of situations and the personal properties of individuals will jointly affect the use of force or fraud in the pursuit of self-interest.

Gottfredson and Hirschi's concept of criminality – low self-control – is not confined to criminal acts. It is also causally implicated in many 'analogous' acts, such as promiscuity, alcohol use and smoking. Such behaviour is portrayed as the impulsive actions of disorganised individuals seeking quick gratification.

Gottfredson and Hirschi turn to predestined actor model explanations in order to account for the variation in self-control among individuals, arguing that the main cause is 'ineffective parenting'. This failure to instil self-control early in life cannot easily be remedied later, any more than effective control, once established, can be later undone. According to this 'stability postulate', levels of self-control will remain stable throughout the life course and 'differences between people in the likelihood that they will commit criminal acts persist over time' (1990: 107).

The *General Theory of Crime* is essentially a radical restatement of the control theory set out by Hirschi in his earlier work, successfully addressing many of the key criticisms aimed at the original. It is more explicitly grounded in a rational actor model conception of crime;

therefore offering a more consistent notion of criminal motivation than has been the case with previous control theories. By asserting that crime is essentially interchangeable while the propensity to commit crime remains stable throughout the life course, the theory has no need to provide separate explanations for different *types* of crime, nor for *primary* or persistent *secondary* deviation.

The theory does, however. deny the relevance of structural or sociological variables, including those included in Hirschi's original theory. The types of bonds an individual establishes with other people and institutions are now said to be a function of that same individual's level of self-control. Thus, those who have self-control are more likely to form constraining social relationships, whereas those who lack it will tend to 'avoid attachments to or involvement in all social institutions' (1990: 168).

Gottfredson and Hirschi describe their theory as 'general', claiming that it 'is meant to explain all crime, at all times' (1990: 117). Whether it does, however, depends on the extent to which the observed nature of crime corresponds with that presented as typical by the authors. Depicting all crime as impulsive, unplanned and of little or no real benefit to the perpetrator poses particular problems in the case of white-collar – or business – crime. There is much evidence that high-ranking governmental and corporate officials, acting independently or on behalf of the organisations they serve, use fraud and force in carefully planned ways to enrich themselves and maintain their positions. As Barlow (1991: 238) observes:

> Compared to low-end crime, high-end crime is much more likely to involve planning, special expertise, organisation, delayed gratification, and persistence – as well as considerably larger potential gains.

The existence of high-level crime also seems to cast considerable doubt on Gottfredson and Hirschi's 'stability postulate', that is, the notion that levels of self-control remain constant throughout the life course. Since low self-control is also incompatible with the discipline and effort normally required to attain high office, it is difficult to see how corporate offenders managed to climb the corporate ladder in the first place!

Even if the proposition that low self-control is a causal factor in some, or even most, types of crime is accepted, can we also accept the straightforward association Gottfredson and Hirschi propose between low self-control and ineffective parenting? Although the literature discussed elsewhere in this book does suggest a relationship between parenting and delinquency, this is compromised and complicated when structural factors are considered. For example, while her study of socially deprived families in Birmingham did find that parental supervision was an important factor in determining adolescent offending behaviour, Harriet Wilson warned against the misinterpretation of her findings:

> The essential point of our findings is the very close association of lax parenting methods with severe social handicap. Lax parenting methods are often the result of chronic stress ... frequent or prolonged spells of unemployment, physical or mental disabilities amongst members of the family, and an often-permanent condition of poverty. It is the position of the most disadvantaged groups in society, and not the individual, which needs improvement in the first place.
>
> (Wilson, 1980: 233–4)

These findings show quite clearly that even by relocating the source of control from the nature of an individual's bond to society back to within the individual himself or herself, Gottfredson and Hirschi cannot escape the need to incorporate some sense of underlying structural context into their analysis.

Gender differences in criminal behaviour

There is almost complete agreement among scholars that gender is a major, persistent correlate to criminality. Downes and Rock (1998: 283) have observed:

> ... that females commit markedly fewer crimes than males, of a generally less serious character, and are less likely to persist after a first conviction, has been acknowledged by criminologists ... for most of the past century.

Until fairly recently, however, the possible reasons for this, and the related question of whether theories designed to account for men's criminality are also applicable to women, have not been addressed. In observing this neglect some writers have pointed to the fact that most criminological theorising has been 'crime-led' and thus its subject matter has tended to be the economically deprived young males who apparently commit the bulk of criminal offences (Downes and Rock, 1998). Given that control theory takes the opposite approach and seeks to explain *conformity* rather than deviance, it would appear to be ideally suited to the task of accounting for female criminality, or more particularly, the striking degree of female conformity.

Unfortunately, despite this potential, in its actual application control theory has often been as male-centred and biased as most traditional theories. For example, the most influential model of control theory developed by Hirschi (1969) was presented as gender-neutral. Naffine (1987) notes, however, that in his survey of nearly 4,000 adolescents – in which, in terms of social class and ethnicity at least, he took care to make the sample representative – he did not include a single female. It is difficult to escape the conclusion that Hirschi was not interested in conformity *per se*, but rather with providing an account of *male conformity*. Naffine also argues that the factors in conformity presented by Hirschi all relate to the typical male role of 'breadwinner', such as hard work, responsibility and commitment to employment. Moreover, that conformity in males is depicted as positive. In contrast, female conformity is seen as a function of their passivity and thus, however unintended, takes on negative connotations.

Other tests of control theory, however, have not involved this strong gendering and negative view of the female. For example, Hindelang (1979) replicated Hirschi's study but included females. He found that although the prediction for males was slightly stronger, control theory could predict conformity in both girls and boys. Hindelang attributed the greater conformity of females to the fact that they were more closely controlled within the home and denied full access to the outside world, which was seen largely as a male preserve. Box (1981) certainly did not view control theory as gender-neutral but an invaluable tool in explaining the greater conformity of females. He claimed that stronger social bonding, a more acute awareness of the risks involved in delinquency, and greater peer support for conformity all encourage female conformity and make the choice to conform a rational and thus positive choice.

Heidensohn (1985) – as we saw in Chapter 10 – also maintained that control theory provides the most useful approach to understanding female conformity and deviance. She argued that females' dependency and their 'caring' roles – that is, mother, wife – and the way these aspects of women's experience are reinforced through social/welfare interventions and ideologies and legitimised by the state, all help control women in the home.

A critique of social control theories

In the thirty plus years since Hirschi introduced his control theory it has gained in popularity and influence. Box (1987) observes that this is not difficult to explain. First, social control theory lends itself remarkably well to empirical research and has become *the* most tested theory of crime causation. Moreover, it is very well supported empirically. Second, because it has avoided implicating social structural issues such as poverty and unemployment as a cause of criminal behaviour, it was to become very popular with the 'right wing' in the USA and thus extremely attractive for research funds. It was on the basis of these factors that Box justified his inclusion of control theory in his integrated theory.

While 'popular' support for a particular perspective on crime is, of itself, no proof of worth, extensive empirical support clearly is. Despite its impressive empirical support *vis-à-vis* other theories, however, one could argue, as Downes and Rock (1998) have done, that control theory is not addressing the same problems as its rivals. Alternative sociological theories attempt to account for the character of offending behaviour and to construct models of motivation that account for its typical forms. In control theory, by contrast, deviance has no meaning other than as a means of gratifying basic appetites, be they acquisitive, aggressive or sexual.

Even if we can accept the underlying assumptions of control theory about human nature, that we would all be deviant but for the controls that rein in our natural tendencies, the question still remains: 'in what ways would we be deviant?' By redefining the problem of motivation out of existence, it becomes difficult, if not impossible, for control theory to account for the very phenomena that other theories specifically set out to address. In other words,

> … why delinquency is so often non-utilitarian; why aggression is so frequently ritualised and non-violent in its outcome; why sexual gratification takes such complex forms. In short, control theorists make far too little of both deviance and conformity.
>
> (Downes and Rock, 1998: 238)

There is little doubt that in redirecting attention to the previously overlooked issue of conformity, and how this is 'caused' and sustained, control theory has made a significant contribution to the project of explaining crime and criminal behaviour. It simply fails to supply the complete explanation claimed by Gottfredson and Hirschi.

215

Suggested further reading

Key texts in social control theory written from a US perspective are Gottfredson and Hirschi, *A General Theory of Crime* (1990) and Hirschi, *Causes of Delinquency* (1969). Wilson, 'Parental Supervision: a Neglected Aspect of Delinquency' (1980) provides a classic use of the theory in a UK context. Box, *Deviance, Reality and Society* (1981) and *Recession, Crime and Punishment* (1987), Braithwaite, (1989) and Elliot *et al* (1979) have all produced important texts that have integrated social control theory with other theoretical perspectives. Heidensohn, *Women and Crime* (1985) discusses the value of social control theory in the study of women and crime.

Chapter 15

Left realism

Left realism is unlike the theoretically integrated approaches discussed in the previous three chapters of this fourth part of the book. It is not really an attempt to integrate and synthesize elements from different theories in order to provide a stronger integrated and comprehensive theoretical tool. It is rather more recognition of the validity of explanatory elements contained in each of the three models of crime and criminal behaviour that we have so far encountered and their practical value as part of a comprehensive strategy for dealing with crime both at a macro societal level and at the level of practice.

The origins of left realism

Left realism has it origins in the writings of a group of British criminologists some of whom had been in the forefront of the radical criminology of the 1970s. These texts emerged principally in response to four closely interconnected factors. First, there was a reaction to what they had come to term 'left idealism', the extreme positions that their previous confederates in the radical/critical criminological tradition had now taken up. Second, there was a response to the rising tide of criminal victimisation that was becoming increasingly apparent in British society and where poor people were overwhelmingly the victims.

It seems extremely unlikely, however, that these writers and researchers would have so readily discovered this new reality but for the important impetus provided by the other two factors. These were the rise to prominence and power of the populist conservatives or the 'new right' and the simultaneous rediscovery by right realist criminologists of the rational actor model of crime and criminal behaviour.

This significant shift in the intellectual climate of radical criminology had centred on a debate around the issue of policing the inner city and the notion of moral panics. One prominent view amongst left criminologists was that a 'new realist' view on crime was required. It was time to 'take crime seriously' (Lea and Young, 1984). From this viewpoint it was now argued that crime is not purely a social construction, nor is the fear of crime that is shared by many people. To put the latter down solely to the manipulations of the 'capitalist media' or 'the system' is, again, politically and morally irresponsible. Moreover, as was becoming readily apparent from the findings of victimisation studies – such as the British Crime Surveys – to regard criminal statistics as mere inventions is not acceptable either. Broad patterns of offences can be established after all, and a disproportionate amount of personally hurtful crime is undeniably committed by the more 'marginalised' sectors of the urban working-class, for example, young black males. Quite simply, the lives of many ordinary citizens are seriously disrupted by this kind of offence, and it is in no way 'pro-state' to argue for effective policing in these areas.

This group of criminologists on the left of the political spectrum – such as Jock Young, John Lea and Roger Matthews – became increasingly worried during the 1980s that the debate on crime control was slipping away from them. Critical criminologists were – by denying that working-class crime was a real problem and concentrating instead on 'crimes of the powerful', it was argued – ignoring the plight of working-class victims of predatory crime. Successive defeats of the British Labour Party moreover convinced them that they had allowed the political high ground to be captured by the new populist conservative theorists. The rediscovered rational actor model was gaining favour with government, while administrative criminologists in the Home Office were, as we have seen elsewhere in this book, concentrating on small-scale empirical investigation.

Young detected a need for a 'radical realist' response: one, which recognised the impact of crime but which at the same time addressed the context in which it occurred. The first statement of his dissatisfaction with radical orthodoxy came in a book written with his contemporary John Lea, *What is to be Done About Law and Order?* (1984). In this text they stressed the evidence of victim studies, which showed that official statistics presented an incomplete and even inaccurate picture of the impact of crime. Victim studies had two major advantages: first, they revealed offences and incivilities, which, although not reported to the police, nevertheless caused great misery to those who suffered them. Second, because many of the studies were localised, they gave a truer impression of the situation in particular areas where offending might be concentrated.

Lea and Young were concerned to highlight differences in victimisation levels within groups. For example, national statistics suggest that women as a group are far less likely than men to be victims of homicide, but a closer examination shows that the chances of a black woman being murdered are greater than that of a white male. They also drew attention to the disparity between the impact of crime on different groups: men generally feel anger against aggressors, whereas women tend to suffer shock and fear. Moreover, the impact of crime cannot be measured in absolute terms: £50 stolen from a middle-class home is likely to have less effect on the victims than the same sum taken from a poor household.

For left realists, crime then is a real problem that must be addressed. Lea and Young deal with the argument that corporate crime is more important: yes, 'crimes of the powerful' do exist and are to be condemned, but the effects of corporate crime are generally widespread, while those of direct-contact crime are concentrated. Corporate crime may indeed cause financial loss and even death and danger, but the real problem for those living in high crime areas is posed by predatory offenders in their midst. Left realism takes into account the immediate fears that people have and seeks to deal with them.

Lea and Young were also keen to address the peripheral problems around the central issue. People living in high crime areas suffer individual offences that they may or may not report to the police. But they also suffer a range of incivilities, such as vandalism where they are not directly victimised, threats, vulgarity, sexual harassment, noise and swearing, all of which taken together further reduce quality of life and increase despair.

Police excesses are also identified as causing crime, in two ways. First, police harassment of minority groups causes resentment and feelings of helplessness that may actually encourage offending. Second, 'military-style policing', such as that noted in the run-up to the Brixton riots in April 1981, creates a siege mentality among the residents of an area that discourages them from assisting the police in their investigations. Moreover, aggressive policing further brutalizes crime areas, which in turn leads to more crime.

Left realists have also responded to the claim of critical criminologists that the apparent propensity of black youths to commit predatory crime is solely a result of racist police stereotyping and targeting. While recognising that such stereotyping does exist, and deploring it, Lea and

Young point out that young black males do in fact commit more of these offences. In the USA they are more represented in this category of offenders than Asians, Hispanics and Mexicans who suffer comparative levels of poverty and discrimination. In fact, in Britain, police had at first refused to accept that there was a 'black crime problem', instead pointing out that young black males were over-represented in areas where crime tended to be highest.

Left realism, however, draws on the lessons of anomie theory and proposes that young second-generation African Caribbeans in Britain commit more crime than other ethnic groups because they have been fully integrated into the surrounding culture and have consequently been led to expect a fair slice of the economic cake. Not being able to achieve their promised position through legitimate means, because of discrimination, they turn to crime. Other ethnic minorities, having integrated less, retain strong family and cultural ties that subject them to stronger social control and help them to achieve without offending.

Moreover, left realists doubt the existence of the simple relationship between crime and unemployment that has been so central to the critical criminology perspective. Women, who have been unable until recently to enter the workplace in large numbers, have always been massively under-represented in the ranks of offenders. It is only now, when women are finding opportunities for work, that the female crime rate is starting to rise more quickly.

Critical criminologists are simply accused of being 'schizophrenic' about crime. It is observed that feminists have forced them to take seriously the fear of women about rape and sexual assault, while racial attacks are naturally deplored. Other crime, however, is depicted as being understandable and a symptom of the class struggle. However:

> The tide is turning for radical criminology. For over two decades it has neglected the effect of crime upon the victim and concentrated on the impact of the state – through the process of labelling – on the criminal. … It became an advocate for the indefensible: the criminal became the victim, the state the solitary focus of attention, while the real victim remained off-stage.
>
> (Matthews and Young, 1986: Introduction)

Young also turned his sights on the limited adequacy of the 'new administrative criminology' that had come to dominate the British Home Office and the research departments of the larger universities:

The new administrative criminologists seek to construct a system of punishment and surveillance which discards rehabilitation and replaces it with a social behaviourism worthy of the management of white rats in laboratory cages.

(Young, 1986b: 28)

While criminologists had often been arguing amongst themselves in the pursuit of the 'holy grail' of an all-encompassing explanation of crime and criminal behaviour, there is evidence that governments had lost patience with a discipline that seemed no closer than it ever was to solving the crime problem. One of the world's leading criminologists, the Australian John Braithwaite, had perceptively observed as recently as 1989:

The present state of criminology is one of abject failure in its own terms. We cannot say anything convincing to the community about the causes of crime; we cannot prescribe policies that will work to reduce crime; we cannot in all honesty say that societies spending more on criminological research get better criminal justice policies than those that spend little or nothing on criminology.

(Braithwaite, quoted in Matthews and Young, 1992: 3–4)

In Britain, as we have seen elsewhere in this book, (see in particular Chapter 4 but also Chapter 11), government pessimism at ever being able to solve the crime problem through an understanding and ability to deal with the origins and motivations for offending had shifted the focus of research. Spending since the late 1970s has been devoted more to finding and evaluating pragmatic solutions to particular offences than to developing criminological theory. Most professional crime prevention practitioners enjoying government patronage had come to accept that crime is a function of opportunity. Whatever motives offenders might have, removal of opportunities for offending will, says the assumption, reduce the incidence of crime. The response of the left realists was to be in reality an attempt to develop an all-encompassing crime control strategy which while accepting the need for the practical, pragmatic and certainly the empirical, managed to locate this all within both a macro and micro theoretical context.

A balance of intervention

Central to the left realist crime control strategy is the proposition that crime requires a comprehensive solution: there must be a 'balance of intervention'. Both crime and the causes of crime must be tackled. Their argument is illustrated with the 'square of crime' (see below).

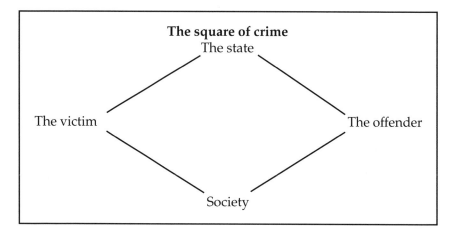

The square of crime is designed as a reminder that crime is the result of a number of lines of force and that intervention to prevent it must therefore take place at different levels in order to be effective. Left realists propose that crime is a function of four factors. First, there is *the state*, principally through the capacity of its front-line agents to label individuals and groups as offenders. Second, there is *the victim* who may actually encourage offenders through inadequate defence or may even precipitate crime through his or her life-style or personality. Third, there is *society*, through which the various forces of social control are exercised. Fourth, there are *the offenders* themselves (their number, their rate of offending, the type of crimes they commit, etc.).

Crime occurs not only as a product of these individual four factors, but also as an outcome of the relationship between them. The relationship between the police and the public that left and indeed right realists argue, determines the effectiveness of the former in preventing crime, can be described as a state–society interplay. The actions of the criminal justice system are a state–offender interplay. Fundamentally, all crime prevention efforts, of whatever type, involve some relationship between the four corners of the square. In short,

> To control crime from a realist perspective involves intervention at each part of the square of crime: at the level of the factors which

give rise to the putative offender (such as structural unemployment), the informal system (such as lack of public mobilisation),
the victim (such as inadequate target hardening), and the formal
system (such as ineffective policing).

(Young, 1986b: 41)

Essentially, all that the left realists are really saying is that there is
something to be said for most explanations of crime and criminal
behaviour. The problem with most theorists, they argue, is that by
occupying entrenched positions on the causes of crime, they are not able
to step back and look at the wider picture.

Critical criminologists accept that the 'new realist' perspective has
much in common with both Engels' (1845) and Bonger's (1916) much
earlier Marxist versions of 'demoralisation' theory. These classical
Marxists had argued that capitalism is a social system that dehumanises
and alienates people, particularly sections of the working class, who
inevitably become at times desperate and antisocial in their strategies for
personal survival. From this perspective, crime statistics are considered
to be an index of the general moral malaise of a society that – in its
legitimate as well as illegitimate business – thrives on greed and self-
interest. It therefore follows that certain kinds of crime, criminal and
victim are not to be 'explained away' as if they are somehow unreal or
merely a product of repressive bourgeois law.

Consequently, both the older Marxists and the new realists see a
positive element in the 'rule of law'. In particular, some need is
recognised for effective policing, for example, in declining urban areas.
More positively, a socialist strategy is held to require the extension and
defence of certain civil rights, which are, nominally at least, available
within liberal capitalist society (Hirst, 1980). The politics of law and
order, for the left, should consequently be less to do with the denial of
street crime and sympathy with marginalised groups, and more to do
with the elaboration of a responsible, rights-based notion of order.

Left realism has been be criticised nonetheless for presenting a
caricature of a supposedly antagonistic 'left idealist' position. The
equation is made that 'the police are part of the state, are a part of
capitalism', or that in 'true socialism, when it comes, there will be no
problems of order, crime or dissent'. Critical theorists such as Phil
Scraton and Joe Sim acknowledge that elements of that position crept
into 1960s and 1970s theorising but assert that virtually no one would
maintain these caricatured assertions in the early twenty-first century. At
the same time, they have quite serious and legitimate reservations about
the drift into left realism that require a response.

223

Critical criminologists have argued that in a phase of capitalism which displays increasingly harsh traits, it is not at all 'idealist' to argue that the main focus and priority should be on the nature of police coercion and authoritarian tendencies in the state (Scraton, 1985; Sim, Scraton and Gordon, 1987). They argue that the most striking fact about law and order today is not so much the fear of crime and street offences. Rather, we are seeing – if only we look in the right places – a massive growth in the powers of the armed and surveillance branches of the state, limbs of the body politic that are becoming dangerously unaccountable. To concentrate on the 'problem of crime' in this context is to reverse the proper order of priorities.

It would be wrong, however, to say – despite some parallels – that left and right realism are the same. The left would strenuously dispute references to Victorian values and the virtues of traditional authority – highlighted by the right – on the grounds that a restricted conception of human autonomy has been based on historical myth. Yet the political right instigated a moral climate during its long period of electoral dominance in the 1980s and 1990s that established an apparent new social consensus. The 'New' Labour Government elected in 1997 was subsequently criticised by many traditionalists on the political left, in particular by critical criminologists, for merely carrying on with the law and order project instigated by their predecessors and supposedly political opponents.

Left realism and 'New' Labour

We have seen above and elsewhere in this book that during the 1980s the British Home Office came to promote what Jock Young has termed the new 'administrative criminology'. The emphasis on reducing the opportunity to offend through small-scale situational crime prevention schemes was in perfect accord with the ideological viewpoint of a Conservative Government in the period 1979–1997 committed to notions of rational choice and making people take responsibility for their actions. But there had also been good practical reasons for this shift in emphasis.

The previous rehabilitative orthodoxy of the predestined actor model of criminal behaviour and its emphasis on treatment and changing criminals (the biological or psychological versions) or their environment (the sociological version) had been widely seen not to work. A considerable sum of money had been spent over the years on rehabilative measures while at the same time the ever-increasing official crime statistics painted a picture of expensive failure.

The new administrative orthodoxy proposed that if none of these causal explanations of criminal behaviour and their corresponding policy interventions worked then there was little point in pursuing this approach. Conservative populists – or 'right realists' – proposed reducing the opportunity to offend, while catching, incarcerating and incapacitating those who did transgress. Nonetheless, this had not been an entirely successful strategy.

The jury is still unquestionably out on the success of situational crime prevention measures. Evaluations of schemes suggest ambiguous outcomes (Hughes, 1998) but crime has definitely been reduced on occasion in certain situations. Problematically, however, while there remains a population of potentially determined and available criminals there will continue to be an issue of crime displacement. In short, locking all doors and bolting all windows might be a good idea but it is apparently no universal panacea for the problem of crime. Situational crime prevention is undoubtedly a sensible but incomplete crime control strategy.

If we accept the latter point then we have to recognise that some attempt has to be made to address the motivations of offenders or – to use the language of the predestined actor model – to locate the causes of crime and do something about them. The solution for the left realists is a 'balanced intervention' that addresses all sides of the crime problem. For the British 'New' Labour government – or the populist socialists – unquestionably influenced by this criminological discourse, it is an approach to crime and criminal behaviour summarised and popularised by the oft-quoted soundbite of Prime Minister Tony Blair when Shadow Home Secretary: 'tough on crime, tough on the causes of crime'.

Being 'tough on crime' suggests that offenders should take responsibility for their actions, this being in theoretical accordance with the prescriptions of the rational actor model of crime and criminal behaviour. Taking a tough stance on the causes of crime suggests a targeting of both those individual and structural factors that in some way encourage criminality and is thus in accordance with not only the predestined actor model, but also – and most appropriately for a socialist political party, however much they might like to disguise that fact – rooted most firmly in the victimised actor model. The theoretical justification for that governmental approach – and it is one that sets it apart from its political opponents and predecessors in government – is offered by the following realist case study of an apparently criminal 'underclass'.

Social exclusion and the 'underclass': a case study

An analysis of a socially excluded 'underclass' whose members are over-represented among the ranks of convicted offenders conducted from a left realist perspective requires that we consider theoretical inputs from each of the three models of crime and criminal behaviour introduced in this book. Two principal academic explanations can be found for the existence of this 'underclass' (Crowther, 1998) and these encompass theoretical insights from each of the three models. Structural accounts – for example, those offered by Dahrendorf (1985), Field (1989) and Jordan (1996) – are normally associated with the political 'left' and have their theoretical foundations firmly located in both the conflict, radical and critical variants of the victimised actor tradition *and* the sociological tradition within the predestined actor model. Primarily various forms of social exclusion, poverty, material deprivation and patterns of inequality are highlighted. Entry into and membership of this class is explained by the inadequacy of state-provided welfare services, changes in the labour market and exclusion from full citizenship. Behavioural accounts, on the other hand – for example, Wilson and Herrnstein (1985) Murray (1990; 1994), and Herrnstein and Murray (1995) – are normally associated with the new political 'right' or populist conservatives and have their theoretical foundations in the rational actor model *and* the biological variant of the predestined actor model (see Chapter 12). This form of explanation came to prominence during the 1980s following the rise in the number of long-term unemployed, the burgeoning lone parent population, increased welfare dependency and rising crime and disorder. From this perspective it is argued that the provision of state welfare erodes individual responsibility by giving people incentives not to work and provide for themselves and their family. Moreover, it is argued that those 'controls' – identified in the previous chapter (see Hirschi, 1969) – that stop individuals and communities from behaving badly, such as, stable family backgrounds and in particular positive male role models – do not exist for many members of this 'underclass'.

Now evidence suggests that non-participation in the labour market fails to contribute, in any simple way, to the creation of a distinctive sub-culture (Westergaard, 1995; Marshall *et al*, 1996; Levitas, 1996; Crowther, 1998). People can remain unemployed for many years, surviving on a very limited income while remaining law-abiding citizens. On the other hand, it has to be recognised that there has been a real problem of crime and antisocial behaviour inflicted on some invariably poor working-class communities by gangs of socially excluded males living in their midst (Campbell, 1993; Jordan, 1996).

This author has proposed elsewhere that a left realist analysis requires the development of a process model that both locates the *structural* pre-conditions for the emergence of this social grouping while at the same time examining the nature of their *behavioural* response to their found predicament (Hopkins Burke, 1999a). It is an analysis that can provide the basis of a balanced intervention in their lives.

The structural preconditions for the emergence of an underclass were undoubtedly the collapse of the unwritten post-war social contract between governments and the unskilled working class in advanced industrial societies. This had been fundamentally founded on the pro-vision of full employment and a fallback position – or safety net – of a relatively generous welfare state. However, with the major economic restructuring that occurred during the late 1970s and the 1980s non-skilled young people – in particular young males – entering into the labour market became increasingly over-represented among the ranks of the unemployed. At the same time, changes to social security entitlement in 1988 – instigated by the populist conservatives with the conscious intention of eradicating welfare dependency – had meant that 16 and 17 year olds lost their automatic right to benefits while 18 to 24 year olds saw a dramatic reduction in the amount of money they could claim. Caroline Adams from the charity 'Action for Children' estimated that this was a contributory reason why 75,000 16 to 17 year olds had no source of income whatsoever (Hopkins Burke, 1998a). In short, the collapse of the economic basis of their existence provides the structural element of a process model of the creation of an underclass (Hopkins Burke, 2000).

The behavioural response of this group has its origins in changes to familial living arrangements encouraged by that economic upheaval. The ideal type nuclear family of industrial modernity (Parsons, 1951) been based on a division of labour and interdependency between men and women that had made considerable sense. The man had invariably been the main breadwinner while the woman had provided the home conditions to support him and nurture and socialise the next generation. It was a rational arrangement because there were very few, if any, realistic alternatives available to either man or woman. In changed socio-economic circumstances it was, however, a form of social arrange-ment that was becoming less of a rational choice for the potential participants.

Feminists have observed that stripped of their role as the breadwinner 'workless' men now had little to offer women and their children other than the erratic affection, violence and child abuse that had often been present in working-class families (Campbell, 1993). Moreover, in a situation where the modernist state was quite understandably prepared to place women and children at the head of the queue for welfare benefits and 'social' housing provision, the former had relinquished their economic dependency on men to become dependent upon an increasingly inadequate welfare state (Field, 1989).

Many young men were now stripped of the informal controls of waged employment and family responsibilities that had previously restrained their wilder excesses and brought them back into the fold of conforming non-offending by their early 20s. Unskilled and poorly educated, they were now completely superfluous to the long-term requirements of post-industrial society. Excluded from legitimate employment opportunities and presenting themselves as unattractive propositions to young women as partners in long-term relationships many of these young men found themselves 'frozen in a state of persistent adolescence' (Pitts, 1996: 260). These restricted life chances had important implications for their involvement in crime because all the evidence suggests that 'growing up' also means growing out of crime (Rutherford, 1992). Now stripped of legitimate access to adulthood these young men were trapped in a limbo world somewhere between childhood and adulthood long after the 'developmental tasks' of adolescence had been completed (Graham and Bowling, 1995).

'New' Labour criminal justice policy revisited

Left realism was to be extremely influential with the 'New' Labour Government elected in 1997. There was a readily identified need for a balanced intervention that tackled both offending behaviour and the social and environmental conditions that supported and encouraged that behaviour. The bottom line, however, would be an attempt to reintegrate back into included society the socially excluded 'underclass' identified above, as a part of a major government project – or 'big idea' – that this author has elsewhere termed 'reintegrative tutelage' (Hopkins Burke, 1999a).

In order to achieve that ambition it would be necessary to incorporate theoretical insights from each of the three substantive models of crime and criminal behaviour outlined in this book. It is the youth justice provisions, in particular, contained in that government's initial flagship criminal justice legislation, the Crime and Disorder Act 1998, that provides us with an unequivocal demonstration of that strategy.

The influence of the rational actor model is indicated in that legislation by the emphasis on the notion that young offenders must take responsibility for their actions. First, the rule of *doli incapax* that had presumed that a child under the age of 14 does not know the difference between serious right and wrong was revised. Second, the courts were given powers to impose a new reparation order, requiring young offenders to make some form of reparation to their victims. It was the crucial intention of these legislative changes that young offenders would encounter the consequences of their actions and recognise the harm they had caused their victims (Home Office, 1997).

Evidence of the influence of the predestined actor model is contained in legislative strategies to identify young people at risk of becoming involved in criminal activity. First, the child safety order was introduced to intervene in the lives of children aged under 10 who are considered to be at risk of becoming involved in crime; for example if they are found wandering the streets unsupervised late at night, or are failing to attend school. Second, local authorities are empowered to impose a temporary curfew on children aged under 10 in a specified public area.

These legislative initiatives contained in the Crime and Disorder Act 1998 were however located in the context of a range of other policy initiatives devised to tackle the causes of crime and criminality amongst young people, while at the same time recognising their status as victims of serious social and economic exclusion. There is a clear resonance here with victimised actor model. First, measures were introduced to support families including assistance for single parents to get off benefits and return to work, to help prevent marriage and family breakdown and to deal with such breakdown. Second, policies were introduced with the intention of helping children achieve at school. These measures included the provision of nursery education for all 4 year olds; an emphasis on higher school standards, with a particular focus on literacy and numeracy skills in primary schools; with steps taken to tackle truancy and prevent exclusions; and the provision of study support out of school hours. Third, there was the provision of opportunities for jobs, training, and leisure, through the New Start strategy aimed at re-engaging in education or training youngsters up to 17 who have dropped out of the system. Moreover, there was the welfare-to-work 'New Deal' for un-employed 18–24 year olds. Fourth, action was taken to tackle drug misuse with new initiatives in the criminal justice system, innovative projects showing what schools and the wider community can do and through the work of the new UK Anti-Drugs Co-ordinator in putting forward a new strategy aimed at young people.

In short, there was to be a comprehensive 'balance of intervention' in the lives of young offenders – or those at serious risk of becoming offenders – with the intention of tackling both their offending behaviour while at the same time challenging the socio-economic structural conditions that had contributed to making such behaviour a rational choice for many.

Suggested further reading

For a comprehensive introduction to the basic tenets of left realism you should consult Lea and Young, *What is to be Done about Law and Order?* (1984), Matthews and Young (eds), *Confronting Crime* (1986) and *Issues in Realist Criminology* (1992) and Young, 'Incessant Chatter: Recent Paradigms in Criminology' (1994) and *The Exclusive Society* (1997). Hopkins Burke, *Youth Justice and the Fragmentation of Modernity* (1999a) extends the discussion of the process model of the underclass.

Chapter 16

Conclusion: crime and postmodernity

In this book we have examined the different ways that crime and criminal behaviour have been explained during the past 200 years. While these explanations have been proposed at various times by, among others, legal philosophers, biologists, psychologists, sociologists, political scientists and geographers, it is possible to locate these many and varied explanations – or criminological theories – in terms of one of three different general models or traditions. These were the focus of the first three parts of this book.

The first tradition – the rational actor model – proposes that human beings enjoy free will and that this enables them to choose whether or not to engage in criminal activities. From this perspective, it is argued that crime can be controlled by making the costs of offending – that is, punishment – sufficient to discourage the pursuit of the rewards of criminality. In other words, the choice of criminal activity would be an irrational one.

The second tradition – the predestined actor model – proposes that criminal behaviour can be explained in terms of factors that exist either within the individual or their environment that cause that person to act in ways over which they have little or no control. It is by identifying these factors and eradicating them through some form of treatment process that crime can be controlled. Thus, biological and psychological variants of this model propose that the individual should be changed, while sociological versions propose that it is the criminogenic environment that should be transformed.

The third tradition – the victimised actor model – denies neither entirely the prescriptions of the rational actor nor the predestined actor models. It is recognised that people make decisions to behave in ways that may well be perfectly rational for them in the circumstances in which they find themselves. On the hand, it is the activities of the economically poor and politically powerless that are criminalised; a process conducted in the interests of those with power and wealth. Individuals can be labelled and criminalised by coming into contact with front-line agents of the state working in the criminal justice and welfare systems, while, at a macro societal level it is those with economic power and the control of authority that are in a position to influence the legislative agenda. From this perspective, crime is seen to be a social construction; it can be controlled or reduced by not criminalising unfortunate individuals and by abolishing legislation that criminalises their activities.

The fourth part of this book has discussed those attempts to produce a synthesis of different theoretical perspectives – some of these being internal to one particular model of criminal behaviour, others in-corporating elements that cross model boundaries – in order to provide a bigger, better, all-encompassing theory that seeks to explain as much crime and criminal behaviour as possible. Indeed, these integrated perspectives invariably seek to explain *all* criminal behaviour, an approach clearly in line with modernist social scientific thinking.

Now, it was explained in the introductory chapter that each of the theories introduced in this book – and, indeed, their particular host model or explanatory tradition – have a common central characteristic. Each is a product of what has come to be termed the modern age. It was observed that prior to the rise of modernity, religion and other forms of pre-scientific knowledge had crucially influenced explanations of crime. At that time, criminal justice and its administration was non-codified, capricious, invariably brutal and at the cynical discretion of the agents of monarchical regimes. In contrast, modern societies are secular, in-dustrialised, rationalised, codified and rule-bound with at least some pretence to widely participative democracy. Science is the dominant – and for a long time unchallenged – form of knowledge. Thus, crime and criminal behaviour – as we have seen in this book – has been explained by reference to scientific discourses or theories.

In the last decades of the twentieth century however there arose increasing doubts about the sustainability of that modernist project in an increasingly fragmented and diverse social world. It is a situation that some social scientists have come to refer as the postmodern condition (See Lyotard, 1984; but also Baudrillard 1988; Bauman, 1989, 1991, 1993).

Postmodernity and criminological explanation

It is possible to identify three main sources for the idea of the post-modern. The first source was the emergence and consolidation of an intellectual current articulated by the publication of two books by Daniel Bell, *The End of Ideology* (1960) and *The Coming of Post-Industrial Society* (1973). It was an emerging worldview that contained two subcurrents. There was the ideological exhaustion of the post-war world with the retreat from the pre-war ideologies of communism and national socialism that had seemed to lead to only totalitarianism, world war and holocaust. At the same time, there was a growing interest in the idea of a post-industrial – or later 'post-Fordist' – society. Manufacturing was giving way to the service industry, primary production was being displaced by secondary exploitation, especially of science and technology, and consumers were coming to outperform producers in the economy. In this changed context, the old radical class analyses seemed to make little sense. In short, the intellectual categories around which modernism had been built appeared to have lost their explanatory power.

The second source was that of poststructuralism, a movement that had flourished mainly in France during the late 1960s and 1970s. As its name suggests, it succeeded structuralism, which had flourished a decade or so earlier, most notably in the work of Claude Levi-Strauss, but could be traced back to the nineteenth century. While structuralists had been preoccupied with the 'deep structures' of language and society, poststructuralists were sceptical of efforts to attach meanings to words. Michel Foucault has contributed significantly to poststructuralism's wider popular influence by arguing that knowledge and language – and so the categories derived from them – cannot be regarded as anything other than subjective and relative (Foucault, 1980). Thus, by emphasising the subjectivity of language, poststructuralism contributed to what can be identified as the central belief of postmodernism, that there is no intellectual tradition that can be considered to have privileged authority over another.

The third source was an aesthetic movement with its foundations in an architectural controversy centred on the rejection of the so-called 'international style' of austere unadorned modernism epitomised by 1960s tower blocks and multi-storey car parks.

In summary, there are three significant characteristics that appear to distinguish postmodernism from modernism. First, there is an aversion to 'metadiscourses', grand self-legitimating theories that it is observed can lead to intellectual sterility and political oppression. Second, there is an awareness of the indeterminacy of knowledge and the impossibility of absolute truth, which has been inherited from the poststructuralists. Third, there is an enthusiasm for eclecticism and variety, which has been derived from art, architecture and literature but which has come to have much stronger intellectual reverberations.

The idea of the postmodern, therefore, involves claims that modernist features of society are under challenge. This can be seen in the realm of culture, where self-proclaimed modern thinkers and artists were challenged from the mid-1960s by anti-modernist ideas. These attacked the dehumanisation of modern society, questioned the authority of technical experts and celebrated human diversity in place of the pressure to encourage rationalised, standardised, human conformity to systems developed by 'experts' and technicians (see Marcuse, 1964). These concerns were reflected in the field of the social sciences by the emergence of radical efforts to challenge orthodox, positivist forms of thought whose claims to objective scientific status were rejected. There is a resonance here with Taylor, Walton and Young's (1973) call for the abolition of the power to criminalise human diversity in the concluding chapter of *The New Criminology*.

Underlying these changes was the beginning of an economic and political transformation manifest in a breakdown of the Keynesian and Fordist practices of the post-war world in the industrial West. This had been prompted by the oil crisis of the early 1970s, an abandonment of full employment policies with a decline in economic competitiveness, and a restructuring of the world economy with the rise in the productive capacity of the nations of the Pacific Rim. Thus, in all three areas, the economy, the political system and culture, there began to emerge increasingly diverse and fragmented social structures which heralded the beginning of postmodernism.

Economically, postmodernity is thus often described as post-Fordism. This involves the rejection of mass production-line technology in favour of flexible working patterns and a flexible labour force. This in turn involves a weakening of trade unions, greater reliance on peripheral and secondary labour markets, the development of a low-paid and part-time, often female, labour force, and the shift towards a service, rather than manufacturing, economy. On the side of capital-owning and controlling interests, it involves a greater stress on enterprise and entrepreneurialism, corporate restructuring and the growth of small businesses acting as subcontractors to larger firms. These trends are often seen as evidence of deindustrialisation and the disorganisation of capitalism.

Politically, postmodernity is complex and is difficult to categorise in traditional terms. An interesting development has been Michel Foucault's (1980) conceptualisation of power, which he argues is not simply the prerogative of the state. For Foucault, strategies of power are pervasive in society and the state is only one location of the points of control and resistance. In this view, there should be a move away from a restricted chain of criminological references – 'state–law–crime–criminals' – to a wider chain of associations that need to be addressed. For Foucault, particular areas of social life, such as medicine, law and sexuality, are colonised and defined by the norms and control strategies which a variety of institutions and experts devise and abide by (Foucault, 1971, 1976). These networks of power and control are governed as much by the *knowledge* and concepts that define them as by the definite intentions of individuals and groups.

The state, for its part, is implicated in this matrix of power–knowledge, but it is only part of it. In this vein it has been argued that within civil society there are numerous 'semi-autonomous' realms and relations, such as communities, occupations, organisations and families, where certain kinds of 'policing' and 'order' are indeed present, but where the state administration and police force are technically absent. These semi-autonomous arenas within society are often appropriately negotiated and resisted by their participants in ways that even now, the state has little jurisdiction over. To some, it may seem ironic that this emphasis comes at a time when many of the traditional coercive and regulatory roles of the state are being *enhanced* politically and technologically.

Postmodernity has been expressed in neo-conservative ideas, such as those promoted by the British Prime Minister, Margaret Thatcher and the American President, Ronald Reagan, and termed *Thatcherism* and *Reaganomics*. These ideologies included the offering of tax cuts as means to facilitate consumer choice, and the dismantling of elaborate state planning and provision in the fields of welfare. At the same time the diversity of interests becoming apparent in western societies placed strains on conventional representative democratic systems. Most long-standing democracies demonstrated themselves to be inadequate to the task of representing myriad interest groups as diverse as major industrialists and financiers, small business proprietors, the unemployed and dispossessed, wide-ranging gender and sexual preference interests, environmentalists and the homeless.

Modernity was essentially an era characterised by moral certainty. There was a confidence and belief in the superiority and infallibility of natural science that had filtered through into the social sciences, in particular, social and political theory. There was a confidence in the explanatory power of grand theories to solve the problems of humanity. There may be competing theories – for example, the many criminological theories introduced in this book – but the devotees of each of these had confidence in the fundamental capacity of their doctrine to solve the problem of crime and criminal behaviour in society. This might well – as we have seen particularly in Part 4 of this book – entail revisions to the theory, the incorporation of concepts from other theoretical perspectives and indeed other models of criminal behaviour, but in the final analysis the intention is the same, the creation of a criminological theory that explains most, if not all, criminal activity.

Postmodern societies are, in contrast to modern societies, characterised by moral ambiguity. Now this condition should not be confused with a period of moral uncertainty where reconsideration and rebuilding of theoretical perspectives can rekindle the moral certainty of old. It is a condition characterised by a terminal loss of certainty with absolutely no expectation that it will ever return.

Postmodern social scientists thus recognise the complexity of society and the moral ambiguities that are inherent within it. There is recognition of a range of different discourses that can be legitimate and hence right for different people, at different times, in different contexts. It is a perspective founded on cultural relativism, the notion that there are a series of legitimate discourses on a particular issue and that it is difficult, if not impossible, to objectively choose between them. Essentially, the objective truth – or the competing objective realities – of modernity, are replaced by recognition of the multiple realities or moral ambiguities of postmodernity. These realities are invariably complex, highly susceptible to inconsistent interpretation and are contested by individuals – politicians and members of the general public – who often make short-term, pragmatic and inconsistent judgements without reference to any coherent body of knowledge.

Whereas modernists had attempted to develop large-scale theories to explain society in terms of enduring, identifiable social structures, postmodernists have followed in the poststructuralist tradition emphasising the redundancy and futility of such efforts and contested the entire concept of truth. The social sciences, since their very inception in modern societies, had made efforts to transcend the relativity of social situations and identify 'what is going on' systematically and objectively, while philosophers had attempted to establish some rational standpoint from which reality could be described. The postmodern writers have on the other hand celebrated the failure of the modern project to establish rational foundations for knowledge and have themselves embraced the trend towards human diversity and social fragmentation. They have argued that there is no objective reality behind the plethora of social meanings. Accounts and definitions have no objective or external reference. They are merely elements in a free-floating system of images that are produced and reproduced through the medium of popular mass communication that come to define reality to consumers.

To some readers postmodernism will undoubtedly appear a nightmare vision; others may embrace and celebrate its implications. The fragmentation of social institutions such as social class and status may increase our uncertainty in our knowledge of how we understand society. However, the same trends also allow the expression of the diversity of human needs, interests and sensitivities. By challenging the validity of modern claims to privileged forms of knowledge for the powerful, postmodernism gives a voice to the less powerful and oppressed. It is hardly surprising, therefore, that some branches of the feminist movement have embraced the approach.

Postmodernists have also celebrated the development of new social movements such as travelling communities as they make efforts to live a lifestyle outside the constraints and dictates of the modern world. In the western world, gay and what were formerly regarded as other unconventional sexual interest groups have also been celebrated for their efforts to break down restrictive stereotypes and 'expert' knowledge surrounding the pursuit of sexual pleasure. The ideas and interests of animal rights groups and environmental concerns are also welcomed. These challenge the adequacy of representation in long-established representative democracies in which party systems commonly only represent the interests of people as members of a social class and, hence, give rise to a restricted form of political agenda which fails to address other interests. The celebration and acceptance of diversity, therefore, is taken as a positive thing.

Lyotard reflects on some of the horrors of the past two centuries of modernist society when people have controlled and killed others in their pursuit of a rational, scientific world order that, in a criminological context, had led from the biological notions of Lombroso via Goring to Auschwitz. Lyotard (1984: 81–2) notes:

> The nineteenth and twentieth centuries have given us as much terror as we can take. We have paid a high enough price for the nostalgia of the whole and the one, for the reconciliation of the concept and the sensible, of the transparent and the communicable experience. Under the general demand for slackening and for appeasement, we can hear the mutterings of the desire for a return to terror, for the realisation of the fantasy to seize reality. The

answer is: Let us wage war on totality; let us be witness to the unrepresentable; let us activate the differences and save the honour of the name.

The philosopher of the social sciences, Feyerabend had also celebrated a non-rationalist, even anarchistic approach to the manner in which we study the world. Highly critical of efforts to unify and control the limits of science and the potential for knowledge as authoritarian and inhumane he argues that 'science is an essentially anarchistic enterprise: theoretical anarchism is more humanitarian and more likely to encourage progress than its "law and order" alternatives' (Feyerabend, 1975: 17).

Problematically, given this general approach, we might legitimately ask how Feyerabend makes a judgement as to what is 'more humanitarian' and more 'progressive', and why this should be the case? He nonetheless asserts:

History generally, and the history of revolutions (in ideas) in particular, is always richer in content, more varied, more many-sided, more lively and more subtle than even the best historian and the best methodologist can imagine. History is full of accidents and conjectures and curious juxtapositions of events and it demonstrates to us the complexity of human change and the unpredictable character of the ultimate consequences of any given act or decision of men. Are we really to believe that the naive and simple-minded rules which methodologists take as their guide are capable of accounting for such a 'maze of interactions'? And is it not clear that successful participation in a process of this kind is possible only for a ruthless opportunist who is not tied to any particular philosophy and who adapts whatever procedure seems to fit the occasion?

(Feyerabend, 1975: 17–18)

The implication of this anarchistic enterprise of Feyerabend for criminological theorising and research appears to be that we should not be slaves to dominant paradigms of how we see the world but be prepared to take risks – perhaps even be prepared to consider the previously unthinkable at least in terms of contemporary orthodoxy – and be prepared to consider the potential of a whole range of often neglected theoretical perspectives.

There is, however, potentially a very negative side to postmodernism. For if there is no such thing as the truth of the human condition how can one provide an argument for basic human rights? Moreover, what foundations are there for law if the human experience is to be seen as reflexive and relative? The relativism implied by postmodernism denies the possibility of truth, and hence of justice, in anything other than a purely subjective form, which inevitably consigns us to the prospect of conflict.

Thus, politically, postmodernism can carry us right the way across the traditional political spectrum from the libertarian right-wing assumption of a war of all against all, resonant of the work of Thomas Hobbes, to a libertarianism of the left which celebrates and tolerates all human diversity and activity. Postmodernism therefore appears contemptuous of the possibility of developing an objective normative (moral) order which human beings can attempt to translate into enforceable norms or laws. Hence, while intellectually challenging and providing a possible explanation for the nature of social change in the contemporary West, the movement appears to provide no basis for the development of a plausible criminological strategy.

Sceptical and affirmative postmodernity

By regarding postmodernism in two distinct ways it is possible to accept some of its power to explain the enormous diversity in contemporary society without accepting some of the baggage of philosophical relativism. Pauline-Marie Rosenau (1992: 15) offers this option identifying what she terms *sceptical* and *affirmative* postmodernism:

> The sceptical post-modernism (or merely sceptics), offering a pessimistic, negative, gloomy assessment, argues that the post-modern age is one of fragmentation, disintegration, malaise, meaninglessness, a vagueness, or even absence of moral parameters and societal chaos. ... this is the dark side of post-modernism, the post-modernism of despair, the post-modernism that speaks of the immediacy of death, the demise of the subject, the end of the author, the impossibility of truth. They argue that the destructive nature of modernity makes the post-modern age one of 'radical, unsuppressible uncertainty' ... characterised by all that is grim, cruel, alienating, hopeless, tired and ambiguous. In this period no social or political project is worthy of commitment. If, as the sceptics claim, there is no truth, then all that is left is play, the play of words and meaning.

Acknowledging that there is no clear-cut divide between the approaches, Rosenau (1992: 15–16) identifies an alternative and more positive tendency in the postmodern movement:

> Although the affirmative postmodernists … agree with the sceptical post-modern critique of modernity, they have a more hopeful, optimistic view of the post-modern age. More indigenous to Anglo-North American culture than to the [European] continent, the generally optimistic affirmatives are oriented towards process. They are either open to positive political action (struggle and resistance) or content with the recognition of visionary, celebratory, personal, non-dogmatic projects that range from New Age religion to New Wave lifestyles and include a whole spectrum of post-modern social movements. Most affirmatives seek a philosophical and intellectual practice that is non-dogmatic, tentative and non-ideological. These postmodernists do not, however, shy away from affirming an ethic, making normative choices, and striving to build issue-specific political coalitions. Many affirmatives argue that certain value choices are superior to others, a line of reasoning that would incur the disapproval of the sceptical postmodernists.

The essential problem for the development of legislation and explanations of crime and criminal behaviour in the postmodern condition remains the difficulty of making any objective claims for truth, goodness and morality. This is, however, less the case for the affirmatives than for the sceptics. On the issue of the foundations of knowledge (epistemology), Rosenau (1992: 137) notes:

> Post-modern social science … announces the end of all paradigms. Only an absence of knowledge claims, an affirmation of multiple realities, and an acceptance of divergent interpretations remain. We can convince those who agree with us, but we have no basis for convincing those who dissent and no criteria to employ in arguing for the superiority of any particular view. Those who disagree with us can always argue that different interpretations must be accepted and that in a postmodern world one interpretation is as good as another. Postmodernists have no interest in convincing others that their view is best – the most just, appropriate, or true. In the end the problem with most postmodern social science is that you can say anything you want, but so can everyone else. Some of what is said will be interesting and fascinating, but some will also be ridiculous

and absurd. Postmodernism provides no means to distinguish between the two.

There are, however, clearly some fundamental logical intellectual difficulties posed for those seeking to research and explain criminal behaviour. First, there is little available empirical evidence to support the assumption that we have already reached a post-ideological climate. To argue that we can achieve the position that no intellectual tradition can be considered to have privileged authority over another is problematic as the reality is that particular traditions are usually seen to be more authorative. Second, whilst postmodernism may advocate giving a voice to the oppressed and less powerful – and may celebrate diversity – it could be argued that in practice power relations and political decisions are fundamentally important and may restrict this ideal. Indeed, it could be argued that recent criminal justice policy – both in the UK and the USA – and the politics that have informed it have tended to encourage less tolerance of difference rather than more. These observations should be borne in mind as in the final section we consider the implications of the postmodern condition for the future of criminological explanation.

The future of criminological explanation

The implications of the debates surrounding postmodernism for how we explain – or indeed respond to – crime and criminal behaviour are not at all certain or readily apparent. Indeed, as one might expect from the nature of the debate they are highly dependent upon a range of often countervailing flexible factors and ambiguities. It is, therefore, certainly not the purpose here to propose a definitive answer to that question, merely to indicate briefly some of the possibilities of the postmodern debate for the future of the criminological project.

The first possibility is that we dismiss the whole notion of post-modernism as non-productive and highly irrelevant to the crimi-nological project. Crime is unquestionably a reality to which its many victims can readily testify. These debates might make for interesting intellectual prognostication in the academy – or even better saloon bars and cafes – but they hardly help to alleviate that victimisation. Improved locks and bolts, increased technological surveillance, and an increased use of incarceration of those offenders who are apprehended are practical if not perfect pragmatic solutions. And it is a widely popular viewpoint. It is nonetheless an extremely expensive and increasingly prohibitive response. The USA, for example, currently has a prison population of in excess of 1.5 million and rising (Hughes, 1998), a situation to which the eminent left realist criminologist Jock Young (1999) refers to as 'Gulag USA', while virtually all western industrial societies are currently engaged in large-scale prison-building programmes.

The spread of modern technological surveillance and private security – allied to zero tolerance style public sector policing strategies – has enabled the affluent and predominantly business areas to protect and defend themselves by excluding the poor and dispossessed from their precincts (Davis, 1990; Hopkins Burke, 1998b, 1999b). Crime rates in major US cities are undoubtedly lower than ten years ago. However, the implications of the social exclusion of whole, and increasingly large, sectors of the population from the material good life while at the same time failing to adequately protect them from the predators in their midst is undoubtedly storing up barely imaginable problems for the future.

Thus, the second possibility of simply accepting the nihilist proposition of sceptical postmodernism and acknowledging that there is little we can do to control crime is neither a politically responsible nor practical criminological project. Something has to be done. Some criminologists observe a usually pessimistic vision that the future of a rather different discipline of criminology might simply be to manage the *risks* associated with such a scenario (Hughes, 1998; Walklate, 1998).

The contemporary notion of *risk management* is very much in vogue in the social sciences. It has its origins in the work of Ulrich Beck (1992) who has written about the consequences of scientific and industrial development during the twentieth century releasing a set of risks that threaten humanity. It is therefore necessary to identify and then manage, or control, those risks in order to ensure the future of our civilisation. David Garland (1996:4) observes that from this perspective crime is no longer seen as an aberration but rather 'an everyday risk to be managed like air pollution and road traffic' with high rates of crime viewed as normal (there are indeed echoes of Durkheim one hundred years previously here). Moreover, he notes that with the ever-decreasing confidence in the capacity of the state to provide security, law and order and crime control, new modes of governing crime – or governance – have emerged. First, there has been the increasing involvement of the private sector, especially in the area of policing and security. Second, there has been – in contrast to the modernist orthodoxy that crime is an abnormality that needs to be identified in all its manifestations and eradicated – the development of the notion of crime as a risk 'condition' to be calculated, or an accident to be avoided. Third, there has been the development of the situational crime prevention strategies identified in this book that have sought to restrict the criminal opportunities available to the potential miscreant. Fourth, there has been the development of strategies to make citizens feel responsibility for crime. Fifth, there has been the emergence of a managerial ethos of 'performance indicators' that judge criminal justice and crime control agencies in terms of measures that have absolutely nothing to do with actually reducing crime.

Hughes (1998: 156) comments that there is a real possibility that in twenty years' time the modes of thought that have been discussed in this book and located in the discipline of criminology will have been superseded by the knowledges of forensic psychology and geography brought together into what he terms a 'pseudo science' of risk management studies. He nonetheless observes that should this be the case, there will still be a need for a critical social science that is able to relate such new discourses to wider questions of social order, social justice and social control.

Certainly a revitalisation of the victimised actor model of crime and criminal behaviour is suggested in such a case. Further research into the variable experiences of different oppressed groups in their relationship to the criminal justice system whether as perpetrators or victims – whether these be women, members of ethnic minorities, young people or children – is likely to make an extremely important contribution to criminological theorising in the early years of the twenty-first century. Although the earlier critical criminologist notion that crime is simply a social construction of the dominant classes in society tends now to be widely regarded as overly simplistic, it is important to remember that some activities once considered criminal are now legal, for example, sexual acts between males, while the converse is also true and some activities that were once legal have subsequently been criminalised, for example, the driving of cars while under the influence of alcohol. We might from a contemporary vantage point consider the future legal status of cannabis smoking (possibly legalised or at least decriminalised) and fox hunting (possibly criminalised).

The third possibility suggested by the postmodern debate for the future of criminological theorising is suggested by the left realist approach that concluded the fourth part of this book. The theoretical foundations of that perspective are of course firmly located in the modernist tradition. It is, moreover, on the whole promoted by those with a strong sense of anathema towards the whole notion of post-modernity. The undoubted explicit intention of left realists is to build a new moral certainty – or even new teleological project – from the contemporary condition which they define as being one of moral uncertainty. To be acceptable to them, it would be a certainty where there was a substantial reduction, or even eradication, of socio-economic inequality. Not for them, the apparent uncontrollable anarchy and even acceptable inequalities of moral ambiguity.

The left realist strategy nevertheless *implicitly* suggests an enthusiasm for the postmodern notion of rejecting grand theoretical solutions. There is certainly a willingness to consider explanatory elements from all perspectives in an attempt to provide a comprehensive crime solution. It is indeed recognised that most criminological theories have something legitimate to say about *some* forms of crime and criminal behaviour, and thus due consideration should be given to these in the appropriate circumstances. It is, however, an approach that certainly does not exclude the further integration of theories if this were to lead to the development of an improved explanatory tool, albeit one with readily recognised limits of generalisability.

It is a strategy that seems to be in harmony with the election of a 'New' Labour Government in 1997 that proposed a 'new politics' beyond doctrinal dogma and which has appeared to be willing to consider policy options from a wide range of perspectives. This strategy, while not entirely non-ideological and undoubtedly part of a much wider strategy of attempting to build a new moral certainty (indeed, it is hard to imagine at this time a possible government that would not attempt that project), fundamentally recognises that good ideas – and for that matter, bad ones – are not the preserve of one side of the traditional left/ right political dichotomy. They can emerge from many different sources and there can be a diverse range of motivations for implementing a policy or strategy (Giddens, 1994, 1998). In terms of criminology, this would appear to be a sensible long-term approach to both under-standing crime and criminal behaviour in all its many manifestations and for the development of flexible strategies for dealing with what this book has clearly demonstrated to be a multifaceted and far from straightforward social problem. Only time will tell.

Suggested further reading

The following texts are recommended for those seeking an introduction to the notion of the postmodern condition: Baudrillard, *Selected Writings* (1988), Bauman, *Modernity and Ambivalence* (1991) and *Postmodern Ethics* (1993), Harvey, *The Condition of Postmodernity* (1989), Lyotard, *The Post-Modern Condition* (1984). Rosenau, *Post-Modernism and the Social Sciences* (1992) is essential reading on the relationship of postmodernity to the social sciences. Both Davis, *The City of Quartz* (1990) and Young, *The Exclusive Society* (1999) provide rather different accounts of contemporary post-industrial societies and the significance for criminology. The notion of risk society in general is discussed by Beck, *Risk Society* (1992) and the significance of this analysis for controlling crime and the notion of governance with the decline of the sovereign state by Garland, 'The Limits of the Sovereign State' (1996). Giddens, *Beyond Left and Right* (1994) and *The Third Way* (1998) attempts to square the circle between the postmodern condition (for him late modernity), left realism and the 'third way' political strategy of New Labour.

References

Adler, F. (1975) *Sisters in Crime: The Rise of the New Female Criminal*, New York: McGraw-Hill.

Adler, Z. (1982) 'Rape – The Intention of Parliament and the Practice of the Courts', *Modern Law Review*, 45: 664.

Aichhorn, A. (1925) *Wayward Youth*, New York: Meridian Books.

Ainsworth, P. (2001) *Offender Profiling and Crime Analysis*, Cullompton: Willan Publishing.

Akers, R.L. (1985) *Deviant Behaviour: A Social Learning Approach, Third Edition*, Belmont, CA: Wadsworth.

Akers, R.L. (1992) 'Linking Sociology and its Specialities', *Social Forces*, 71: 1–16.

Akers, R.L. (1997) *Criminological Theories: Introduction and Evaluation*, Los Angles, CA: Roxbury.

Akers, R.L., Krohn, M.D., Lanza-Kaduce, L. and Radosevich, M. (1979) 'Social Learning and Deviant Behaviour: A Specific Test of a General Theory', *American Sociological Review*, 44: 635–55.

Allsopp, J.F. and Feldman, M.P. (1975) 'Extroversion, Neuroticism and Psychoticism and Antisocial Behaviour in Schoolgirls', *Social Behaviour and Personality* 2: 184.

Allsopp, J.F. and Feldman, M.P. (1976) 'Personality and Antisocial Behaviour in Schoolboys', *British Journal of Criminology*, 16: 337–51.

American Psychiatric Association (1968) *Diagnostic and Statistical Manual of Mental Disorders*, Washington, DC: American Psychiatric Association.

Anderson, E. (1990) *Street Wise*, Chicago: University of Chicago Press.

Andry, R.G. (1957) 'Faulty Paternal and Maternal Child Relationships, Affection and Delinquency', *British Journal of Delinquency*, VIII: 34–48.

Arendt, H. (1964) *Eichmann in Jerusalem: A Report on the Banality of Evil*, New York: Viking Press.

Aubert, W. (1952) 'White Collar Crime and Social Structure', *American Journal of Sociology*, 58: 263–71.

Baldwin, J.D. (1990) 'The Role of Sensory Stimulation in Criminal Behaviour, with Special Attention to the Age Peak in Crime', in L. Ellis and H. Hoffman (eds) *Crime in Biological, Social, and Moral Contexts*, New York: Praeger.

Barlow, H. (1991) 'Review Essay of *A General Theory of Crime*', *Journal of Criminal Law and Criminology*, 1: 82–96.

Bandura, A. (1973) *Aggression: A Social Learning Analysis*, Englewood Cliffs: Prentice Hall.

Bandura, A. and Walters, R.H. (1959) *Adolescent Aggression*, New York: Ronald Press.

Baudrillard, J. (1988) *Selected Writings*, Stanford, CA: Stanford University Press.

Bauman, Z. (1989) *Modernity and the Holocaust*, Cambridge: Polity Press.

Bauman, Z. (1991) *Modernity and Ambivalence*, Cambridge: Polity Press.

Bauman, Z. (1993) *Postmodern Ethics*, Oxford: Blackwell.

Baumhart, R.C. (1961) 'How Ethical are Businessmen?', *Harvard Business Review*, 39: 156–76.

Beccaria, C. (1963, first English edition 1767) *On Crimes and Punishments*, translated by H. Paolucci, Indianapolis: Bobbs-Merrill Educational.

Beck. U. (1992) *Risk Society*, London: Sage.

Becker, G.S. (1968) 'Crime and Punishment: An Economic Approach', *Journal of Political Economy* 76(2): 169–217.

Becker, H. (1963) *Outsiders: Studies in the Sociology of Deviance*, New York: Free Press.

Becker, H. (1967) 'Whose Side Are We On?', *Social Problems* 14(3): 239–47.

Bedau, H. (1964) *The Death Penalty in America*, Garden City, NY: Anchor Books.

Beechey, V. (1977) 'Some Notes on Female Wage Labour in Capitalist Production', *Capital and Class* (Autumn): 45–66.

Bell, D. (1960) *The End of Ideology*, Glencoe, Illinois: Free Press.

Bell, D. (1973) *The Coming of Post-Industrial Society: A Venture in Social Forecasting*, London: Heinemann.

Bennett, T. (1986) 'Situational Crime Prevention from the Offender's Perspective', in K. Heal and G. Laycock (eds) *Situational Crime Prevention: From Theory into Practice*, London: HMSO.

Bentham, J. (1970) *An Introduction to the Principles of Morals and Legislation*, edited by J.H. Burns and H.L.A. Hart, London: Athlone Press.

Bertrand, M. (1967) 'The Myth of Sexual Equality Before the Law', in *Proceedings of the Fifth Research Conference on Delinquency and Criminality*, Montreal: Quebec Society of Criminology.

Beyleveld, D. (1978) *The Effectiveness of General Deterrents Against Crime: An Annotated Bibliography of Evaluative Research*, Cambridge: Cambridge Institute of Criminology.

Beyleveld, D. (1979) 'Deterrence Research as a Basis for Deterrence Policies', *Howard Journal*, 18: 135.

Blackburn, R. and Maybury, C. (1985) 'Identifying the Psychopath: The Relation of Cleckley's Criteria to the Interpersonal Domain', *Personality and Individual Differences* 6: 375–86.

Bonger, W. (1916) *Criminality and Economic Conditions*, reissued 1969, Bloomington: Indiana University Press.

Bottomley, A.K. and Coleman, C. (1981) *Understanding Crime Rates*, Farnborough: Gower.

Bowlby, J. (1952) *Maternal Care and Mental Health*, 2nd edn, Geneva: World Health Organisation.

Box, S. (1981) *Deviance, Reality and Society*, 2nd edn, London: Rinehart and Winston.

Box, S. (1983) *Crime, Power and Mystification*, London: Sage.

Box, S. (1987) *Recession, Crime and Punishment*, London: Macmillan.

Box, S. and Hale, C. (1983) 'Liberation and Female Criminality in England and Wales', *British Journal of Criminology*, 23(1).

Braithwaite, J. (1984) *Corporate Crime in the Pharmaceutical Industry*, London: Routledge.

Braithwaite, J. (1989) *Crime, Shame and Reintegration*, Cambridge: Cambridge University Press.

Brantingham, P.J. and Brantingham, P.L. (eds) (1981) *Environmental Criminology*, Beverley Hills: Sage.

Brantingham, P.J. and Brantingham, P.L. (1994) 'Burglar Mobility and Crime Prevention Planning', in R.V.G. Clarke and T. Hope (eds) *Coping with Burglary*, Boston: Kluwer-Nijhoff.

Brown, B. (1986) 'Women and Crime: The Dark Figures of Criminology', *Economy and Society*, 15(3): 355–402.

Brown, G.W. and Harris, T. (1978) *Social Origins of Depression*, London: Tavistock.

Brown, S. (1998) *Understanding Youth and Crime: Listening to Youth?* Buckingham: Open University Press.

Bruegel, I. (1978) 'Women as a Reserve Army of Labour: A Note on Recent British Experience', *Feminist Review*, 3: 12–23.

Burgess, E.W. (1928) 'The Growth of the City', in R. Park, E.W. Burgess and R.D. McKenzie, *The City*, Chicago: University of Chicago Press.

Burgess, R.L. and Akers, R.L. (1968) 'A Differential Association-Reinforcement Theory of Criminal Behaviour', *Social Problems* 14: 128–47.

Burke, R.D. and Sunley, R. (1996) *'Hanging Out' in the 1990s: Young People and the Postmodern Condition*, Occasional Paper 11, COP Series, Scarman Centre for the Study of Public Order, University of Leicester.

Burke, R.D. and Sunley R. (1998) 'Youth Subcultures in Contemporary Britain', in K. Hazelhurst and C. Hazlehurst (eds) *Gangs and Youth Subcultures: International Explorations*, New Jersey: Transaction Press.

Burt, C. (1945) *The Young Delinquent*, London: University of London Press.

Burton, R.V., Maccoby, E. and Allinsmith, W. (1961) 'Antecedents of Resistance to Temptation in Four-year-old Children', *Child Development* 32: 689.

Cain, M. (ed.) (1989) *Growing Up Good*, London: Sage.

Cain, M. (1990) 'Towards Transgression: New Directions in Feminist Criminology', *International Journal of the Sociology of the Law*, 18(1): 1–18.

Campbell, A. (1981) *Girl Delinquents*, Oxford: Basil Blackwell.

Campbell, B. (1993) *Goliath: Britain's Dangerous Places*. London: Methuen.

Carlen, P. (1983) *Women's Imprisonment*, London: Routledge & Kegan Paul.

Carlen, P. (1988) *Women, Crime and Poverty*, Buckingham: Open University Press.

Carlen, P. (1992) 'Criminal Women and Criminal Justice: The Limits to and Potential of Feminist and Left Realist Perspectives', in R. Matthews and J. Young (eds), *Issues in Realist Criminology*, London: Sage.

Carson, W.G. (1980) 'White-collar Crime and the Institutionalisation of Ambiguity: The Case of the Early Factory Acts', in G. Geis and E. Stotland (eds) *White Collar Crime: Theory and Research*, Beverley Hills, Sage.

Chambliss, W.J. (1964) 'A Sociological Analysis of the Law of Vagrancy', *Social Problems*, 12: 67–70.

Chambliss, W.J. (1969) *Crime and the Legal Process*, New York: McGraw-Hill.

Chambliss, W.J. (1975) 'Toward a Political Economy of Crime', *Theory and Society*, 2: 152–3.

Chambliss, W.J. and Seidman, R.T. (1971) *Law, Order, and Power*, Reading, MA: Addison-Wesley.

Chilton, R.J. and Markle, G.E. (1972) 'Family Disruption, Delinquent Conduct, and the Effect of Subclassification', *American Sociological Review*, 37: 93–108.

Christiansen, K.O. (1968) 'Threshold of Tolerance in Various Population Groups Illustrated by Results from the Danish Criminologic Twin Study', in A.V.S. de Reuck and R. Porter (eds) *The Mentally Abnormal Offender*, Boston: Little, Brown.

Christiansen, K.O. (1974) 'Seriousness of Criminality and Concordance Among Danish Twins', in R. Hood (ed.) *Crime, Criminology and Public Policy*, New York: Free Press.

Christie, N. (1993) *Crime Control as Industry: Towards Gulags, Western Style?* London: Routledge.

Ciba Foundation Symposium (1996) *Genetics of Criminal and Antisocial Behaviour*, Chichester: Wiley.

Cicourel, A. (1968) *The Social Organisation of Juvenile Justice*, New York: Wiley.

Clapham, B. (1989) 'A Case of Hypoglycaemia', *The Criminologist*, 13: 2–15.

Clarke, R.V.G. (1980) ' "Situational" Crime Prevention: Theory and Practice', *British Journal of Criminology*, 20: 132–45.

Clarke, R.V.G. (1987) 'Rational Choice Theory and Prison Psychology', in B.J. McGurk and R.E. McGurk (eds) *Applying Psychology to Imprisonment: Theory and Practice*, London: HMSO.

Clarke, R.V.G. and Mayhew, P. (eds) (1980) *Designing Out Crime*, London: HMSO.

Cleckley, H. (1964 and 1976) *The Mask of Sanity*, St Louis, MO: C.V. Mosby.

Clinard, M.B. (1952) *The Black Market: A Study of White Collar Crime*, New York: Holt, Rinehart and Winston.

Clinard, M.B. and Yeager P.C. (1980) *Corporate Crime*, New York: Free Press.

Cloninger, C.R. and Gottesman, I.I. (1987) 'Genetic and Environmental Factors in Antisocial Behaviour Disorders', in S.A. Mednick, T.E. Moffit and S. Stack, *The Causes of Crime: New Biological Approaches*, Cambridge: Cambridge University Press.

Cloward, R.A. and Ohlin, L.E. (1960) *Delinquency and Opportunity: A Theory of Delinquent Gangs*, New York: Free Press.

Cohen, A.K. (1955) *Delinquent Boys: The Culture of the Gang*, New York: Free Press.

Cohen, L.E. and Felson, M. (1979) 'Social Inequality and Predatory Criminal Victimization: An Exposition and Test of a Formal Theory', *American Sociological Review,* 44: 588–608.

Cohen, L.E., Kluegel, J. and Land, K. (1981) 'Social Inequality and Predatory Criminal Victimisation: An Exposition and Test of a Formal Theory', *American Sociological Review* 46: 505–24.

Cohen, S. (1973) *Folk Devils and Moral Panics: The Creation of the Mods and Rockers*, London: Paladin.

Cohen, S. (1980, new edition) *Folk Devils and Moral Panics*, Oxford: Martin Robertson.

Cohen, S. (1985) *Visions of Social Control*, Cambridge: Polity Press.

Collins, J.J. (1988) 'Alcohol and Interpersonal Violence: Less than Meets the Eye', in A. Weiner and M.E. Wolfgang (eds) *Pathways to Criminal Violence*, Newbury Park, CA: Sage.

Comte, A. (1976) *The Foundations of Sociology* (readings edited and with an introduction by K. Thompson), London: Nelson.

Conklin, J.E. (1977) *Illegal But Not Criminal*, New Jersey: Spectrum.

Connell, R.W. (1987) *Gender and Power*, Cambridge: Polity.

Connell, R.W. (1995) *Masculinities*, Cambridge: Polity.

Cornish, D.B. and Clarke, R.V.G. (1986) *The Reasoning Criminal*, New York: Springer-Verlag.

Cortes, J.B. and Gatti, F.M. (1972) *Delinquency and Crime: A Biopsychological Approach*, New York: Seminar Press.

Croall, H. (1992) *White-collar Crime*, Buckingham: Open University Press.

Croall, H. (1998) *Crime and Society in Britain*, Harlow: Longman.

Cromwell, P.F., Durham, R., Akers, R.L., and Lanza-Kaduce, L. (1995) 'Routine Activities and Social Control in the Aftermath of a Natural Catastrophe', *European Journal on Criminal Policy and Research*, 3: 56–69.

Crowe, R.R. (1972) 'The Adopted Offspring of Women Criminal Offenders', *Archives of General Psychiatry* 27(5): 600–3.

Crowther, C. (1998) 'Policing the Excluded Society', in R.D. Hopkins Burke *Zero Tolerance Policing*, Leicester: Perpetuity Press.

Curtis, L.A. (1975) *Violence, Race and Culture*, Lexington, MA: Heath.

Dahrendorf, R. (1958) 'Out of Utopia: Toward a Reconstruction of Sociological Analysis', *American Journal of Sociology*, 67 (September): 115–27.

Dahrendorf, R. (1959) *Class and Class Conflict in an Industrial Society*, London: Routledge & Kegan Paul.

Dahrendorf, R. (1985) *Law and Order*, London: Stevens.

Dale, D. (1984) 'The Politics of Crime', *Salisbury Review*, October.

Dalgard, S.O. and Kringlen, E. (1976) 'Norwegian Twin Study of Criminality', *British Journal of Criminology*, 16: 213–32.

Dalton, K. (1961) 'Menstruation and Crime', *British Medical Journal*, 2: 1752–3.

Dalton, K. (1964) *The Pre-menstrual Syndrome and Progesterone Therapy*, London: Heinemann Medical.

Daly, K. and Chesney-Lind, M. (1988) 'Feminism and Criminology', *Justice Quarterly*, 5(4): 487–535.

Damer, S. (1974) 'Wine Alley: The Sociology of a Dreadful Enclosure', *Sociological Review*, 22: 221–48.

Darwin, C. (1968) *On the Origin of the Species*, New York: Penguin.

Darwin, C. (1871) *The Descent of Man*, London: John Murray.

Darwin, C. (1872) *The Expression of Emotions in Man and Animals*, Philosophical Library.

Davis, M. (1990) *The City of Quartz: Evacuating the Future in Los Angeles*. London: Verso.

DeLuca, J.R. (ed) (1981) *Fourth Special Report to the US Congress on Alcohol and Health*, Rockville, Maryland: National Institute on Alcohol Abuse and Alcoholism.

Dobash, R.E. and Dobash, R.P. (1980) *Violence against Wives*, London: Open Books.

Dobash, R.E. and Dobash, R.P. (1992) *Women, Violence and Social Change*, London: Routledge & Kegan Paul.

Downes, D. (1966) *The Delinquent Solution*, London: Routledge & Kegan Paul.

Downes, D. and Rock, P. (1998) *Understanding Deviance*, 3rd edn, Oxford: Oxford University Press.

Dugdale, R.L. (1877) *The Jukes*, New York: Putnam.

Durkheim, E. (1933 originally published in 1893) *The Division of Labour in Society*, Glencoe, IL: Free Press.

Durkheim, E. (1951, originally published in 1897) *Suicide*, New York: Free Press.

Durkheim, E. (1964 originally published 1915) *The Elementary Forms of Religious Life*, Glencoe, IL: Free Press.

Ehrenkranz, J. Bliss, E. and Sheard, M.H. (1974) 'Plasma Testosterone: Correlation with Aggressive Behaviour and Social Dominance in Man', *Psychosomatic Medicine*, 36: 469–83.

Ehrlich, I. (1975) 'The Deterrent Effect of Capital Punishment: A Question of Life or Death', *American Economic Review*, 65: 397.

Einstadter, W. and Henry, S. (1995) *Criminological Theory*, Fort Worth, TX: Harcourt Brace.

Elliot, D., Ageton, S. and Canter, J. (1979) 'An Integrated Theoretical Perspective on Delinquent Behaviour', *Journal of Research in Crime and Delinquency*, 16: 126–49.

Ellis, L. (1990) 'The Evolution of Violent Criminal Behaviour and its Non-Legal Equivalent', in L. Ellis and H. Hoffman (eds) *Crime in Biological, Social and Moral Contexts*, New York: Praeger.

Ellis, L. and Cronz, P.D. (1990) 'Androgens, Brain Functioning, and Criminality: The Neurohormonal Foundations of Antisociality', in L. Ellis and H. Hoffman (eds) *Crime in Biological, Social, and Moral Contexts*, New York: Praeger.

Erikson, K. (1962) 'Notes on the Sociology of Deviance', *Social Problems*, 9: 309–14.

Erikson, K. (1966) *Wayward Puritans: A Study in the Sociology of Deviance*, New York: Wiley.

Etzioni, A. (1961) *A Comparative Analysis of Complex Organisations*, Glencoe: Free Press.

Evans, D.J., Fyfe, N.R. and Herbert, D.T. (eds) (1992) *Crime, Policing and Place: Essays in Environmental Criminology*, London: Routledge.

Eysenck, H.J. (1959) *Manual of the Maudsley Personality Inventory*, London: University of London Press.

Eysenck, H.J. (1963) 'On the Dual Nature of Extroversion', *British Journal of Social Clinical Psychology*, 2: 46.

Eysenck, H.J. (1970) *Crime and Personality*, London: Granada.

Eysenck, H.J. (1977) *Crime and Personality*, 3rd edn, London: Routledge & Kegan Paul.

Eysenck, H.J. and Eysenck, S.B.J. (1970) 'Crime and Personality: An Empirical Study of the Three-factor Theory', *British Journal of Criminology* 10: 225.

Eysenck, S.B.J., Rust, J. and Eysenck, H.J. (1977) 'Personality and the Classification of Adult Offenders', *British Journal of Criminology*, 17: 169–70.

Faberman, H.A. (1975) 'A Criminogenic Market Structure: The Automobile Industry', *Sociological Quarterly*, 16: 438–57.

Fagan, J. (1990) 'Intoxication and Aggression', in M. Tonry and J.Q. Wilson (eds) *Crime and Justice: A Review of Research*, 13, Chicago: University of Chicago Press.

Farrington, D.P. (1992) 'Juvenile Delinquency', in J.C. Coleman (ed.) *The School Years*, 2nd edn, London: Routledge.

Farrington, D.P. (1994) 'Introduction', in D.P. Farrington (ed.), *Psychological Explanations of Crime*, Aldershot: Dartmouth.

Farrington, D.P. and Morris, A.M. (1983) 'Sex, Sentencing and Reconviction', *British Journal of Criminology*, 23(3).

Farnsworth, M. (1989) 'Theory Integration versus Model Building', in S.F. Messner, M.D. Krohn and A.E. Liska (eds) *Theoretical Integration in the Study of Deviance and Crime*, Albany, New York: State University of New York Press.

Feldman, M.P. (1977) *Criminal Behaviour: A Psychological Analysis*, Bath: Pitman Press.

Felson, M. (1994) *Crime and Everyday Life*, Thousand Oaks, CA: Pine Forge.

Ferri, E. (1895) *Criminal Sociology*, London: Unwin.

Ferri, E. (1968, originally 1901) *Three Lectures by Enrico Ferri*, Pittsburgh, PA: University of Pittsburgh Press.

Feyerabend, P. (1975) *Against Method: Outline of an Anarchistic Theory of Knowledge*, London: New Left Books.

Field, F. (1989) *Losing Out: The Emergence of Britain's Underclass*, Oxford: Blackwell.

Fishbein, D.H. and Pease, S.E. (1990) 'Neurological Links between Substance Abuse and Crime', in L. Ellis and H. Hoffman (eds) *Crime in Biological, Social, and Moral Contexts*, New York: Praeger.

Fishbein, D.H. and Pease, S.E. (1996) *The Dynamic of Drug Abuse*, Boston: Allyn Bacon.

Flanzer, J. (1981) 'The Vicious Circle of Alcoholism and Family Violence', *Alcoholism*, 1(3): 30–45.

Foucault, M. (1971) *Madness and Civilisation: A History of Insanity in the Age of Reason,* London: Tavistock.

Foucault, M. (1976) *The History of Sexuality*, London: Allen Lane.

Foucault, M. (1977) *Discipline and Punish – the Birth of the Prison*, London: Allen Lane.

Foucault, M. (1980) *Power/Knowledge: Selected Interviews and Other Writings 1972–77,* (ed.) C. Gordon, Brighton: Harvester Press.

Fowler, F.J., McCall, M.E. and Mangione, T.W. (1979) *Reducing Residential Crime and Fear: The Hartford Neighborhood Crime Prevention Program*, Washington, DC: US Government Printing Office.

Fowler, F.J. and Mangione, T.W. (1982) *Neighborhood Crime, Fear and Social Control: A Second Look at the Hartford Program*, Washington, DC: US Government Printing Office

Freud, S. (1920) *A General Introduction to Psychoanalysis*, New York: Boni and Liveright.

Freud, S. (1927) *The Ego and the Id*, London: Hogarth.

Friedlander, K. (1949) 'Latent Delinquency and Ego Development', in K.R. Eissler (ed.) *Searchlights on Delinquency*, New York: International University Press, 205–15.

Garfinkel, H. (1984) *Studies in Ethnomethodology*, Oxford: Basil Blackwell.

Garland, D. (1996) 'The Limits of the Sovereign State: Strategies of Crime Control in Contemporary Society', *British Journal of Criminology*, 34(4): 445–71.

Garland, D. (1997) 'The Development of British Criminology', in M. Maguire, R. Morgan and R. Reiner (eds) *The Oxford Handbook of Criminology*, Oxford: Clarendon Press.

Garofalo, R. (1914) *Criminology*, Boston: Little, Brown.

Geis, G. (1967), 'The Heavy Electrical Equipment Anti-trust Cases of 1961', in M.B. Clinard and R. Quinney (eds) *Criminal Behaviour Systems*, New York: Holt, Rinehart & Winston.

Geis, G. (1968) *White-collar Crime: The Offender in Business and the Professions*, New York: Atherton.

Geis, G. and Goff, C. (1983) 'Introduction' in E. Sutherland, *White-Collar Crime: The Uncut Version*, New Haven: Yale University Press.

Geis, G. and Maier, R.F. (eds) (1977) *White-collar Crime: Offences in Business, Politics and the Professions – Classic and Contemporary Views*, New York: Free Press.

Gelsthorpe, L. and Morris, A. (1980) *Feminist Perspectives in Criminology*, Buckingham: Open University Press.

Gelsthorpe, L. and Morris, A. (1988) 'Feminism and Criminology in Britain', *British Journal of Criminology*, 28: 83–110.

Gibbens, T.C.N. (1963) *Psychiatric Studies of Borstal Lads*, Oxford: Oxford University Press.

Gibbons, D.C. (1970) *Delinquent Behaviour*, Englewood Cliffs, NJ: Prentice-Hall.

Gibbs, J. (1966) 'Conceptions of Deviant Behaviour', *Pacific Sociological Review*, (Spring) 9: 9–14.

Gibbs, J. (1975) *Crime, Punishment, and Deterrence*, New York: Elsevier.

Giddens, A. (1994) *Beyond Left and Right: The Future of Radical Politics*, Cambridge: Polity Press.

Giddens, A. (1998) *The Third Way: The Renewal of Social Democracy*, Cambridge: Polity Press.

Gill, O. (1977) *Luke Street: Housing Policy, Conflict and the Creation of the Delinquency Area*, London: Macmillan.

Glueck, S. and Glueck, E. (1950) *Unravelling Juvenile Delinquency*, Oxford: Oxford University Press.

Goddard, H.H. (1914) *Feeblemindedness: Its Causes and Consequences*, New York: Macmillan.

Gordon, R.A (1986) 'Scientific Justification and the Race–IQ–Delinquency Model', in T. Hartnagel and R. Silverman (eds) *Critique and Explanation: Essays in Honor of Gwynne Nettler*, New Brunswick, NJ: Transaction.

Goring, C. (1913) *The English Convict: A Statistical Study*, London: HMSO.

Gottfredson, M.R. and Hirschi, T. (1990) *A General Theory of Crime*, Stanford, CA: Stanford University Press.

Gouldner, A. (1968) 'The Sociologist as Partisan: Sociology and the Welfare State', *The American Sociologist*, May: 103–16.

Graham, J. and Bowling, B. (1995) *Young People and Crime*, Home Office Research Study No. 145, London: HMSO.

Gramsci, A. (1977, 1978) *Selections from the Political Writings*, London: Lawrence & Wiseheart.

Gregory, J. (1986) 'Sex, Class and Crime: Towards a Non-Sexist Criminology', in R. Matthews and J. Young (eds) *Confronting Crime*, London: Sage.

Gross, E. (1978) 'Organisations as Criminal Actors', in J. Braithwaite and P. Wilson (eds) *Two Faces of Deviance: Crimes of the Powerless and the Powerful*, Brisbane: University of Queensland Press.

Guerry, A.M. (1833) *Essai sur la Statisque Morale de la France*, Paris: Crochard.

Hagan, J. (1994) *Crime and Disrepute,* California: Pine Forge Press.

Hagedorn, J. (1992) 'Gangs, Neighbourhoods, and Public Policy', *Social Problems,* 38 (4): 529–42.

Hall, S. and Jefferson, T. (eds) (1976) *Resistance Through Rituals,* London: Hutchinson.

Hall, S., Critcher, C., Jefferson, T., Clarke, J. and Roberts, B. (1978) *Policing the Crisis,* London: Macmillan.

Hall, S., and Scraton, P. (1981) 'Law, Class and Control', in M. Fitzgerald, G. McLennan and J. Pawson (eds) *Crime and Society: Readings in History and Theory,* London: Routledge and Kegan Paul & The Open University Press.

Hanmer, J. and Saunders, S. (1984) *Well-Founded Fear,* London: Hutchinson.

Hare, D.R. (1970) *Psychopathy: Theory and Research,* New York: Wiley.

Hare, D.R. (1980) 'A Research Scale for the Assessment of Psychopathy in Criminal Populations', *Personality and Individual Differences,* 1: 111–19.

Hare, D.R. (1982) 'Psychopathy and Physiological Activity During Anticipation of An Aversive Stimulus in a Distraction Paradigm', *Psychophysiology,* 19: 266–80.

Hare, D.R. and Jutari, J.W. (1986) 'Twenty Years of Experience with the Cleckley Psychopath', in W.H. Reid, D. Dorr, J.I. Walker and J.W. Bonner (eds) *Unmasking the Psychopath: Antisocial Personality and Related Syndromes,* New York: Norton.

Hartmann, H. (1981) 'The Family as a Locus of Class, Gender and Political Struggle: The Example of Housework', *Signs,* 6.

Harvey, D. (1989) *The Condition of Postmodernity: An Enquiry into the Origins of Cultural Change,* Oxford: Blackwell.

Hay, D. (1981) 'Property, Authority and the Criminal Law', in M. Fitzgerald, G. McLennan and J. Pawson (eds), *Crime and Society: Readings in History and Theory,* London: Open University Press/Routledge.

Heal, K. and Laycock, G. (eds) (1986) *Situational Crime Prevention – From Theory into Practice,* London: HMSO.

Healy, W. and Bronner, A.F. (1936) *New Light on Delinquency and its Treatment,* New Haven: Yale University Press.

Heidensohn, F. (1968) 'The Deviance of Women: A Critique and an Enquiry', *British Journal of Criminology,* 19(2): 160–76.

Heidensohn, F.M. (1985) *Women and Crime,* London: Macmillan.

Heidensohn, F. (1987) 'Women and Crime: Questions for Criminology', in P. Carlen and A. Worrall (eds) *Gender, Crime and Justice,* Buckingham: Open University Press.

Heidensohn, F. (1994) 'Gender and Crime', in M. Maguire, R. Morgan and R. Reiner (eds) *The Oxford Handbook of Criminology,* Oxford: Oxford University Press.

Henle, M. (1985) 'Rediscovering Gestalt Psychology', in S. Koch and D.E. Leary (eds), *A Century of Psychology as a Science,* New York: McGraw-Hill.

Herrnstein, R.J. and Murray, C. (1994) *The Bell Curve,* New York: Basic Books.

Hillyard, P. (1987) 'The Normalisation of Special Powers: From Northern Ireland to Britain', in P. Scraton (ed.) *Law, Order and the Authoritarian State*, Buckingham: Open University Press.

Hindelang, M.J. and Weis, J.G. (1972) 'Personality and Self-reported Delinquency: An Application of Cluster Analysis', *Criminology* 10: 268–94.

Hindelang, M. (1979) 'Sex Differences in Criminal Activity', *Social Problems*, 27: 15–36.

Hirschi, T. (1969) *Causes of Delinquency*, Berkeley, CA: University of California Press.

Hirschi, T. and Hindelang, M.J. (1977) 'Intelligence and Delinquency: A Revisionist Review', *American Sociological Review* 42: 572–87.

Hirst, P.Q. (1980) 'Law, Socialism and Rights', in P. Carlen and M. Collinson (eds) *Radical Issues in Criminology*, Oxford: Martin Robertson.

Hobbes, T. (1968 originally 1651) *Leviathan*, edited by C.B. Macpherson, Harmondsworth: Penguin.

Hoffman, M.L. and Saltzstein, H.D. (1967) 'Parent Discipline and the Child's Moral Development', *Journal of Personality and Social Psychology*, 5: 45.

Hoghughi, M.S. and Forrest, A.R. (1970) 'Eysenck's Theory of Criminality: An Examination with Approved School Boys', *British Journal of Criminology* 10: 240.

Hooks, b. (1988) *Talking Back, Thinking Feminist, Thinking Black*, Boston: South End Press.

Hollin, C.R. (1989) *Psychology and Crime: An Introduction to Criminological Psychology*, London: Routledge.

Holmes, R.M. and De Burger, J. (1989) *Serial Murder*, Newbury Park, CA: Sage.

Home Office (1997) *Aspects of Crime: Young Offenders*, London: Home Office.

Hooton, E.A. (1939) *The American Criminal: An Anthropological Study*, Cambridge, MA: Harvard University Press.

Hopkins Burke, R. (1998a) 'Begging, Vagrancy and Disorder', in R. Hopkins Burke (ed.) *Zero Tolerance Policing*, Leicester: Perpetuity Press.

Hopkins Burke, R. (1998b) 'The Contextualisation of Zero Tolerance Policing Strategies', in R. Hopkins Burke (ed.) *Zero Tolerance Policing*, Leicester: Perpetuity Press.

Hopkins Burke, R. (1999a) *Youth Justice and the Fragmentation of Modernity*, Scarman Centre for the Study of Public Order Occasional Paper Series, The University of Leicester.

Hopkins Burke, R. (1999b) 'The Socio-Political Context of Zero Tolerance Policing Strategies', *Policing: An International Journal of Police Strategies and Management*, 21(4): 666–82.

Hopkins Burke, R. (2000) 'The Regulation of Begging and Vagrancy: A Critical Discussion', *Crime Prevention and Community Safety: An International Journal* 2(2): 43–52.

Hough, M., Clarke, R.V.G. and Mayhew, P. (1980) 'Introduction', in R.V.G. Clarke and P. Mayhew (eds), *Designing Out Crime*, London: HMSO.

Hughes, G. (1998) *Understanding Crime Prevention: Social Control, Risk and Late Modernity*, Buckingham: Open University Press.

Hutchings, B. and Mednick, S.A. (1977) 'Criminality in Adoptees and their Adoptive and Biological Parents: A Pilot Study', in S.A. Mednick and K.O. Christiansen (eds) *Biosocial Bases of Criminal Behaviour*, New York: Gardner.

Ignatieff, M. (1978) *A Just Measure of Pain: The Penitentiary and the Industrial Revolution*, London: Macmillan.
Institute of Race Relations (1987) *Policing Against Black People*, London: Institute of Race Relations.

Jacobs, J. (1965) *The Death and Life of Great American Cities*, Harmondsworth: Penguin.
Jaggar, A. (1983) *Feminist Politics and Human Nature*, New Jersey: Rowman and Littlefield.
Jefferson, T. (1997) 'Masculinities and Crime', in M. Maguire, R. Morgan and R. Reiner (eds) *The Oxford Handbook of Criminology* Second Edition, Oxford: Oxford University Press.
Jeffery, C.R. (1977) *Crime Prevention Through Environmental Design*, Beverly Hills: Sage.
Jeffery, C.R. (ed.) (1979) *Biology and Crime*, Beverly Hills: Sage.
Jensen, A.R. (1969) 'How Much can we Boost IQ and Scholastic Achievement?', *Harvard Educational Review* 39: 1–23.
Jones, G. (1980) *Social Darwinism and English Thought – The Interaction between Biological and Social Theory*, Brighton: Harvester Press.
Jones, S. (1993) *The Language of the Genes*, London: Harper Collins.
Jones, T., Newburn, T. and Smith, D. (1994) *Democracy and Policing*, London: Policy Studies Institute.
Jordan, B. (1996) *A Theory of Social Exclusion and Poverty*, Cambridge: Polity.

Katz, J. (1988) *Seductions of Crime: Moral and Sensual Attractions in Doing Evil*, New York: Basic Books.
Keverne, E.B., Meller, R.E. and Eberhart, J.A. (1982) 'Social Influences on Behaviour and Neuroendocrine Responsiveness in Talapoin Monkeys', in *Scandinavian Journal of Psychology*, 1: 37–54.
Kendler, H.H. (1985) 'Behaviourism and Psychology: An Uneasy Alliance', in S. Koch and D.E. Leary (eds) *A Century of Psychology as Science*, New York: McGraw-Hill.
King, M. (1981) *The Framework of Criminal Justice*, London: Croom Helm.
Kitsuse, J.I. (1962) 'Societal Reaction to Deviant Behaviour: Problems of Theory and Method', *Social Problems*, 9: 247–56.
Kitsuse, J.I. and Dietrick, D.C. (1959) 'Delinquent Boys: A Critique', *American Sociological Review*, 24: 208–15.
Klein, D. (1973, 1976) 'The Aetiology of Female Crime: A Review of the Literature', in L. Crites (eds) *The Female Offender*, Massachusetts: Lexington.
Klinefelter, H.F., Reifenstein, E.C., Albright, F. (1942) 'Syndrome Characterized by Gynecomastia, Aspermatogenesis without Aleydigism and Increased

Excretion of Follicle-Stimulating Hormone' *Journal of Clinical Endocrinology* 2: 615–27.

Knights, B. (1998) "'The Slide to Ashes': An Antidote to Zero Tolerance' in R. Hopkins Burke (ed.) *Zero Tolerance Policing*. Leicester: Perpetuity Press.

Kolvin, I., Miller, F.J.W., Scott, D.M., Gatzanis, S.R.M. and Fleeting, M. (1990) *Continuities of Deprivation?* Aldershot: Avebury.

Koestler, A. and Rolph, C.H. (1961) *Hanged by the Neck*, Harmondsworth: Penguin.

Kozol, H.L., Boucher, R.J. and Garofalo, R.F. (1972) 'The Diagnosis and Treatment of Dangerousness', *Crime and Delinquency* 18: 371–92.

Kramer, R.C. (1984) 'Corporate Criminality: The Development of An Idea', in E. Hochstedler.

Kretschmer, E. (1964) *Physique and Character*, Translation by W.J.H. Sprott, New York: Cooper Square.

Kreuz, L.E. and Rose, R.M. (1972) 'Assessment of Aggressive Behaviour and Plasma Testosterone in a Young Criminal Population', *Psychosomatic Medicine*, 34: 321–33.

Krisberg, B. (1974) 'Gang Youth and Hustling: The Psychology of Survival', *Issues in Criminology* 9 (Spring 1): 115–131.

Lacey, N., Wells, C. and Meure, D. (1990) *Reconstructing Criminal Law: Critical Social Perspectives on Crime and the Criminal Process*. London: Weidenfeld and Nicolson.

Laing, R.D. (1960) *The Divided Self*, Harmondsworth: Penguin.

Lambert, J.R. (1970) *Crime, Police and Race Relations*, London: Institute of Race Relations/Oxford University Press.

Lange, J. (1930) *Crime as Destiny*, London: Allen and Unwin.

Lea, J. and Young, J. (1984) *What is to be Done about Law and Order?* Harmondsworth: Penguin.

Lemert, E. (1951) *Social Pathology: A Systematic Approach to the Theory of Sociopathic Behavior*, New York: McGraw-Hill.

Lemert, E. (1972) *Human Deviance, Social Problems and Social Control*, 2nd edn, Englewood Cliffs, NJ: Prentice-Hall.

Leonard, E. (1983) *Women, Crime and Society*, London: Longmans.

Lesser, M. (1980) *Nutrition and Vitamin Therapy*, New York: Bantam.

Levitas, R. (1996) 'The Concept of Social Exclusion and the New Durkheimian Hegemony', *Critical Social Policy*. 16 (1): 5–20.

Liazos, A. (1972) 'The Poverty of the Sociology of Deviance: "Nuts, Sluts and Perverts" ', *Social Problems* 20: 103–20.

Lilly, J.R., Cullen, F.T. and Ball, R.A. (1986) *Criminological Theory: Context and Consequences*, London: Sage.

Liska, A.E. (1987) *Perspectives on Deviance*, Englewood Cliffs, NJ: Prentice-Hall.

Liska, A.E.; Krohn, M.D. and Messner, S.F. (1989) 'Strategies and Requisites for Theoretical Intervention in the Study of Crime and Deviance', in S.F. Messner, M.D. Krohn and A.E. Liska (eds) *Theoretical Integration in the Study of Deviance and Crime*, Albany, NY: State University of New York Press.

Little, A. (1963) 'Professor Eysenck's Theory of Crime: An Empirical Test on Adolescent Offenders', *British Journal of Criminology* 4: 152.

Locke, J. (1970) *Two Treatises of Government*, edited by P. Laslett, Cambridge: Cambridge University Press.

Locke, J. (1975) *An Essay Concerning Human Understanding*, edited by P.M. Nidditch, Oxford: Clarendon Press.

Loeber, R. and Dishion, T. (1983) 'Early Predictors of Male Delinquency: A Review', *Psychological Bulletin* 94(1): 68–91.

Lofland, L.H. (1973) *A World of Strangers: Order and Action in Urban Public Space*, New York: Basic Books.

Lombroso, C. (1876) *L'uomo delinquente* (*The Criminal Man*), Milan: Hoepli.

Lombroso, C. and Ferrero, W. (1885) *The Female Offender*, London: Unwin.

Lyotard, J.-F. (1984) *The Post-Modern Condition: A Report on Knowledge*, Manchester: Manchester University Press.

McCord, W. and McCord, J. (1964) *The Psychopath: An Essay on the Criminal Mind*, New York: Van Nostrand Reinhold.

McCord, W., McCord, J. and Zola, I.K. (1959) *Origins of Crime: A New Evaluation of the Cambridge-Somerville Youth Study*, New York: Columbia University Press.

McEwan, A.W. (1983) 'Eysenck's Theory of Criminality and the Personality Types and Offences of Young Delinquents', *Personality and Individual Differences*, 4: 201–4.

McEwan, A.W. and Knowles, C. (1984) 'Delinquent Personality Types and the Situational Contexts of their Crimes', *Personality and Individual Differences* 5: 339–44.

McGurk, B.J. and McDougall, C. (1981) 'A New Approach to Eysenck's Theory of Criminality', *Personality and Individual Differences*, 13: 338–40.

Mannheim, H. (1948) *Juvenile Delinquency in an English Middletown*, London: Kegan Paul, Turner, Trubner and Co. Ltd.

Mannheim, H. (1955) *Group Problems in Crime and Punishment*, London: Routledge & Kegan Paul.

Marcuse, H. (1964) *One Dimensional Man*. Boston: Beacon.

Mark, V.H. and Ervin, F.R. (1970) *Violence and the Brain*, New York: Harper Row.

Mars, G. (1982) *Cheats at Work: An Anthology of Workplace Crime*, London: George Allen and Unwin.

Marshall, G., Roberts, S. and Burgoyne, C. (1996) 'Social Class and the Underclass in Britain and the USA', *British Journal of Sociology*, 47 (10): 22–44.

Martin, J.P. and Webster, D. (1971) *The Social Consequences of Conviction*, London: Heinemann.

Martinson, R. (1974) 'What Works? – Questions and Answers About Prison Reform', *The Public Interest*, 35: 22–54.

Matza, D.M. (1964) *Delinquency and Drift*, New York: Wiley.

Matthews, R. (1992) 'Replacing "Broken Windows": Crime, Incivilities and Urban Change', in R. Matthews and J. Young (eds) *Issues in Realist Criminology*, London: Sage.

Matthews, R. and Young, J. (eds) (1986) *Confronting Crime*, London: Sage.

Matthews, R. and Young, J. (eds) (1992) *Issues in Realist Criminology*, London: Sage.

Maxson, C.L. and Klein, M.W. (1990) 'Street Gang Violence: Twice as Great or Half as Great?' in C.R. Huff (ed.) *Gangs in America*, Newbury Park, CA: Sage, pp. 71–102.

Mayhew, H. (1968) *London Labour and the London Poor, Vol. IV: Those That Will Not Work, Comprising Prostitutes, Thieves, Swindlers and Beggars*, New York: Dover Publications.

Mayhew, P., Clarke, R.V.G., Sturman, A. and Hough, J.M. (1976) *Crime as Opportunity*, London: HMSO.

Mayhew, P. (1984) 'Target-Hardening: How Much of an Answer?' in R.V.G. Clarke and T. Hope (eds) *Coping with Burglary*, Boston: Kluwer-Nighoff.

Mays, J.B. (1954) *Growing Up in the City: A Study of Juvenile Delinquency in an Urban Neighbourhood*, Liverpool: Liverpool University Press.

Mead, G. (1934) *Mind, Self and Society*, Chicago: University of Chicago Press.

Mednick, S.A. (1977) 'A Biosocial Theory of the Learning of Law-Abiding Behavior', in S.A. Mednick and K.O Christiansen (eds) *Biosocial Bases of Criminal Behavior*, New York: Gardner.

Mednick, S.A. and Christiansen, K.O. (eds) (1977) *Biosocial Bases of Criminal Behavior*, New York: Gardner.

Mednick, S.A., Pollock, V. Volavka, J. and Gabrielli, W.F. (1982) 'Biology and Violence', in M.E. Wolfgang and N.A. Weiner (eds) *Criminal Violence*, Beverly Hills, CA: Sage.

Mednick, S.A., Gabrielli, T., William, F. and Hutchings, B. (1984), 'Genetic Influences on Criminal Convictions: Evidence from an Adoption Cohort', *Science*, 224.

Mednick, S.A., Moffit, T.E. and Stack, S. (eds) (1987) *The Causes of Crime: New Biological Approaches*, Cambridge: Cambridge University Press.

Mednick, S.A. and Volavka, J. (1980) 'Biology and Crime', in N. Morris and M. Tonry (eds) *Crime and Justice: An Annual Review of Research*, Vol. 2, Chicago: University of Chicago Press.

Menard, S. and Morse, B. (1984) 'A Structuralist Critique of the IQ-Delinquency Hypothesis: Theory and Evidence', *American Journal of Sociology* 89: 1347–78.

Merry, S.E. (1981) 'Defensible Space Undefended', *Urban Affairs Quarterly*, 16: 397–422.

Merton, R.K. (1938) 'Social Structure and Anomie', *American Sociological Review*, 3 (October): 672–82.

Messerschmidt, J.W. (1993) *Masculinities and Crime*, Lanham, MD: Rowman and Littlefield.

Mill, J.S. (1963–84) *The Collected Works of John Stuart Mill*, edited by F.E.L. Priestly, Toronto: University of Toronto Press.

Miller, W.B. (1958) 'Lower Class Culture as a Generalising Milieu of Gang Delinquency' *Journal of Social Issues,* 14: 5–19.

Monahan, T.P. (1957) 'Family Status and the Delinquent Child: A Reappraisal and Some New Findings', *New Forces,* 35: 250–66.

Monahan, J. (1981) *Predicting Violent Behaviour,* Beverly Hills, CA: Sage.

Moore, J.W. (1991) *Going Down to the Barrio,* Philadelphia: Temple University Press.

Morash, M. and Rucker, L. (1989) 'An Exploratory Study of the Connection of Mother's Age at Childbearing to her Children's Delinquency in Four Data Sets', *Crime and Delinquency,* 35: 45–58.

Morgan, P. (1975) *Child Care: Sense and Fable,* London: Temple Smith.

Morgan, P. (1978) *Delinquent Fantasies,* London: Temple Smith.

Morris, A. (1987) *Women, Crime and Criminal Justice,* Oxford: Blackwell.

Morris, T. and Blom-Cooper, L. (1979) *Murder in England and Wales Since 1957,* The Observer.

Morris, T.P. (1957) 'The Criminal Area: A Study in Social Ecology', London: Routledge & Kegan Paul.

Morrison, W. (1995) *Theoretical Criminology: From Modernity to Post-modernity,* London: Cavendish.

Muncie, J. (1999) *Youth Crime: A Critical Introduction,* London: Sage.

Mukjurkee, S.K. and Fitzgerald, M.K. (1981) 'The Myth of Rising Crime', in S.K. Mukjurkee and J.A. Scutt (eds) *Women and Crime,* London: Allen & Unwin.

Murray, C. (ed.) (1990) *The Emerging British Underclass,* London: Institute of Economic Affairs Health and Welfare Unit.

Murray, C. (1994) *Underclass: The Crisis Deepens,* London: Institute of Economic Affairs.

Naess, S. (1959) 'Mother–Child Separation and Delinquency', *British Journal of Delinquency* 10: 22.

Naess, S. (1962) 'Mother–Child Separation and Delinquency: Further Evidence', *British Journal of Criminology* 2: 361.

Naffine, N. (1987) *Female Crime,* Sydney: Allen and Unwin.

Newman, O. (1972) *Defensible Space: Crime Prevention Through Urban Design,* New York: Macmillan.

Newman, O. (1976) *Defensible Space: People and Design in the Violent City,* London: The Architectural Press.

Nye, F.I. (1958) *Family Relationships and Delinquent Behavior,* New York: Wiley.

Olwens, D. (1987) 'Testosterone and Adrenaline: Aggressive and Antisocial Behaviour in Normal Adolescent Males', in S.A. Mednick, T.E. Moffit and S. Stack (eds) *The Causes of Crime: New Biological Approaches,* Cambridge: Cambridge University Press.

Omerod, D. (1996) 'The Evidential Implications of Psychological Profiling', *Criminal Law Review.* 863.

Packer, H. (1968) *The Limits of the Criminal Sanction*, Stanford, CA: Stanford University Press.

Park, R.E. (1921) *Introduction to the Study of Sociology*, Chicago: University of Chicago Press.

Parker, H. (1974) *View From the Boys*, Newton Abbot: David and Charles.

Parsons, T. (1937) *The Structure of Social Action*, New York: McGraw-Hill.

Parsons, T. (1951) *The Social System*, London: Routledge & Kegan Paul.

Pearce, F. and Tombs, S. (1993) 'US Capital versus the Third World: Union Carbide and Bhopal', in F. Pearce and M. Woodiwiss (eds) *Global Crime Connections*, Basingstoke: Macmillan.

Persky, H. Smith, K.D. and Basu, G.K. (1971) 'Relation of Psychological Measures of Aggression and Hostility to Testosterone Production in Man', *Psychosomatic Medicine*, 33: 265–75.

Piaget, J. (1980) *Adaptation and Intelligence: Organic Selection and Phenocopy* (trans. W. Mays), Chicago, IL: University of Chicago Press.

Pihl, R.O. (1982) 'Hair Element Levels of Violent Criminals', *Canadian Journal of Psychiatry*, 27: 533–45.

Pihl, R.O. and Peterson, J.B. (1993) 'Alcohol/Drug Use and Aggressive Behavior', in S. Hodgins (ed.) *Moral Disorder and Crime*, Newbury Park, CA: Sage.

Piliavin, I. and Briar, B. (1964) 'Police Encounters with Juveniles', *American Journal of Sociology*, 69: 153–62.

Pitts, J. (1986) 'Black Young People and Juvenile Crime: Some Unanswered Questions', in R. Matthews and J. Young (eds) *Confronting Crime*, London: Sage.

Pitts, J. (1996) 'The Politics and Practice of Youth Crime', in E. McLaughlin and J. Muncie, *Controlling Crime*, London: Sage in Association with the Open University.

Platt, A.M. (1969) *The Child Savers: The Invention of Delinquency*, Chicago: University of Chicago Press.

Plint T. (1851) *Crime in England*, London: Charles Gilpin.

Plummer, K. (1975) *Sexual Stigma*, London: Routledge & Kegan Paul.

Plummer, K. (1979) 'Misunderstanding Labelling Perspectives', in D. Downes and P. Rock (eds) *Deviant Interpretations*, London: Martin Robertson.

Pollak, O. (1950, 1961) *The Criminality of Women*, New York: Barnes.

Presdee, M. (1994) 'Young People, Culture and the Construction of Crime: Doing Wrong versus Doing Crime', in G. Barak (ed.) *Varieties of Criminology*, Westport, CT: Praeger.

Price, W.H. and Whatmore, P.B. (1967) 'Behaviour Disorders and Patterns of Crime Among XYY Males Identified at a Maximum Security Hospital', *British Medical Journal* 1: 533.

Prinz, R.J. Roberts, W.A. and Hantman, E. (1980) 'Dietary Correlates of Hyperactive Behaviour in Children', *Journal of Consulting and Clinical Psychology*, 48: 760–85.

Pryce, K. (1979) *Endless Pressure: A Study of West Indian Life-styles in Bristol*, Harmondsworth: Penguin.

Quételet, M.A. (1842) *A Treatise on Man*, Edinburgh: William and Robert Chalmers.

Quinney, R. (1970) *The Social Reality of Crime*, Boston: Little, Brown.

Radzinowicz, L. (1948–86) *A History of English Criminal Law and its Administration from 1750*, 5 volumes: (i) (1948) *The Movement for Reform*; (ii) (1956) *The Clash Between Private Initiative and Public Interest in the Enforcement of the Law*; (iii) (1956) *Cross Currents in the Movement of the Reform of the Police*; (iv) (1968) *Grappling for Control*; (v) (with R. Hood, 1986) *The Emergence of Penal Policy in Victorian and Edwardian England*, London: Stevens and Sons.

Rafter, N.H. and Heidensohn, F. (eds) (1985) *International Feminist Perspectives: Engendering a Discipline*, Buckingham: Open University Press.

Raloff, J. (1983) 'Locks – a Key to Violence', *Science News*, 124: 122–36.

Reckless, W. (1961) *The Crime Problem*, 3rd edn, New York: Appleton Century Crofts.

Reckless, W. (1967) *The Crime Problem*, 4th edn, New York: Appleton Century Crofts.

Redl, F. and Wineman, D. (1951) *Children Who Hate*, New York: Free Press.

Reiman, J. (1979) *The Rich Get Richer and the Poor Get Prison*, New York: John Wiley.

Reiss, A. (1951) 'Delinquency as the Failure of Personal and Social Controls', *American Sociological Review*, 16: 213–39.

Rex, J. and Moore, R. (1967) *Race, Community and Conflict: A Study in Sparkbrook*, London: Institute of Race Relations/OUP.

Rock, P. (1973) *Deviant Behaviour*, London: Hutchinson.

Rose, R.M. (1974) Bernstein, I.S. Gorden, T.P. and Catlin, S.E. (1974) 'Androgens and Aggression: A Review and Recent Findings in Primates', in R.L. Holloway (ed.), *Primate Aggression: Territoriality and Xenophobia*, New York: Academia Press.

Rosenau, P.-M. (1992) *Post-Modernism and the Social Sciences: Insights, Inroads and Intrusions*, Princeton, NJ: Princeton University Press.

Rousseau, J. (1964) *First and Second Discourses*, edited by R.D. Masters, New York: St Martin's Press.

Rousseau, J. (1978) *The Social Contract*, edited by R.D. Masters, New York: St Martin's Press.

Rowe, D.C. and Rogers, J.L. (1989) 'Behaviour Genetics, Adolescent Deviance, and "d": Contributions and Issues', in G.R. Adams, R. Montemayor and T.P. Gullotta (eds), *Advances in Adolescent Development*, Newbury Park, CA: Sage: 38–67.

Rutherford, A. (1992) *Growing Out of Crime*, 2nd edn, London: Waterside Press.

Rutter, M. (1981) *Maternal Deprivation Reassessed*, Harmondsworth: Penguin.

Saunders, W. (1984) *Alcohol Use in Britain; How Much is Too Much?* Edinburgh: Scottish Health Education Unit.

Scarmella, T.J. and Brown, W.A. (1978) 'Serum Testosterone and Aggressiveness in Hockey Players', *Psychosomatic Medicine*, 40: 262–75.

Schalling, D. (1987) 'Personality Correlates of Plasma Testosterone Levels in Young Delinquents: An Example of Person-Situation Interaction', in S.A. Mednick, T.E. Moffit and S.A. Stack (eds) *The Causes of Crime: New Biological Approaches*, Cambridge: Cambridge University Press.

Schlapp, M.G. and Smith, E. (1928) *The New Criminology*, New York: Boni and Liveright.

Schlossman, S., Zellman, G. and Shavelson, R. (1984) *Delinquency Prevention in South Chicago: A Fifty-Year Assessment of the Chicago Area Project*, Santa Monica, CA: Rand.

Schraeger, L.S. and Short, J.F. (1978) 'Towards a Sociology of Organisational Crime', *Social Problems*, 25: 407–19.

Schur, E. (1971) *Labelling Deviant Behaviour: Its Sociological Implications*, New York: Harper and Row.

Schutz, A. (1962) *The Problem of Social Reality*, The Hague: Martinus Nijhoff.

Schwatz, M.D. and DeKeseredy, W.S. (1991) 'Left Realist Criminology: Strengths, Weaknesses and the Feminist Critique', *Crime, Law and Social Change*, 15: 51.

Schwendinger, H. and Schwendinger, J. (1970) 'Defenders of Order or Guardians of Human Rights', *Issues in Criminology* 7: 72–81.

Scraton, P. (1985) *The State of the Police*, London: Pluto.

Scraton, P. and Chadwick, K. (1996 originally 1992) 'The Theoretical Priorities of Critical Criminology', in J. Muncie, E. McLaughlin, and M. Langan (eds) (1996) *Criminological Perspectives: A Reader*, London: Sage.

Scruton, R. (1980) *The Meaning of Conservatism*, Harmondsworth: Pelican.

Scruton, R. (1985) *Thinkers of the New Left*, London: Longman.

Sellin, T. (1959) *The Death Penalty*, Philadelphia: American Law Institute.

Sellin, T. (1973) 'Enrico Ferri' in H. Mannheim (ed.), *Pioneers in Criminology*, 2nd edn, Montclair, NJ: Patterson-Smith.

Shah, S.A. and Roth, L.H. (1974) 'Biological and Psychophysiological Factors in Criminality', in D. Glaser (ed.) *Handbook of Criminology*, London: Rand McNally.

Shaw, C.R. (1930) *The Jack-Roller: A Delinquent Boy's Own Story*, Chicago: University of Chicago Press.

Shaw, C.R. (1931) *The Natural History of a Delinquent Career*, Chicago: University of Chicago Press.

Shaw, C.R. (1938) *Brothers in Crime*, Chicago: University of Chicago Press.

Shaw, C.R. and McKay, H.D. (1972) *Juvenile Delinquency and Urban Areas*, Chicago: University of Chicago Press.

Sheldon, W.H. (1949) *Varieties of Delinquent Youth*, London: Harper.

Shoenthaler, S.J. (1982) 'The Effects of Blood Sugar on the Treatment and Control of Antisocial Behaviour: A Double-Blind Study of an Incarcerated Juvenile Population', *International Journal for Biosocial Research*, 3: 1–15.

Shockley, W. (1967) 'A "Try Simplest Cases" Approach to the Heredity-Poverty-Crime Problem', *Proceedings of the National Academy of Sciences* 57: 1767–74.

Skinner, B.F. (1938) *The Behaviour of Organisms*, New York: Appleton-Century-Crofts.

Skinner, B.F. (1981) 'Selection by Consequences', *Science*, 213: 501–04.

Sim, J. Scraton, P. and Gordon, P. (1987) 'Introduction: Crime, the State, and Critical Analysis', in P. Scraton, (ed.) (1987) *Law, Order and the Authoritarian State: Readings in Critical Criminology*, Buckingham: Open University Press.

Simon, R. J. (1975) *Women and Crime*, London: Lexington Books.

Smart, C. (1977) *Women, Crime and Criminology*, London: Routledge & Kegan Paul.

Smart, C. (1981) 'Response to Greenwood', in A. Morris and L. Gelsthorpe (eds) *Women and Crime*, Cambridge: Cropwood Conference Series.

Smart, C. (1990) 'Feminist Approaches to Criminology; or Post-Modern Woman Meets Atavistic Man', in L. Gelsthorpe and A. Morris (eds) *Feminist Perspectives in Criminology*, Buckingham: Open University Press.

Smart, J. (1981) 'Undernutrition and Aggression', in P.F. Brain and D. Benton (eds) *Multidisciplinary Approaches to Aggression Research*, Amsterdam: Elsevier/North Holland.

Smith, Adam (1910) *The Wealth of Nations*, London: Dent.

Smith, D. and Gray, J. (1986) *Police and People in London*, London: Policy Studies Institute.

Smith, D.E. and Smith, D.D. (1977) 'Eysenck's Psychoticism Scale and Reconviction', *British Journal of Criminology* 17: 387.

Spencer, H. (1876–1896) *Principles of Sociology* (3 vols), London: Williams and Norgate.

Spencer, H. (1971) *Structure, Function and Evolution,* readings, edited with an introduction by S. Andreski, London: Nelson.

Spergel, I.A. (1964) *Racketsville, Slumtown, Haulburg*, Chicago: University of Chicago Press.

Spergel, I.A. (1995) *The Youth Gang Problem: A Community Approach*, Oxford: Oxford University Press.

Staw, B.M. and Szwajkowski, E. (1975) 'The Scarcity-Munificence Component of Organizational Environments and the Commission of Illegal Acts', *Administrative Science Quarterly*, 20: 345–54.

Stumpfl, F. (1936) *Die Ursprunge des Verbrechens im Lebenslauf von Zwillengen*, Leipzig: Verlag.

Sullivan, R.F. (1973) 'The Economics of Crime: An Introduction to the Literature', *Crime and Delinquency*, 19: 138–49.

Sutherland, E.H. (1937) *The Professional Thief: By a Professional Thief*, Chicago: University of Chicago Press.

Sutherland, E.H. (1940) 'White-collar Criminality', *American Sociological Review*, 5: 1–12.

Sutherland, E.H. (1947) *Principles of Criminology*, 4th edn, Philadelphia: Lippincott.

Swartz, J. (1975) 'Silent Killers at Work', *Crime and Social Justice*, 3: 15–20.

Syndulko, K. (1978) 'Electrocortical Investigations of Sociopathy', in R.D. Hare and D. Schalling (eds) *Psychopathic Behaviour: Approaches to Research*, Chichester: Wiley.

Tannenbaum, F. (1938) *Crime and the Community*, New York: Columbia University Press.

Tappan, P.W. (1960) *Crime, Justice and Correction*, New York: McGraw-Hill.

Taylor, C.S. (1990) *Dangerous Society*, East Lansing, MI: Michigan State University Press.

Taylor, I. (1981) *Law and Order: Arguments for Socialism*, London: Macmillan.

Taylor, I., Walton, P. and Young, J. (1973) *The New Criminology: For a Social Theory of Deviance*, London: Routledge & Kegan Paul.

Taylor, I., Walton, P. and Young, J. (eds) (1975) *Critical Criminology*, London: Routledge & Kegan Paul.

Thomas, D.W. and Hyman, J.M. (1978) 'Compliance, Theory, Control Theory and Juvenile Delinquency', in M. Krohn and R.L. Acker (eds) *Crime, Law and Sanctions*, London: Sage.

Thomas, W.I. (1907) *Sex and Society*, Boston: Little, Brown.

Thomas, W.I. (1923,1867) *The Unadjusted Girl*, New York: Harper & Row.

Thompson, E.P. (1975) *Whigs and Hunters*, London: Allen Lane.

Thrasher, F. (1947) *The Gang*, Chicago: University of Chicago Press.

Tierney, K. (1982) 'The Battered Women Movement and the Creation of the Wife Beating Problem', *Social Problems*, 29 (February): 207–20.

Tolman, E.C. (1959) 'Principles of Purposive Behaviour', in S. Koch and D.E. Leary (eds), *A Century of Psychology as a Science*, New York, NY: McGraw-Hill.

Tong, R. (1988) *Feminist Thought: A Comprehensive Introduction*, London: Routledge.

Trasler, G. (1986) 'Situational Crime Control and Rational Choice: A Critique', in K. Heal and G. Laycock (eds) *Situational Crime Prevention: From Theory into Practice*, London: HMSO.

Turk, A.T. (1969) *Criminality and the Social Order*, Chicago: Rand-McNally.

Virkkunen, M. (1987) 'Metabolic Dysfunctions Amongst Habitually Violent Offenders: Reactive Hypoglycaemia and Cholesterol Levels', in S.A. Mednick, T.E. Moffit and S.A. Stack (eds) *The Causes of Crime: New Biological Approaches*, Cambridge: Cambridge University Press.

Volavka, J. (1987) 'Electroencephalogram Among Criminals' in S.A. Mednick, T.E. Moffit and S.A. Stack (eds) *The Causes of Crime: New Biological Approaches*, Cambridge: Cambridge University Press.

Vold, G.B. (1958) *Theoretical Criminology*, Oxford: Oxford University Press.

Vold, G.B., Bernard, T.J. and Snipes, J.B. (1998) *Theoretical Criminology*, 4th edn, Oxford: Oxford University Press.

von Hirsch, A. (1976) *Doing Justice: The Choice of Punishments. Report of the Committee for the Study of Incarceration*, New York: Hill and Wang.

Walker, N. (1980) *Punishment, Danger and Stigma: The Morality of Criminal Justice,* Oxford: Basil Blackwell.

Walker, N. (1985) *Sentencing: Theory, Law and Practice,* London: Butterworth.

Walklate, S. (1998) *Understanding Criminology: Current Theoretical Debates,* Buckingham: Open University Press.

Wells, C. (1993) *Corporations and Criminal Responsibility.* Oxford: Clarendon Press.

West, D.J. (1969) *Present Conduct and Future Delinquency,* London: Heinemann.

West, D.J. and Farrington, D.P. (1973) *Who Becomes Delinquent?* London: Heinemann.

Westergaard, J. (1995) *Who Gets What? The Hardening of Class Inequality in the Late Twentieth Century.* Cambridge: Polity Press.

Wilkins, L. (1964) *Social Deviance,* London: Tavistock.

Wilmott, P. (1966) *Adolescent Boys in East London,* London: Routledge & Kegan Paul.

Wilson, H. (1980) 'Parental Supervision: a Neglected Aspect of Delinquency', *British Journal of Criminology,* 20: 315–27.

Wilson, J.Q. (1975) *Thinking About Crime,* New York: Basic Books.

Wilson, J.Q. and Herrnstein, R.J. (1985) *Crime and Human Nature,* New York: Simon and Schuster.

Wilson, J.Q. and Kelling, G.L. (1982) 'Broken Windows', *Atlantic Monthly,* March, 29–38.

Wilson, W.J. (1991) 'Public Policy Research and the Truly Disadvantaged', in C. Jencks and P.E. Peterson (eds) *The Urban Underclass,* Washington, DC: The Brookings Institution, 460–81.

Witkin, H.A., Mednick, S.A. and Schulsinger, F. (1977) 'XYY and XXY Men: Criminality and Aggression', in S.A. Mednick and K.O. Christiansen (eds), *Biosocial Bases of Criminal Behaviour,* New York: Gardner Press.

Wolfgang, M.E. and Ferracuti, F. (1967) *The Sub-culture of Violence: Towards an Integrated Theory in Criminology,* Beverly Hills: Sage.

Wootton, B. (1959) *Social Science and Social Pathology,* London: Allen & Unwin.

Wootton, B. (1962) 'A Social Scientist's Approach to Maternal Deprivation', in M.D. Ainsworth (ed.) *Deprivation of Maternal Care: A Reassessment of its Effects,* Geneva: World Health Organisation.

Wright, M. (1982) *Making Good: Prisons, Punishment and Beyond,* London: Burnett.

Wright, R.A. (1993) 'A Socially Sensitive Criminal Justice System', in J.W. Murphy and D.L. Peck (eds) *Open Institutions: The Hope for Democracy.* Westport, CT: Praeger.

Yablonsky, L. (1962) *The Violent Gang,* New York: Macmillan.

Young, J. (1971) *The Drug Takers: The Social Meaning of Drugtaking,* London: Paladin.

Young, J. (1986a) 'The Failure of Criminology: The Need for a Radical Realism', in R. Matthews and J. Young (eds) *Confronting Crime,* London: Sage.

Young, J. (1986b) 'Ten Points of Realism', in R. Matthews and J. Young (eds) *Issues in Realist Criminology*, London: Sage.

Young, J. (1994) 'Incessant Chatter: Recent Paradigms in Criminology', in M. Maguire, R. Morgan and R. Reiner (eds) *The Oxford Handbook of Criminology*, Oxford: Clarendon Press.

Young, J. (1999) *The Exclusive Society: Social Exclusion, Crime and Difference in Late Modernity*, London: Sage.

Zimring, F. and Hawkins, G. (1968) 'Deterrence and Marginal Groups', *Journal of Research in Crime and Delinquency*, 5: 110–15.

Zimring, F. and Hawkins, G. (1973) *Deterrence*, Chicago: University of Chicago.

Glossary

administrative criminology: emphasis on reducing the opportunity to offend by the creation and evaluation of usually small-scale situational crime prevention schemes.

anomie theories: there are two variants; the first, developed by Emile Durkheim, proposes that anomie is a condition of normlessness experienced by individuals during periods of rapid socio-economic change when previous forms of control and restraint have broken down; the second, developed by Robert Merton, proposes that individuals use alternative means – including criminal activities – to gain access to socially created needs that they are unable to obtain through legitimate behaviour.

antisocial personality disorder: relatively recent term that it is interchangeable with that of psychopathy. There are various definitions of this condition that in general emphasise such traits as an incapacity for loyalty, selfishness, irresponsibility, impulsiveness, inability to feel guilt and failure to learn from experience.

behavioural learning theories: a variant of psychological positivism that proposes that criminal behaviour is conditioned learned behaviour.

biological positivism: proposes that human beings commit crime because of internal physiological factors over which they have little or no control.

biosocial theory: contemporary biologists who propose that physiological characteristics of an individual are only part of the explanation of criminal behaviour; factors in the physical and social environment are also influential.

'bloody code': a body of legislation that during the seventeenth to the early eighteenth century prescribed the death penalty for a vast number of property crimes.

Chicago school: a group of sociologists based at the University of Chicago during the 1920s and 1930s who developed the ecological explanation of crime which proposes that people engage in criminal activities because of determining factors in their immediate environment.

Classical criminology: the foundations of the rational actor model of explaining criminal behaviour – people are rational human beings who choose to commit criminal behaviour and can be dissuaded from doing so by the threat of punishment.

cognitive learning theories: reject much of the positivist psychological tradition of explaining criminal behaviour by incorporating notions of creative thinking and thus choice, in many ways more akin to the rational actor model.

conflict theories: a variant of the victimised actor model that proposes that definitions of criminality – and the decision to act against certain activities and groups – are made by those with control of authority in a pluralist but equal society.

corporate crime: involves illegal acts carried out in the furtherance of the goals of an organisation.

crime control: model of criminal justice that prioritises efficiency and getting results with emphasis on catching, convicting and punishing the offender (see 'due process').

critical criminology: or 'left idealists' to their former cohorts in the radical tradition (see 'left realism') that proposes that crime is defined in terms of the concept of oppression, that some groups in society are seen to be the most likely to suffer oppressive social relations based upon class division, sexism and racism.

deterrence: a doctrine that punishment must be both swift and certain in order to dissuade people not to commit crime.

deviancy amplification: a concept which suggests that the less tolerance there is to an initial act of group deviance, the more acts will be defined as deviant (see 'moral panics').

deviant subculture theories: there are many different variants – mostly positivist but latterly incorporating notions of choice – that propose that (predominantly young) people commit crime and deviant behaviour in the company of others for whom this is seen as the normal thing to do.

differential association theory: offending behaviour is likely to occur when individuals acquire sufficient inclinations towards law breaking that outweigh their associations with non-criminal tendencies.

due process: it is the purpose of the criminal justice system to prove the guilt of a defendant beyond a reasonable doubt in a public trial as a condition for the imposition of a sentence; the state has a duty to seek out and punish the guilty but must prove the guilt of the accused (see 'crime control').

environmental criminology: the study of where and when crimes occur.

environmental design: it is proposed that the nature of the built environment can affect the level of crime both by influencing potential offenders and by affecting the ability of a person to exercise control over their surroundings.

environmental management: it is argued that if evidence that crime has been committed is allowed to remain in place this will itself lead to further offences being committed because it sends out a message that no-one cares.

ethnomethodology: a method of sociological analysis concerned with how individuals experience and make sense of social interaction.

European Enlightenment: philosophical movement that occurred in western

Europe during the seventeenth and eighteen centuries which proposed that the social world could be explained and regulated by natural laws; political systems should be developed that embraced new ideas of individual rationality and free will.

feminism: there are different versions but all observe that it is men who are the dominant group in society and it is privileged males who make and enforce the rules to the detriment of women.

folk devils: see 'moral panic'.

integrated criminological theories: an incorporation of elements from different approaches in an attempt to provide a stronger explanatory tool than that offered by one individual theory.

Italian school: early biological positivists who developed the influential notion that the criminal is a physical type distinct from the non-criminal.

just deserts: a philosophy that eschews individual discretion and rehabilitation as legitimate aims of the justice system, that justice must be both done and seen to be done (see 'due process').

labelling theories: propose that crime is a product of the social reaction to an activity; if the action is ignored or not discovered the person does not become a criminal; this only happens when the person is processed by the criminal justice system and sets off on the path to a criminal career.

latent delinquency theory: proposed that the absence of an intimate attachment with parents could lead to later criminality.

left realism: a response to populist conservatism and right realism that proposes the need for a balance of intervention to address both the crime and the conditions that have caused it, influential with the 'New' Labour Government elected in the UK in 1997.

maternal deprivation theory: suggested that a lack of a close mother/child relationship in the early years could lead to criminal behaviour.

modernism or modernity: a secular society based on rationality and reason with science as the dominant form of social explanation.

moral panic: a frenzy of popular societal indignation usually whipped up about a particular activity that is seen to threaten the very fabric of civilisation; once labelled as such, those engaged in the activity become ostracised and targeted as 'folk devils'.

multiple masculinities: there are different masculinities that are all are subject to challenge and change over time.

neo-Classical criminology: the recognition that there is a limitation on the level of rationality enjoyed by some people such as children and the mentally ill, and this is a justification for mitigating circumstances in the courtroom.

new criminology: sought an explanation of criminal behaviour based on a theoretical synthesis of Marxism and labelling perspectives.

offender profiling: used, particularly in the USA, to help detect particular types of criminals, has been most useful in the detection of serial murders.

opportunity theory: a more formalised version of routine activities theory that considers elements of exposure, proximity, guardianship and target attractiveness as variables that increase the risk of criminal victimisation.

phenomenology: a philosophical approach that proposes that phenomena are only 'real' if they are defined as such by individuals who then act on the basis of those definitions.

postmodernism or postmodernity: a challenge to rationality, reason and science as the dominant forms of social explanation.

popular conservative criminology: came to prominence with the rise of the political 'new right' in the UK and USA during the late 1970s and the 1980s, based predominantly on 'right realist' theory.

positivism: a crucial element of the predestined actor model that proposes that human behaviour is determined by factors – either internal (as in the case of biological and psychological positivism) or external (as in the case of sociological positivism) – that are outside the control of the person.

predatory crime: direct contact, personal or property, crime.

predestined actor model of crime and criminal behaviour: based on the positivist doctrine of determinism where criminal behaviour is explained in terms of factors, either internal or external to the human being, that cause people to act in ways over which they have little or no control.

pre-modernism or pre-modernity: pre-scientific society where religion and spirituality are the dominant forms of explanation.

psychodynamic theories: a variant of psychological positivism that proposes that criminal behaviour is in some way determined by the psychosexual development of the individual during childhood.

psychological positivism: people commit crime because of internal psychological factors over which they have little or no control; there is a criminal personality.

psychopathy: (see 'antisocial personality disorder'.)

radical criminology: usually informed by some version of Marxist socio-economic theory, this variant of the victimised actor model proposes that there are deeply inherent inequalities in society that provide those with economic and political power the opportunity to criminalise the activities of the poor and powerless.

rational actor model of crime and criminal behaviour: based on the notion of free will, it proposes that human beings choose to commit criminal behaviour and can be deterred through the threat of punishment.

rational choice theory: contemporary variant of the rational actor model that provides the theoretical foundations of situational crime prevention and which proposes that human beings commit crime when the opportunity arises and that this can be thwarted by removing that opportunity.

reintegrative shaming: proposes that the key to crime control is a cultural commitment to shaming in ways that are positive rather than negative.

right realism: based on a rediscovery of the rational actor model of crime and criminal behaviour and the notion that human beings choose to commit criminal behaviour just like any other and can be deterred by the threat of punishment.

routine activities theory: proposes that for a personal or property crime to occur, there must be at the same time and place a perpetrator, a victim, and/or an object of property.

self-fulfilling prophecy: a false definition of a situation, evoking a new behaviour that makes the original false assumption come true.

serial murder: a repetitive event where the murderer kills at a number of different times, frequently spanning a matter of months or years, and often committed at different locations.

situational crime prevention: (see 'administrative criminology'.)

social construction of crime: highly influential concept within the victimised actor model that proposes that criminal behaviour only occurs because those with power and authority define certain activities – usually engaged in by the poor and powerless – as criminal while those of the powerful are ignored.

social contract theories: challenged the notion of the 'natural' political authority previously asserted by the aristocracy, arguing that human beings should freely enter into contracts with others to perform interpersonal or civic duties.

social control theories: contemporary versions propose that people commit crime when their social bond to society is broken.

social disorganisation theory: has its origins in the notion developed by Emile Durkheim that imperfect social regulation leads to a variety of different social problems, including crime; as developed by the Chicago school there was call for efforts to reorganise communities to emphasise non-criminal activities.

social evolutionism: the notion that human beings develop as part of a process of interaction with the world they inhabit.

sociological positivism: people commit crime because of determining factors in their environment over which they have little or no control.

square of crime: a left realist notion that proposes crime to be the result of a number of lines of force and that intervention to prevent it must therefore take place at different levels in order to be effective.

symbolic interactionism: primarily analyses the way individuals conceptualise themselves and others around them with whom they interact.

techniques of neutralisation: the ways in which offenders may justify their deviant activities to themselves and others.

underclass theory: groups in socially isolated neighbourhoods have few legitimate employment opportunities and this increases the chances that they turn to illegal or deviant activities for income.

utilitarianism: assesses the applicability of policies and legislation to promote the 'happiness' of those citizens affected by them.

victimised actor model of crime and criminal behaviour: people commit crime because they have in some way been the victims of an unjust society; they can have choices but these are constrained by their structural situation.

white-collar crime: occurs when an individual commits crime against an organisation within which they work.

Author index

Adler, F., 15, 167, 246
Adler, Z., 166, 246
Aichhorn, A., 11, 79, 246
Akers, R.L., 12, 40, 46, 93–5, 185, 246
Akers, R.L., Krohn, M.D., Lanza-Kaduce, L. and Radosevich, M., 94, 246
Allsopp, J.F. and Feldman, M.P., 85–6, 246
Anderson, E., 125, 246
Andry, R.G., 80, 246
Arendt, H., 76, 246
Aubert, W., 118, 246

Baldwin, J.D., 11, 69, 195, 247
Bandura, A., 122, 247
Bandura, A. and Walters, R.H., 11, 81, 247
Barlow, H., 212, 247
Baudrillard, J., 232, 244, 247
Bauman, Z., 76, 232, 244, 247
Baumhart, R.C., 93, 247
Beccaria, C., 27–8, 34, 247
Beck, U., 242–4, 247
Becker, G.S., 9, 43, 247
Becker, H., 13, 131, 136–39, 142, 146, 154, 247
Bedau, H., 41, 247
Beechey, V., 160, 247

Bell, D., 233, 247
Bennett, T., 49, 247
Bentham, J., 8, 25–9, 202, 247
Bertrand, M., 162, 247
Beyleveld, D., 41, 247
Binet, A., 58, 247
Blackburn, R. and Maybury, C., 87, 247
Bonger, W., 154, 223, 248
Bottomley, A.K. and Coleman, C., 41, 248
Bowlby, J., 11, 80–2, 164, 248
Box, S., 15, 17, 110–11, 122, 128, 167, 177, 181, 207–10, 214–16, 248
Braithwaite, J., 6, 18, 111, 118, 122, 176–7, 181, 297, 210–11, 216, 221, 248
Brantingham, P.J. and Brantingham, P.L., 17, 44, 192, 195, 198, 200, 248
Brown, G.W. and Harris, T., 168, 248
Brown, S., 169, 248
Bruegel, I., 160, 248
Burgess, E.W., 103, 248
Burgess, R.L. and Akers, R.L., 93, 248
Burke, R.D. and Sunley, R., 124, 126–7, 248
Burt, C., 11, 82, 248

275

Subject index

absolute poverty, 178
actual deprivation, 179
administrative criminology, 175, 220, 224–5, 268
adopted children, 10, 60–2
adrenaline sensitivity, 69
affectional bonds, 205–7
affirmative postmodernism, 240
aggression, 66, 68, 81
alcohol, 39, 56, 69, 71, 243
allergies and diet, 70–1,
ancien regime, 25
anomie, 12, 15, 17, 99, 106–13, 116, 165, 171, 203, 208, 210, 220, 268
anomie gap, 117–8
antisocial personality disorder, 11, 69, 71, 268
area studies, 193
asthenics, 64
atavism, 54–5, 162
athletics, 164
Auschwitz, 237
automatic behaviours, 83–4
automatic nervous system, 87–8, 188

balanced intervention, 18, 221–4, 229
begging, 39, 198–9

behavioural learning theories, 11, 83–90, 189, 268
bell curve, the, 75, 226
biochemistry, 67–71, 188
biological positivism, 9–11, 51, 54–76, 162–4, 185, 226
biosocial theory, 16, 187–91, 268
black feminism, 161
Blair, T., 18
blood sugar levels, 69
'bloody code', 2, 267
boundary maintenance mechanisms, 139
brain injuries, 66
brain tumours, 66
British Crime Survey, 199, 218
broken families, 11, 82–3, 141
broken windows thesis, 39, 198
burglary, 41, 44

cannabis, 5, 71, 243
capable guardians, 45–7
capital punishment, 27, 41
capitalism, 51, 154, 173, 176, 223, 234
castration, 72
Centre for Contemporary Cultural Studies, 126, 156
chemotherapy, 72